The Falklands War

The Editors would like to dedicate this volume to their teachers at the University of Virginia, Princeton, and Georgetown without whose example of moral and scholarly excellence this work would not have been possible.

A.R.C. and A.C.A.

The Falklands War

Lessons for Strategy, Diplomacy, and International Law

Edited by

Alberto R. Coll
Georgetown University

and

Anthony C. Arend
University of Virginia

Boston
GEORGE ALLEN & UNWIN
London   Sydney

Allen & Unwin, Inc
Fifty Cross Street, Winchester, Mass. 01890, USA

George Allen & Unwin (Publishers) Ltd,
40 Museum Street, London WC1A, 1LU, UK

George Allen & Unwin (Publishers) Ltd,
Park Lane, Hemel Hempstead, Herts HP2 4TE, UK

George Allen & Unwin Australia Pty Ltd,
8 Napier Street, North Sydney, NSW 2060, Australia

First published in 1985

Library of Congress Cataloging in Publication Data

Main entry under title:
   The Falklands War
Includes index.
1. Falkland Islands War, 1983—Addresses, essays,
lectures. I. Coll, Alberto R. II. Arend, Anthony C.
F3031.5.F34   1985   997'.11   84–18622
ISBN 0-04-327075-1 (alk. paper)
ISBN 0-04-327076-X (pbk. : alk paper)

British Library Cataloguing in Publication Data

The Falklands War: lessons for strategy,
   diplomacy and international law.
1. Falkland Islands—International status
2. Great Britain—Foreign relations—
Argentina 3. Argentina—Foreign relations
—Great Britain
I. Coll, Alberto R.   II. Arend, Anthony C.
341.4'2   JX4084.F3
ISBN 0-04-327075-1
ISBN 0-04-327076-X Pbk

Set in 10 on 11½ point Palatino by Mathematical Composition Setters
Ltd, Salisbury, UK
and printed by Billings and Sons Ltd., London and Worcester.

Contents

CONTENTS

Notes on Contributors

The Editors

Alberto R. Coll is Assistant Professor of International Politics, Law and Organization at Georgetown University. He is a former Newcombe Fellow, Weaver Fellow, Eisenhower Fellow, and the author of *The Western Heritage and American Values: Law, Theology and History* (1982) and *The Wisdom of Statecraft* (1985). In 1984 he was awarded a Leroy Hill Fellowship by the Institute for Humane Studies.

Anthony C. Arend is a Lecturer of International Law at Georgetown University, a consultant to the Center for Law and National Security at the University of Virginia, and the author of several articles on international legal issues. He is a former Articles Editor of the *Virginia Journal of International Law* and a former Weaver Fellow.

Contributors

Inis L. Claude, Jr. is the Edward R. Stettinius, Jr. Professor of Government and Foreign Affairs at the University of Virginia. His works include such classics in the field of international relations theory as *Power and International Relations* (1962) and *Swords into Plowshares: The Problems and Progress of International Organization* (4th ed. 1971).

David A. Colson is Assistant Legal Advisor for Oceans, International Environment, and Science Affairs at the U.S. State Department.

Thomas M. Franck is Professor of Law and Director of the Center for International Studies at New York University. He has served as constitutional advisor to several developing nations, and former Director of the United Nations Institute for Training and Research. His published writings include *African Law, The Structure of Impartiality*, and *Secrecy and Foreign Policy*.

David C. Gompert was Deputy to the Under Secretary of State for Political Affairs and a member of the Haig mission during the Falklands War. He also has served as Deputy Assistant Secretary of State for European Affairs, and Special Assistant to Secretary of State Henry Kissinger. He is the author of many articles on international security issues and editor of *Nuclear Weapons and World Politics*.

Christopher C. Joyner is Associate Professor of Political Science and International Relations at George Washington University. He has been Senior Editor of the *Virginia Journal of International Law* and Co-Director of Florida State University's Center for Peace and Environmental Studies. He is the author of numerous legal publications, including a forthcoming book on the strategic and international legal status of Antarctica.

Douglas Kinney is a U.S. Foreign Service Officer with specializations in European and Latin American politics. In addition to several Embassy posts abroad, he has served in Henry Kissinger's Secretariat, in the Secretaries' Open Forum, in the Office of UN Political Affairs, and most recently as Advisor to Ambassador Kirkpatrick at the U.S. Mission to the United Nations. He is currently at the Institute for the Study of Diplomacy, Georgetown University, where he is doing a study on "National Interests/National Honor: The Diplomacy of the Falklands Crisis."

Monroe Leigh is a partner of the Washington law firm of Steptoe and Johnson, and was Legal Advisor to the U.S. State Department from 1975 to 1977. He was a member of the Permanent Court of Arbitration at The Hague from 1975 to 1980, and was President of the American Society of International Law from 1980 to 1982. He specializes in international law and international trade law.

Howard S. Levie is Professor Emeritus of Law at St. Louis University. He is a leading authority on the laws of war, and the author of *Prisoners of War in International Armed Conflict* (1979) and *Protection of War Victims* (4 vols., 1981).

Srilal Perera is a lawyer and graduate fellow at Georgetown University. He has served in several international organizations, including the United Nations and the World Bank, and specializes on the role of regional law and organizations in international politics and economics.

Alfred P. Rubin is Professor of International Law at the Fletcher School of Law and Diplomacy, Tufts University. In 1981–2 he served as Charles H. Stockton Professor of International Law at the Naval War College. Among his many writings are two books on European imperialism: *The International Personality of the Malay States* and *Piracy, Paramountcy and Protectorates* (both 1974).

Dov S. Zakheim is Assistant Under Secretary for Policy and Resources in the U.S. Department of Defense. He is a former Special Assistant to the Assistant Secretary of Defense for International Security Policy, and principal analyst with the National Security and International Affairs Division of the Congressional Budget Office. He is the author of numerous articles and major policy studies.

Preface

The origins of this book were a conference on the Falklands War co-sponsored by the John Bassett Moore Society of International Law and the Center for Law and National Security at the University of Virginia School of Law in the fall of 1982. Some of the papers presented at the conference are incorporated here, as are also those of several other contributors who, though not present at the conference, agreed to prepare chapters for the book. In their work of editing and preparing the manuscript the editors enjoyed the warm support and encouragement of the Moore Society and its vice-president, Mr. David Whitescarver, and of the Director of the Center for Law and National Security, Professor John Norton Moore. The Department of Government of Georgetown University and its chairman, Professor William V. O'Brien, also provided valuable support, especially through the dedicated and unfailing efforts of the department's secretary, Ms. Sandra Rosenberg, who typed several chapters of the book. Ms. Jennifer Bunch of the University of Virginia School of Law likewise typed, with similar patience and efficiency, some of the other chapters. We also wish to express our appreciation to Ms. Leslie Sherman, University Fellow in the Department of Government at Georgetown University, who critically reviewed the manuscript with care and thoughtfulness. Without all of these concerted efforts, and without the scholarly dedication of this book's contributors, the project could not have been completed.

A differently edited version of Thomas Franck's essay in this book appeared in the *American Journal of International Law* (January 1983); a short version of Inis Claude's was published in *Global Perspectives*, vol. 1 (1983); and some portions of Anthony Arend's main essay appeared in the *Virginia Journal of International Law* (Winter 1983). All these publishers kindly offered their permission, and we extend our thanks to them.

Although the definitive history and political analysis of the Falklands War will not be written for some time to come, the editors hope that this work will be a valuable introduction for any serious student of that conflict, its underlying crisis, and its multiple dimensions. The editors also take certain pride in noting that this book represents a flourishing relationship between Georgetown University and the University of Virginia, a relationship centered around shared concerns for the normative, philosophical, and legal dimensions of international politics.

ALBERTO R. COLL
ANTHONY C. AREND
Washington, D.C.
1 April 1984

The Falklands War

1

The Falklands War: Intersection of Strategy, Diplomacy, and International Law

ANTHONY C. AREND

The Falklands War of 1982 provided diplomats, strategists, and international lawyers with the opportunity to apply their skills to attempt to resolve the conflict and, after the fact, to assess the implications of the war for the international system. Unfortunately, scholars writing on the Falklands War, by necessity, have normally limited their evaluation of the war to its implications for their particular disciplines. A full understanding of the Falklands War, however, requires a multi-disciplined approach; issues relating to politics, diplomacy, strategy, and law are inextricably linked and must be examined together if lessons are to be learned and further conflict is to be avoided.

In an effort to understand the many dimensions of the Falklands Crisis, this study brings together essays by thirteen scholars and practitioners of law, diplomacy, and strategy. These essays are grouped into three parts. Part One examines the "Challenges to International Law." Part Two discusses the "Challenges to Diplomacy" and Part Three looks at the strategic, military, legal, and political implications that the Falklands War of 1982 has for the future of international relations.

Part One begins with an essay by an international legal scholar, Alfred P. Rubin. He sets the tone for the book by

1

describing the historical context out of which the 1982 conflict arose and examining the applicable international law. He begins by discussing the problem of discovery, explaining the various British, Dutch, Portuguese, and Spanish sightings of the Falklands in the 1500s and 1600s. Then he turns to the law regarding questions of title to territory and discusses such concepts as *uti possidetis* and effective occupation. Applying international legal doctrine to the conflicting British and Argentine claims, Rubin concludes that there is still much uncertainty about how a hypothetical tribunal would resolve the sovereignty dispute.

Following this historical and legal overview of the sovereignty question, Thomas M. Franck, another international legal expert, continues the discussion with an examination of the strategic role of legal principles. He takes up the question of the efficacy of legal norms and demonstrates how legal principles played a major role in shaping the response of states to the Falklands War. According to Franck, many states were extremely concerned about the precedent an Argentine victory might set. They were concerned that the Argentine example, if unchecked, would encourage other states to use force unilaterally in areas where they had a direct stake. Thus, legal principles helped to rally some nations to take a stand in the Falklands War. But the problem, Franck explains, is that the principles were unable to *deter* Argentine aggression. This is attributable in part to the long list of violations of article 2 (4) of the UN Charter that have gone unanswered since World War II. Franck contends that the Falklands War illustrates a selective application of principles and concludes that if a principle is invoked only occasionally it loses its power to deter and calls into question the legitimacy of fighting to defend an already emasculated norm.

After Franck's essay, Alberto R. Coll, a lawyer and political scientist, examines the philosophical and legal dimensions of the use of force. Before beginning his analysis of the law, Coll raises an important caveat about legal judgments—they are in reality only relative and never absolute. Although legal pronouncements often seem black and white, they hide the real subtleties of human behavior. Philosophically and theologically speaking, it may be improper to brand one state as the aggressor and the other state as the victim. Corporate responsibility and the fallen nature of all men make it difficult to ascribe absolute wrong or absolute right in most cases. But within the earthly order of things man must make normative judgments

2

about right and wrong—even if they do deviate from the absolute. With this philosophical point in mind, Coll outlines the evolution of the traditional international law of conflict management from the pre-League period to the present. After setting forth the current provisions of the United Nations Charter, he analyzes Argentina's actions in light of the law of the Charter. He also gives a detailed discussion of Argentina's contentions about the legality of its behavior. Following this legal analysis, Coll discusses some larger questions that the Falklands War raises for the efficacy of the existing international norms of conflict management. He concludes by suggesting a possible international mechanism that could, in the future, help resolve conflicts such as the Falklands dispute.

In the third essay of Part One, Anthony C. Arend examines two problems revealed by the Falklands War: the failure of collective enforcement and the illegitimacy of means of peaceful change. He then explores the implications that these problems have for the status of international law. He suggests that in light of the inaction of the collective enforcement provisions of the Charter, there may be a new norm emerging to fill the gap in the law. After describing this possible norm, Arend looks at the significance of the illegitimacy of means of peaceful change; he argues that there has been a continued dilution of the Article 2(4) prohibition against the unilateral use of force as states have sought to take up arms for reasons of "justice."

Following this somewhat stark analysis of the *jus ad bellum*—the law relating to the recourse to hostilities—Part One concludes with a more encouraging discussion of the *jus in bello*—the laws of war. In this essay Howard S. Levie examines the compliance of Argentina and Great Britain with the traditional norms regarding the conduct of hostilities. Levie, a noted specialist in the laws of war, reviews in detail the activities of the belligerents and concludes that compliance was very high. He discusses such important issues as the lawfulness of the maritime exclusion zone, the involvement of fishing vessels, the question of hospital ships, the use of incendiary weapons, the role of protecting powers, the treatment of civilians and prisoners of war, the involvement of mercenaries, and the issue of neutrals and neutrality. Levie concludes his essay by examining the larger implications of the crisis for the future status of the laws of war.

The study of the Falklands War continues with an examination in Part Two of "The Challenges to Diplomacy." Douglas

Kinney, who served as advisor on Latin American affairs to Ambassador Kirkpatrick at the United Nations during the war, introduces this section with a discussion of British–Argentine diplomacy. He provides an overview of the negotiations between Great Britain and Argentina from their beginnings in 1964 through the 1982 conflict. He examines the early diplomatic maneuvers at the United Nations and the seventeen years of bilateral negotiations. Then he turns to a detailed discussion of the mediation efforts by Alexander Haig, President Belaunde-Terry of Peru, and UN Secretary-General Javier Perez de Cuellar. He explains how these efforts were perceived by the parties and why, ultimately, they were unsuccessful.

After Kinney's *tour de force*, David C. Gompert, who was Deputy to the Under secretary of State for Political Affairs and was personally involved in the Haig mission, analyzes the American efforts to mediate the crisis. Based on his first-hand experience, Gompert's contribution describes how the conflict was viewed from the perspective of the Argentines, the British, and the Americans; he examines the frustrations of the Argentines, the British underestimation of the problem, and the conflicting foreign policy goals of the United States. Gompert continues by explaining how the United States sought a political solution to the conflict and examines some of the intricate tactical problems of the Haig mission. He concludes with an extensive examination of the lessons of the war for "national diplomacy and decision-making, international order, and organization."

Gompert's discussion is followed by a more detailed examination of the United Nations' involvement in an essay by international relations and organization theorist, Inis L. Claude, Jr., which explores the general lessons that the Falklands War teaches about the United Nations. He begins by asking why efforts at peaceful settlement failed and discusses some of the theoretical problems involved. He argues that the UN was used less as a "peace conference" than as a "battlefield" in which both sides attempted to gain legitimacy for their particular positions. Claude reviews why Argentina did rather poorly in this battle at the UN, despite previous indications to the contrary. He then discusses why the British initially fared well at the United Nations, but began to lose support once they landed on the islands. This vacillation, Claude concludes, reflects a general tendency of the UN to be committed to peace, but unwilling to act when peace is violated.

4

Moving from the universal to the regional organization, Srilal Perera, a lawyer and political scientist, discusses in detail the origins of the hemispheric system and formal arrangements for establishing Inter-American security and how they figured in the Falklands conflict. Perera begins with a discussion of early efforts at securing American solidarity in the nineteenth century and traces the adoption of legal instruments establishing regional organization in the mid-twentieth century. Perera also explores important provisions of the OAS charter that relate to the regulation of the use of force. He then discusses some historical inter- and intra-continental disputes that have caused division among Latin American states. Having set the historical stage, Perera continues his essay with an exploration of the response of the OAS to the Falklands War and an analysis of the legal problems involved. Perera concludes Part Two of this volume with a discussion of the implications of the Falklands War for the Inter-American system.

Part Three of this book, entitled "Looking into the Future: Strategic, Military, and Political Implications," examines the long-term as well as short-term effects of the Falklands War. In the first essay, Dov S. Zakheim, a military analyst, provides an in-depth exploration of the specific political and military lessons of the Falklands War. He begins at the broadest level by looking at what he terms the "politico-military implications." Here he explores the general strategic implications of the war, examining a number of questions: the problem of deterrence, the role of naval forces in crisis management, the ability to plan for unanticipated conflicts, the role of allies and access to supplies, the problem of arms sales, and the question of home-front support. Zakheim then turns to the more specific implications that the war had for military operations; he looks at the importance of naval surface forces, the amphibious mission, special operation forces, logistics, the conduct of land- and sea-based operations, and a number of other operational issues. Following this discussion, he examines the lessons that can be learned from the performance of particular weapons systems in the Falklands War. Zakheim concludes his essay with some observations about the most important implications of the war for military planners.

Following Zakheim, Christopher C. Joyner focuses on the effect of the Falklands War on another British–Argentine dispute—their conflicting claims to the continent of Antarctica. Joyner, an expert on Antarctica, examines the history of British and Argentine claims to the continent. He then explores the legal regime set up by the Antarctic Treaty of 1959 and the possible sources of rivalry between the two countries. He concludes his discussion by examining whether the current regime is serving the interests of both states and whether either might be tempted to use force to gain Antarctic resources.

Joyner's essay is followed by David A. Colson's discussion on the management of boundary disputes. Colson, an assistant legal advisor for the State Department, takes one of the underlying issues of the crisis, a boundary dispute, and demonstrates how in some instances such disputes have been controlled in the past and explains the role of interim measures in these situations. Colson begins by examining the importance of sovereignty disputes and shows how they have increased as coastal state jurisdiction has expanded. He then discusses three cases where arrangements were made to regulate a boundary dispute. Colson concludes his essay by examining the possible use of interim measures to obtain a *modus vivendi*, even though the actual dispute may take much time to be resolved.

This book draws to an end appropriately by returning to the question of the future of the Falklands themselves. Although a military solution temporarily settled the Falklands issue, the underlying sovereignty dispute has yet to be politically resolved. Monroe Leigh attempts to deal with this problem. Presupposing that UN, OAS, and bilateral methods continue to be unproductive, Leigh, former Legal Advisor to the State Department, suggests that the United States and Great Britain should establish a jointly administered trusteeship. Leigh recognizes the many difficulties that such a proposal would involve, but nevertheless demonstrates how it could be beneficial to the parties involved. He discusses the legal mechanics of such a proposal and, while recognizing that his suggestion is a bit unorthodox, cites examples where trusts have been administered jointly in the past.

In the final essay, Alberto R. Coll draws together many of the important lessons that the Falklands War can teach diplomats, military planners, and students of international law and politics. By reflecting on these lessons, those involved in future conflicts may be better equipped to help prevent or, at least, minimize the destructiveness of armed conflict, while broadening their understanding of the intricate and tragic tapestry of international relations. •

PART ONE

The Challenges
to International Law

2

Historical and Legal Background of the Falkland/Malvinas Dispute

ALFRED P. RUBIN

Argentina's seizure of the Falkland/Malvinas Islands and South Georgia Island[1] on 2 April 1982 caught the major centers of international scholarship by surprise. Only one major account of the competing claims to the Falkland/Malvinas Islands existed, and the almost desperate search of the libraries in New York and Washington for reliable information was the topic of amusing dinner-table conversations. The following study draws much of the historical evidence from that book, *The Struggle for the Falkland Islands*, written by Julius Goebel in 1927.[2] The historical material is supplemented by a legal analysis of the validity of British and Argentine claims to sovereignty.

Discovery: The Facts

The earliest recorded European contact with land that might have been the Falkland/Malvinas Islands appears to have been in 1501, when Amerigo Vespucci, an Italian geographer accompanying a Portuguese exploration, reported a sighting vaguely in the area. The location is doubtful, and the description unclear. Magellan, a Portuguese sea captain sailing under Spanish flag, sighted something in 1519 that might have been the Falkland/Malvinas group, but placed it 75 leagues (about 225 nautical miles) away, where there is nothing. In 1540, a voyage sponsored by the Spanish Bishop of Plasencia under the command of Francisco Camargo might have landed on the Falkland/Malvinas, but again the evidence is thin. The first English seaman who might have sighted the Falkland/Malvinas Islands was John Davis in 1592. The second was Sir Richard Hawkins in 1593. Neither of their descriptions matches the Falkland/Malvinas Islands and there seems to be no basis for giving them greater weight than the equivalent descriptions of Camargo.

The first unmistakable European sighting of the Falkland/Malvinas Islands was probably that of the Dutchman Sebald de Weert in 1600. In 1614 another Dutch expedition, under Le Maire and Schouten, sighted the same land, and the mapmakers' practice of calling the group the "Sebald Islands" began. The "Sebalds" were visited by the Englishmen William Dampier in 1684 and John Strong in 1690. It was Strong who renamed them the "Falkland" Islands after Viscount Anthony Falkland, a commissioner of Admiralty. Captain Woodes Rogers sighted them again in 1708 but did not land there. In the meantime, a Frenchman, Beauchesne Gouin, sailing from St. Malo, "discovered" the islands in 1701, and other French voyagers visited them in 1706, 1708 and 1711. They remained uncolonized.

Discovery: The Law

From 1400 to 1800 there is no clear evidence that any European state regarded mere discovery or sighting as sufficient to establish sovereignty over unclaimed land. Indeed, even temporary landings and the naming of rivers or other geographical features were not regarded as sufficient to exclude the legal claims of later explorers who did more. Instead, unpopulated land was brought into the European system of territorial jurisdiction by other legal means including symbolic acts, the establishment of a colony, or an agreement between contesting European states.

The Falkland/Malvinas might be construed to be within the zone allocated to Spain by the Papal Bull *Inter Caetera Divinae* of 4 May 1493. But the Bull itself did not purport to grant sovereignty to Spain against any adverse claim, only the right to conquer non-Christian princes and otherwise to acquire territory within the Spanish zone to the exclusion of equivalent

Portuguese rights. Moreover, the Bull was the outcome of an arbitration to which only Spain and Portugal were parties. England and France were not involved, and it would be a serious misunderstanding of the politics of the time to suppose that the Catholic monarchs of those two countries, which had not yet entered the competition for overseas empire, considered themselves bound, or were considered by anybody else to be bound, by the results of that arbitration. Indeed, Spain and Portugal themselves quickly relegated the secular aspects of the Bull to the background by concluding in 1494 the Treaty of Tordesillas, which moved the line drawn by the pope some 270 leagues westward. That treaty was not addressed formally by the papacy until twelve years later when Julius II, the successor to Alexander VI, purported to confirm it in what appears to have been an attempt to preserve in formal documents a secular power that had in fact already been rejected by Spain and Portugal. Even if the transaction of which the Bull was a part had been regarded as fixing rights in European law as of 1493, and the Spanish and Portuguese adjustments between themselves of those rights were regarded as wholly within the framework of papal authority, in the light of the massive shifts of sovereignty among European powers in the 500 years that followed 1493 in the area covered by arbitration, and the complete rejection of the Bull's authority by all the states concerned, it seems irrational to attempt now to base a claim of right under current concepts of international law on the Bull's eternal validity.

Until the mid-eighteenth century there appear to have been none of the symbolic acts regarding the Falkland/Malvinas Islands that have frequently signaled the incorporation of unoccupied territory into the European system. Instead, there were complex political maneuverings in Europe among the British, French, and Spanish authorities in which the general language of various attempts to resolve the colonial wars of the seventeenth and eighteenth centuries was interpreted differently by the interested parties. The only significant legal development in this period was the resurgence of *uti possidetis*. This was the practice of fixing a critical date and agreeing by treaty that the actual possessor of the disputed territory at that date had, as far as the parties to the treaty were concerned, absolute rights to it. *Uti possidetis* extinguished legal claims that no longer conformed to facts, even if such claims had some merit. The key transaction purporting to fix rights in the Falkland/Malvinas Islands during this period involved treaties between Spain and England in 1667 and 1670. But there seems to be no credible evidence that either power had actual possession of the islands before, during, or immediately after that time.

Effective occupation

While it can be argued that "effective control" or "occupation" was not necessary in addition to symbolic acts to bring un-populated territory[3] into the legal dominion of a European power under seventeenth- and eighteenth-century international law, it seems clear that in the absence of "symbolic" acts, the open and unopposed exercise of effective control was sufficient to vest sovereignty. Thus it is legally important to know the history of actual occupation.

The first known European settlement was French. A small settlement was made in April of 1764 by Antoine Louis de Bougainville. The settlers were from St. Malo in France. When Commodore John Byron surveyed the islands in 1765 for England, he appears not to have known of the French settle-ment, and not to have noticed it. Whether that is an indication of the insignificance of the settlement or the superficiality of Byron's survey is not clear. But in January 1766 a British colony was established out of sight of the French colony. A clash became likely between the imperial ambitions of the two powers in this desolate area. Apparently no serious thought was given to the possibility of dividing the small archipelago between the two claimants. Instead the French sold their settlement and rights to Spain. The transaction was complex, resulting in the transfer of administration to the Spanish authorities in Buenos Aires. (Since the settlers were from St. Malo, the French called the islands the "Malouines"; in due course the Spaniards called them the "Malvinas.")

Shortly thereafter a Spanish fleet dispatched from Montevideo in June 1770 removed forcefully the entire British settlement. In response, Great Britain threatened to go to war against Spain. Intricate diplomatic maneuverings between the two antagonists led to an agreement dated 22 January 1771 obligating Spain to restore the small British colony on the islands. The two powers openly agreed that this settlement was not an acknowledgment by Spain of the validity of any underlying British claim to sovereignty. In the exchange of diplomatic notes that concluded the agreement, Spain stated that its promise to restore the

British colony "cannot nor ought in any wise to affect the question of the prior right of sovereignty." The British, while not repeating that precise language in their formal response, accepted the promise to restore the colony and the apology for the injury to British honor. In their note, the British stated that the apology "together with the full performance of the said engagement [would be accepted] as a satisfaction for the injury done to the Crown." There was, however, no assertion of a British right to sovereignty over the Falklands.

There is some evidence suggesting that there was more to the agreement. After a review of what survives of the Spanish internal correspondence, and close examination of the events of the next five years (to 1774), it appears that there was an unrecorded British promise to repay the Spanish apology by dismantling the British settlement. If this is so, then the overt Spanish apology and replacement of the settlement would balance the Spanish delict in removing the settlement without British permission; the British "voluntary" removal of the settlement later would balance the publicity surrounding the Spanish apology, and leave the underlying conflict of claims to sovereignty unaffected by the entire transaction. In any case, the British did not immediately remove their settlement and Spain suspected Great Britain of reneging on the unrecorded commitment. Another crisis loomed. It was averted by the action of Great Britain in actually removing the colony on 20 May 1774, leaving in its place a marker recording the British claim to sovereignty.

The Spanish settlement, governed from Buenos Aires, survived two more generations. On the outbreak of the wars of independence in Latin America in 1806, it was abandoned by Spain. The colonists stayed on until 1811. There is no evidence that Spain or the colonists intended their withdrawal to be more significant legally than the British withdrawal of 1774. It seems likely that the failure to leave an equivalent statement of the claim behind was the result of the obvious assumptions of the time; by 1811 it cannot have been suspected by any colonists that a doubt existed any longer about the nature and extent of the Spanish possession regardless of theoretical British claims. There was no need to leave a marker behind because there was no doubt about the legal implications of the withdrawal—it was voluntary, prompted by internal affairs of Spain only, and not the result of any diplomatic bargaining.

By 1816 the colonists of Buenos Aires had established their independence of Spain in fact, if not yet beyond dispute by Spain.

North American adventurers of a seafaring disposition flocked to the standard of Latin American independence, including one Colonel Daniel Jewitt. He took a privateer's commission from the government of Buenos Aires and visited the Falkland/Malvinas Islands. He found around fifty vessels there, mostly American whalers and sealers, stopping for water and rest. He gave them notice of Buenos Aires' claim to sovereignty, but nobody seems to have paid much attention to him.

In 1823 the authorities in Buenos Aires formally appointed a government for the Falkland/Malvinas Islands and after several commissioners of Buenos Aires had been thwarted by weather and the vicissitudes of navigation in establishing a permanent colony there, one Louis Vernet was successful. Vernet seems to have been French by birth, but a resident of Hamburg in his youth.[4] He had resided some time in the United States, but was a national of Buenos Aires by 1828 and acted as such in all that followed. In January 1828 the government of Buenos Aires granted him land tenure and freedom from taxation with regard to his investments in the Falkland/Malvinas for twenty-three years. On 30 August 1829 Vernet was formally installed on the islands as Governor and Commandant of Military Forces for Buenos Aires. Meanwhile, in 1823 Spain had recognized the independence of its former colony and the government of Buenos Aires received diplomatic and consular representatives from many countries including the United States and Great Britain.

The incidents of 1831–3 are complex but can be quickly summarized. Vernet's authority was disputed by some American sailing vessel captains. He seized three American vessels, one of which escaped and made its way back to the United States. President Andrew Jackson did not suffer inhibitions of American activities gladly; he dispatched a naval vessel, the *Lexington*, to the Falkland/Malvinas. Vernet, having sailed to Buenos Aires on one of the arrested vessels to pursue admiralty proceedings against both, found himself instead charged by Captain Davison, the American commander answerable for the conduct of both, with "piracy" and the subject of furious complaint by U.S. Consul Slacum and the British diplomatic chargé d'affaires, Woodbine Parish. Around this time, in December 1831, the *Lexington* entered the Buenos Aires port in the Falkland/Malvinas under a false (French) flag and bodily removed Vernet's lieutenant, an Englishman named Matthew Brisbane, to Montevideo.

In February 1832 the Buenos Aires government refused to deal any longer with Slacum and he was replaced by Francis Baylies. Negotiations proved futile, and the government of Buenos Aires found itself incapable of restoring effective government to the Falkland/Malvinas in the face of American opposition. Finally, on 20 December 1832, two British warships arrived to discover that the new Buenos Aires governor, Don Juan Esteban Mestivier, had been murdered by the colonists. His deputy, Don Jose Maria Pinedo, was told to remove the Buenos Aires flag, which he refused to do. The British then landed a small force and replaced the Argentine flag with the British flag, which flew over the islands continuously until the Argentine expedition of 1982. In the course of a few years, Buenos Aires colonists were peacefully and gradually replaced by British colonists. Buenos Aires, and later Argentina, never ceased to protest openly and loudly against British occupation and administration of the Falkland/Malvinas.

The Law

The allegations of "piracy" against Vernet and Brisbane seem to have been totally baseless by any understanding of the law of the 1830s. The question was submitted in 1832 to the British Law Officers of the Crown when the question arose about British reactions to the American arrest of Matthew Brisbane. The Law Officers concluded that "the United States will not be justified in bringing Matthew Brisbane to trial for Piracy" because he was acting in execution of the orders of a regular and acknowledged government (of Buenos Aires) regardless of the dispute regarding sovereignty in the Falkland/Malvinas Islands.[5]

The Monroe Doctrine, under which the United States announced its opposition to further European colonization of the New World in 1823, is not a legal document binding on Argentina or Great Britain. To the degree British action in the Falkland/Malvinas Islands might seem to violate American policy, there is evidence that Francis Baylies had already advised the British minister in Buenos Aires that the United States would prefer British rule there to the continuance of the horde of "pirates" that threatened American shipping. It is clear that the United States did not in 1832 regard the Monroe Doctrine as any obstacle to British administration of the islands.

The major question as of 1833 was whether the British claim

had been abandoned in 1774; whether the British occupation of the islands was simply the assertion of its old claim on terms familiar to Argentina or was something new. The Spanish departure from the Falkland/Malvinas Islands in 1811 and the "American destruction of Vernet's settlement in 1831" left the islands *res nullius* according to a British writer.[6] That classification of the facts, imputing to Buenos Aires an intention to abandon the islands, seems almost capricious. Can it be seriously argued that the symbolic British plaque left in 1774 was sufficient to preserve a British claim to islands allegedly abandoned voluntarily, while active Argentine protest was not effective to preserve a claim to islands evacuated under the threat of force? Indeed, not only was the British plaque apparently destroyed in 1781, but no British protest over the continued Spanish colony between then and 1811 seems to have occurred. If anybody abandoned a claim, it was the British between 1774 and 1811, and again it was the British whose silence between 1823 and 1832 in the face of open Buenos Aires assertions of sovereignty might be construed to be an acquiescence in Argentine control. Argentine protests after 1833 make it absurd to speak of Argentine aquiescence in the new order of things brought about by the British Navy during a time of political unrest in Argentina and maintained in disregard of Argentine interests ever since.

Thus the tempting route, the application of the rule of the 1928 Isle of Palmas (Miangas) Arbitration to quiet title, is foreclosed. In that well-reasoned landmark award, the Swiss arbitrator, Max Huber, gave sovereignty to the Netherlands over a small island claimed by the United States as successor to Spanish possessions in the Philippines. After holding that both the Dutch and Spanish claims had been historically well-founded but insufficient to exclude the equivalent opposing claims (as the Spanish and English claims to the Falkland/Malvinas Islands seemed to be until 1766 or 1774, or until enough time passed after 1774 for the British claim to lapse by the implication of British acquiescence in the open Spanish administration), Huber argued that the silence of Spain and the United States over many years had vested title in the Netherlands; Spain and the United States had lost their adverse claim by extinctive prescription—the imputation of acquiescence by silence. None of this reasoning applies to the Falkland/Malvinas Islands after 1832 to extinguish the Argentine claim.[7]

A perusal of the other leading cases quieting territorial

disputes leads to the same uncertain conclusion. At the root of the award in the Clipperton Island Arbitration, for example, was the perception of the arbitrator, King Victor Emmanuel III of Italy, that Mexico, the losing claimant, had established no manifestation of sovereignty over the island prior to a French proclamation and visit of 1858.[8] France won the award. But in the case of the Falkland/Malvinas Islands, Spanish occupation had begun in 1766 with the purchase of French rights, and was more or less continued by Spain and Buenos Aires until 1832. Indeed, the Clipperton Island award supports the Argentine position that the hiatus of 1811–23 is legally irrelevant and does not return the Falkland/Malvinas Islands to the status of *res nullius*; the award notes that the French failure to exercise authority in Clipperton Island between 1858 and 1897, when both France and Mexico landed there, did not return the island to the legal situation of *territorium nullius* because France showed no intent to abandon its claim. Given the political and economic vicissitudes of France between 1858 and 1897, this is understandable; so is the equivalent Buenos Aires silence of 1811–23. The situation is distinguishable from the British loss after 1774, because Great Britain's intention to abandon its claim can be derived from its silence in the face of adverse Spanish continuous and peaceful administration. No such continuous and peaceful occupation of Clipperton Island occurred to deprive France of its rights. Thus, assuming the British plaque of 1774 and the French declaration of 1858 to have had equal legal effect, it was subsequent events and the applicability of the notion of extinctive prescription *vel non* that makes the difference. Similarly, the 1953 judgment of the International Court of Justice in the sovereignty dispute between England and France over unpopulated islands in the English Channel rested on considerations inapplicable to the Falklands.[9] The deciding factors in that case were the incorporation of the sovereignty of those islands into the pattern of European landholding in medieval times, and insufficient evidence of a continuous adverse claim to deprive the British of sovereignty derived from the feudal holdings of the ancient Dukedom of Normandy. In the Falkland/Malvinas case, the Spanish possession until 1811 and the Argentine possession until 1832 were notorious.

There are many other cases supporting the conclusion that the international law of territory offers little help in settling the Malvinas problem; it would be tedious to spell out all the analogies and differences among the existing cases. The overriding problem is that in the absence of a legal doctrine making adverse possession sufficient to vest title to territory even in the presence of protest and serious question about the validity of title in the possessor, there is no way for the law to resolve the dispute.

One may want to argue, as Sir Hersch Lauterpacht did fifty years ago, that there are no disputes the law cannot resolve.[10] Aside from various technical modifications of the Lauterpacht logic, however, there is the tendency of judicial and arbitral resolutions, in the absence of modifying instructions defining "equity," to convert a mere likelihood of having a better claim into a complete certainty, and a reasonable but inferior claim into a nullity.[11] Thus, with no one knowing how an arbitrator or properly seized court would weigh Argentine title lost by conquest and maintained only by the underlying threat of force to repel a counter-conquest, it is understandable that neither side is anxious for third-party settlement. Even if one party were convinced that his claim was likely to succeed with 80 percent certainty, he would have to be prepared to risk losing all; if one party were convinced that his likelihood of success before an impartial tribunal was only 20 percent, he would have to face the politically explosive risk of losing that 20 percent by submitting the case to an all-or-nothing judicial procedure.

The United Nations Charter envisages this predicament by not requiring judicial settlement or arbitration of disputes and by focusing instead on the impermissibility of the resort to force to resolve them. Article 2 (3) of the Charter says: "All members of the United Nations shall settle their international disputes by peaceful means in such a manner that international peace and security, and justice, are not endangered." This is the provision Argentina violated in 1982, forcing the United States and others to side with the United Kingdom in its attempt, backed by the United Nations Security Council, to recover administration over the Falkland/Malvinas.[12] Under this provision of positive law, the solution to unresolvable problems seems to be patience and the application of non-forcible pressures. On the other hand, the United Nations has in the past accepted the use of force with minimal fuss, and approved its results when the remnants of colonialism were involved, even in disregard of the will of the people most directly affected. The most egregious case was the Indian invasion of Goa after approximately 450 years of generally peaceful Portuguese sovereignty. There are ironies in applying that precedent to the Falkland/Malvinas situation. If the products of colonialism were to be regarded as illegitimate, all the boundaries of Latin America and the very existence of some states, including Argentina, would be legally doubtful.

One suggested solution is to apply the principles of self-determination. It is possible to argue that if Great Britain never had conquered the islands, but British settlers had become the overwhelmingly dominant element of the population, they might be entitled to self-determination as a political reflection of the need of the international legal order for a cultural and historical link between any identifiable group of people and its government. But this approach is irrelevant to the Falklands. There, the British removed the Argentine colonists and brought in their own settlers, in what amounted to a population transfer. It is legally questionable whether such forcible transfers can create the basis for sovereignty or for the exercise of the right to self-determination.[13]

One final implication might be noted. Since the Falkland/Malvinas Islands are to some degree dependent on Argentina for economic survival, and British investment in the islands is not beyond the reach of compensation, it should be possible to negotiate a compromise. The outlines of such a compromise are easy to draw, involving the transfer of sovereignty and military installations to Argentina on some of the lesser islands, and British administration and economic control on the islands which have already been partially developed by British enterprise. But without the willingness to negotiate, such outlines seem illusions. The problem is that each side must be convinced of the validity of the other's claim before it can have the political backing of its home constituencies to enter into meaningful negotiations. But the events of the 1980s have featured such an exaggerated national pride, to justify the sacrifices which the two governments' policies required their home constituencies to make, that an appreciation of the other's case seems a long way off. The situation is comparable in a sense to that of the Penobscot and Passamoquoddy Indians in the state of Maine, who had to win a series of lawsuits before the governor of the state could explain to the non-Indian electorate why it was necessary to settle the Indian claims; for their part, the Indians had to settle for much less than their court victories entitled them to have. The Indians feared that insistence on their legal rights would lead to legislation nullifying the court rulings. There is, however, no likelihood that any state in the international system would require its population to make the sacrifices of "rights" the Indians made to achieve a politically acceptable result. The failure to achieve such a solution leads, in turn, to heightened tensions, mounting economic burdens, and even, as demonstrated by the 1982 Falklands crisis, to the tragedy of war.

Notes: Chapter 2

1 South Georgia has its own history, and the basis for the Argentine claim to it appears to be merely succession to British administrative powers exercised from the Falkland/Malvinas. The steady Argentine rejection of the legal effect of that British administration as a basis for establishing rights even in the Falkland/Malvinas group itself would seem to justify rejection of the Argentine claims to South Georgia without further analysis.

2 J. Goebel, *The Struggle for the Falkland Islands* (New Haven, Conn.: Yale University Press, 1927).

3 "Unpopulated territory" was the term used by the Europeans to refer even to territory that was populated if the native population was not organized politically in a way acceptable to the Europeans. This normally, but not always, meant that the natives were organized militarily and able to resist European advances. In the Eastern Greenland case, Denmark v. Norway, PCIJ Ser. A/B, no. 53 (1933), for example, the Permanent Court of International Justice treated Greenland as "unpopulated" despite evidence of an Eskimo population capable from time to time of massacring the Viking settlements there. In the Falkland/Malvinas Islands there was no population to 1764 as far as is known.

4 Goebel, *The Struggle for the Falkland Islands*, p.435.

5 A. McNair, *Law Officers' Reports*, 1956, p. 268.

6 J.C.J. Medford, Introduction to 1982 ed. of Goebel, *The Struggle for the Falkland Islands*, p. xii.

7 See The Island of Palmas (Miangas) Arbitration 2 R. Int'l Arb. Awards, 1928, p. 829.

8 The Clipperton Island Arbitration, 2 R. Int'l Arb. Awards, 1931, p. 1107.

9 The Ecrehos and Minquiers Case (United Kingdom v. France), ICJ Reports, 1953, p. 47.

10 H. Lauterpacht, *The Function of Law in the International Community* (Oxford: Clarendon Press, 1933), pp. 100–4.

11 cf. Legal Status of Eastern Greenland (Denmark v. Norway), PCIJ Ser. A/B, no. 53 (1933).

12 Other Charter provisions, such as article 2 (4) and article 51, seem inapplicable to the degree that they presume sovereignty to have vested in the United Kingdom or Argentina. The Security Council did not specify which provisions of the Charter it relied upon in its call for Argentine withdrawal from the islands on 3 April 1982.

13 This issue has implications for the Middle East, where a significant portion of the Israeli population consists of Jews "encouraged" to migrate, and where large numbers of Palestinians left their ancestral homes in the territory now comprising the state of Israel. For an example of how the problem was handled historically, see the series of Advisory Opinions by the PCIJ in 1923; Ser. B, nos. 6, 7, and 8 dealing with ethnic Germans resident in

territory ceded to Poland by the Treaty of Versailles, and with the failure of a plebiscite to determine the boundary between Poland and Czechoslovakia; and Ser. B, no.10 delivered in 1925 concerning the exchange of Greek and Turkish populations under a 1923 treaty.

3

The Strategic Role of Legal Principles

THOMAS M. FRANCK

Since 1945, Britain has relinquished 5,200,000 square miles of colonial possessions with some 800 million inhabitants. Many of these ex-colonies like Malaya, Zambia, and Jamaica contain inestimable billions of dollars' worth of natural resources. Around the globe, from the Caribbean to Fiji, the thin, red line has by and large responded rather gracefully to the recessional, occasioning rarely a shot fired in anger. Then came the Argentine invasion of the Malvinas. To hold those barren, forlorn Falkland Islands, inhabited by a mere 1,800 agoraphiles, the British expended the lives of about 250 of their countrymen and killed nearly 1,000 Argentines. The cost of the operation to Britain has been put at 2·6 billion dollars, including the replacement cost of seven ships.

What is to be made of all this by the international lawyer concerned with world order? Was this a selfless, necessary defense of principles that are the pillars of civilized conduct among states? Or was it a declining world power's sclerotic delusion of Thermopylae? Are we to derive from the Falklands War the moral that principles do matter? Or only, as Samuel Johnson said after the 1770 Falklands War, that an exaggerated sense of patriotism "is the last refuge of scoundrels"?

These questions matter, because, on the one hand, small wars are becoming endemic in a world brittle as a tinder-bed. On the other, the erosion of principled conduct by states is equally alarming, since a decent concern for principle is the cohesive force in building a society. Without it, social interaction is purely random and social evolution directionless. The meaning of the

Falklands War thus affords an insight into the state of the international system.

Observing the unfolding of the Falklands crisis, in Britain and at the United Nations, this lawyer became convinced that principles of international law directly affected strategic outcomes and had a dramatic mobilizing effect on public opinion, particularly in Britain and Western Europe. Principled legal thinking by governments also had significant consequences at the United Nations. Ignoring strategic, geographic, ethnic, social, and economic factors, nations reacted to the crisis by asking "what precedential effect would an Argentine victory have on us?" In a rather dramatic fashion, political-strategic concerns were subordinated to considerations of principle; or, more precisely, principle became a dominant factor in the political-strategic equation. The Falklands crisis thus provides a case study of the potential role of international legal principles in the conduct of world politics. It also illustrates the dangers that arise when principles are neglected or applied selectively.

The importance of the principles at stake undoubtedly conditioned the speedy and unusually coherent policy of the European Community. Speaking on behalf of those nations, Mlle. Edmonde Dever, the Belgian Ambassador to the United Nations, captured that feeling early: "If the use of force were to be rewarded," she said, "this would encourage any state with territorial ambitions to follow suit. Peace in the world would become even more precarious and many countries, no matter what group they belonged to, would feel threatened. The reaction of many small countries in the world to the Argentine invasion demonstrates, furthermore, that this danger has been understood." This perception ensured the early passage, over the opposition only of Panama, of Security Council Resolution 502 calling on Argentine troops to withdraw from the islands. It also facilitated severe Western European economic and military sanctions against Argentina.

What happened at UN Headquarters in May and June—and what did not happen—illustrates the residual power of principles to shape policies and behavior of members of the international community. In the corridors of the General Assembly building, the junta found itself almost without support, except from a few states with interests and ambitions similar to Argentina's. It was clearly impossible for Argentina to summon up the Third World's automatic majority by convening the General Assembly, because there was no such majority in support of

Argentina's action. In speeches at the Security Council, there were *pro forma* invocations of colonialism's evils. But in the delegates' lounge even most Latin Americans distanced themselves from what they called the military "adventurists." Ambassador Munoz Ledo of Mexico—a country which has a better claim to Texas than Argentina has to the Falklands—stated publicly: "We reject the use of force to settle this or any other conflict." His Foreign Ministry condemned the invasion outright. The Bogota delegation was nicknamed "British Colombians" for their perceived posture. At home, public opinion was equally skeptical. Rio de Janeiro's leading newspaper, *Jornal do Brasil*, echoing the sentiments of its government, asked, "why must Argentina's neighbors adopt a continental position as a bloc when the Government of Argentina has demonstrated such little appreciation for what peace on this continent means to them?" (cited in the *New York Times*, 23 May 1982, p. 14).

This new deviation from Third World solidarity could not be explained solely in terms of the Argentine junta's global unpopularity, although this did play a part. Aside from the action of Venezuelan dock workers in refusing to unload Scotch whisky, the junta got very little tangible help, only some watered-down resolutions of the OAS and the Havana meeting of the non-aligned. Even these did not condone the use of force. This can only be understood in the context of states' concern for principles; not a theoretical but highly practical concern that reflects strategic planning and national self-interest.

The principles which moved so many nations during the Falklands crisis are both clear and basic to the system established by the UN Charter. Article 2(3) obliges members to "settle their international disputes by peaceful means" while 2(4) prohibits "the threat or use of force" against a state. These concepts are further embroidered in the landmark "Declaration on Principles of International Law Concerning Friendly Relations and Cooperation Among States" adopted by the General Assembly in 1970. It "solemnly proclaims" that every state "has the duty to refrain from the threat or use of force to violate the existing boundaries of another State or as a means of solving international disputes, including territorial disputes..." Argentina, of course, joined in supporting that Declaration, which also requires states to settle disputes by "negotiation, inquiry, mediation, conciliation, arbitration, judicial settlement, resort to regional agencies, or arrangements or other means of their choice" but never by resort to military force.

Another, more controversial, set of principles evoked by the Falklands crisis has to do with the disposition of the islands, which are a British colony. Under article 73 of the UN Charter, the colonial power is obliged to recognize that "the interests of the inhabitants of these territories are paramount" and to promote, within the UN system, "the well-being of the inhabitants" including the right "to develop self-government, to take due account of the political aspirations of the peoples, and to assist them in the progressive development of their free political institutions . . ." The Declaration on Friendly Relations also purports to give the people of each colony the right freely to choose the "establishment of a sovereign and independent State, the free association or integration with an independent State or the emergence into any political status freely determined by a people. . ." This is important because it makes clear that the decolonization of a territory need not lead to independence or merger with a neighboring state, but that self-determination can take the form of free association with the "mother country," the direction preferred by the Falkland inhabitants.

Diplomatic action at the UN in May and June showed that, for the most part, principles matter in two related senses. First, principles like article 2(4) are perceived to lay down the basic rules of the game. Most states, if they are not themselves parties to a current dispute, tend to "vote for the rules" because they perceive themselves to have a greater national interest in protecting those rules from erosion than in supporting either side. Of course, in many instances it is difficult to tell who violated the rules, which state "started" the crisis. But when that is clear, as it was in the Falklands invasion, then states tend to lean on the violator, as did Mexico, Colombia, Brazil and Chile, even while occasionally genuflecting to the cherished icons of hemispheric solidarity.

There is a second sense in which principles matter. Principles are, after all, the ephemeral strands of extrapolative logic linking one situation with others. Many at the UN with no direct stake in the disposition of the Falklands chose sides because a key issue—whether historic titles may be used to force changes in established national boundaries—reminded them of another situation in which they do have a strong interest. Of course, this works both ways. Venezuela supported Argentina, while Guyana strongly supported Britain, because the former has a claim based on historic title against the latter. Guatemala and Belize saw the issue as similar to their own boundary dispute.

Kenya, a large part of its territory still claimed by Somalia on the basis of historic title, was outspoken in Britain's cause. Addressing Argentina as "a violent member of the United Nations committing naked aggression against its neighbours," Ambassador Maina made it clear that

> whether or not the [Argentine] claims are valid ... they should not be settled at the expense of people who now live on the Falkland Islands. They are paramount, and in our view their interests are paramount. Whatever claims Argentina may have against the British based on history and the imperialism of the past may be settled without treating the people of the Falkland Islands like chattel in real estate ... If we bend the principle of decolonization of peoples to look like the redistribution of territories, this Organization is in real trouble. One has only to look at any map of one's choice to see why ... [A]ny attempt to redraw the maps of the world would lead this planet to endless war and destruction.

The lack of African support for Argentina is also understandable in another sense which illustrates the role of reciprocal principles in a slightly different fashion. As Ambassador Maina pointed out, Argentina, as recently as September 1981, at the meeting of non-aligned foreign ministers, had dissociated itself from a resolution calling for support to Southern African liberation movements insofar as this implied aid to armed struggle, on the stated ground that "resorting to force is incompatible with the Charter of the United Nations." Wryly, Mania asked: "what happened between September 1981 and April 1982 ... to transform Argentina ...?"

The direct connection made by governments between the events in the South Atlantic and matters close to their own national interest was apparent to anyone following the proceedings in the Security Council. Of the fifteen current Members of the Council, eleven are states on one side or another of problems very similar to that of the Falklands. France has a network of fragments of empire, many in the category of "departments d'outre mer," which wish to remain French. The deputy representing one of these overseas departments (St. Pierre et Miquelon in the Gulf of St. Lawrence) made a panicky prediction, in May, of an imminent Canadian invasion of his homeland. Guyana, equally nervous of an oil-rich neighbor which claims two-thirds of its territory, on 11 May notified the

UN that it had been the subject of a "threatening" incursion by Venezuelan soldiers. Both Jeremiads proved, at the least, premature. But they reflected the understandable fear that one event could lead to another, an operational view of principle. Even the United States has ties with Puerto Rico, and expects soon to establish a relationship with the distant Northern Marianas, comparable to that of Britain with the Falklands. "Historic title" forms the basis of claims by Ireland to Northern Ireland, Japan to the Southern Kurile islands currently in the Soviet Union's keep, Togo to British Togoland which was annexed to Ghana, Spain to Gibraltar, and China to those parts of British Hong Kong colony ceded by China in 1842 and 1860. As Panamanian Foreign Minister Jorge Illueca told the Security Council, the Gibraltar case is indistinguishable from the Falklands issue. "These colonial enclaves," he said, "have no justification; they are inadmissible, reprehensible, and stand condemned by the world conscience."

The Panamanian position, too, illustrated the role of a sort of principled thinking. As the voice of this world conscience, Panama, the only hispanic Latin American country then on the Security Council, provided most of the ardent, if eccentric, support for Argentina. Delegates were startled by the temper of Illueca's outbursts, which attributed Prime Minister Thatcher's intractability to "the glandular system of women" and called on the UN to deprive the British Ambassador, Sir Anthony Parsons, of the use of his knighthood since, in the world organization, "we do not have a monarchical system." The Panamanians privately admitted that what occasioned all this verbal excess was not the Malvinas so much as thoughts of the Panama Canal. Here, again, the power of principles, of extrapolative thinking, was at work. Illueca surprised delegates with the theory that the Falkland islanders deserved no right of self-determination because, he contended (wrongly), they are all "employees of a colonial company who are of the same nationality as the oppressor nation." The bigger game he was really stalking, however, was the Panama Canal company and its resident U.S. "zonians." This author asked one Panamanian representative whether he had considered that, if Argentina had succeeded in asserting its historic title, the government of Colombia might have revived its old claim to its isthmus province. "Oh, but they wouldn't," the Panamanian replied, somewhat uncertainly. But how could he be sure? Panama, after all, had been "stolen" from Colombia by the same two colonial powers, Britain and the United States, which, seventy years earlier, had relieved Buenos Aires of the Malvinas.

For most countries, not being the subject of claims based on historic title, the principles at stake in the Falklands were not quite so specifically relevant. Yet they were perceived as no less important. As British historian Hugh Trevor-Roper wrote to the *New York Times*, "if Argentina had kept its spoil today, the rule of law would have been replaced by that of force, and no undefended island would have been secure." Ambassador Jacobs of Antigua and Barbuda said, "as a small island State whose only defence against aggression by those larger and more powerful than ourselves is the Charter of the United Nations and the resolutions of the Security Council, we must deplore Argentina's illegal use of force ..." In a world where sixty-two states have populations of fewer than a million, and thirty-two have fewer than 200,000, Jacobs spoke for a significant constituency. Most of these vulnerable nations agreed with Shridath Ramphal, the Secretary-General of the Commonwealth, who said bluntly: "in making a firm and unambiguous response to Argentina's aggression, Britain is rendering a service to the international community as a whole ... Commonwealth countries, including in particular Commonwealth countries in Latin America, have stood full square behind Britain in this matter."

This was far from public posturing. Nations and territories felt themselves threatened by the ripple effect an Argentine victory would have had. Worried senior officials of the Netherlands Antilles rushed to New York in May to request UN technical assistance in constructing a status that would permit their constitutional link with the Netherlands to continue in peace. "We do not wish to follow Surinam's disastrous experience with premature independence," their spokesperson said. On the other hand, the Antilles did not want the link with Holland to provide an excuse for "liberation" from "colonialism" by a powerful Latin American neighbor. When it was suggested that the islands might escape the "colonial" label by constructing a relationship with the Netherlands which either could terminate on notice, one of the visitors replied, "Oh no. We cannot give the Netherlands the power to rid themselves of us so easily."

But what does all this activity prove about the utility of principles in the international system? Perhaps only that nations may still be moved, or manipulated, by appeals to principle. Reflecting Americans' traditional reserve towards such appeals, Ronald Steel pointed out (*New York Times*, 28 May 1982, p. 32) that what the Argentina junta tried to do in the Falklands follows quite logically from similar acts the international community has tolerated with a mere wink. The geopolitically pragmatic practice, he argued, long ago obliterated the principles. India's seizure of the Portuguese colony of Goa in 1961 was benevolently overlooked by the UN system. Although the Portuguese dictatorship made it impossible to demonstrate the political preference of the Goans, it is probable that the inhabitants of the enclave had no desire, after 450 years as part of Portugal, to be "liberated" by India. When the Goan invasion came to the notice of the Security Council, Ambassador Adlai Stevenson charged that India had violated the Charter principles. But nothing was done, except that U.S. Ambassadors to New Delhi are still instructed not to visit the area in order to avoid legitimizing its annexation. In a similar case, the United States and the UN actually helped to take the western half of the vast island of Papua New Guinea (West Irian) away from Holland and, without the consent of the inhabitants, handed it to Indonesia as a reward for its use of military force against the territory. During the transfer, the UN flag flew over the area for eight months. In 1963, after assuming control, Indonesia conducted a rigged "consultation," which a shamefaced international community accepted as *fait accompli.*

More recent examples are the Indonesian seizures of Portuguese East Timor and the Moroccan taking of the Spanish (Western) Sahara, both in 1975. In each instance, the preferences of the local inhabitants for independence were clearly evidenced and blatantly ignored. In Timor there was bitter resistance to the invaders, which was brutally suppressed. The General Assembly passed a toothless resolution. In the Western Sahara, a visiting UN fact-finding mission reported the overwhelming desire of the indigenous population for independence and the International Court of Justice in its advisory opinion on the legal status of that territory reiterated its assertion that "the subsequent development of international law in regard to non-self-governing territories, as enshrined in the Charter of the United Nations, made the principle of self-determination applicable to all of them." The "right of self-determination requires a free and genuine expression of the will of the people concerned." When all this was ignored by the invading Moroccan army, the General Assembly passed two contradictory resolutions, one recognizing the right of the Saharawis to independence and the other ratifying the *fait accompli.* Both times, the UN ineffectually criticized the usurping government but did nothing more concrete. The British government certainly did not identify with the Timorese, some 50,000 of whom died defending the same right Britain now claims for the Falkland Kelpers. As for the United States, it has made a short shadow-play of restricting military sales to Morocco and Indonesia, but has staunchly supported and supplied both aggressor regimes.

These are dramatic instances of national policy based not on principle but on pragmatic geopolitical strategy. In East Timor and the Western Sahara, the West supported its surrogates, the legions of General Suharto and King Hassan, without much thought for cost to the credibility and deterrent power of the principles at stake. Who could blame Galtieri's anger and confusion at being treated so differently from Suharto and Hassan?

The junta's confusion was further compounded by the unprincipled way in which the Third World previously had dealt with the Falklands issue in the General Assembly and in the councils of the non-aligned. In both settings, the Argentine claim has been essentially recognized since 1965 by resolutions which called for negotiations between Argentina and Britain to terminate the "colonial" presence. In 1973 the Assembly explicitly determined that "the way to put an end to this colonial situation is the peaceful solution of the conflict of sovereignty." This was tantamount to a call for Britain to negotiate the islands' transfer to Argentina, while somehow "bearing in mind" the interests of the inhabitants.

That line of resolutions on the Falklands, paralleling others on Gibraltar, while not sanctioning Argentina's use of force, did implicitly reject the inhabitants' claim to self-determination. It is the most egregious instance of abandonment by the Third World of the very principle to which its member states owe their existence. True, the population of Gibraltar (about 30,000) is small, and that of the Falklands is even smaller. The UN debates, however, show no attempt to make the distinction on that basis, if only because there are other Third World countries with comparably minute populations. Such a line would have been impossible to draw without intense internal squabbling within the Third World bloc. These resolutions did not, of course, invite Argentina to invade the Falklands. But they did encourage the junta to believe they had the Third World in their pocket, a costly mistake for which the Third World must take some responsibility. Why did the Third World for so long go along with such unprincipled principles in which most, as it turned out, did not really believe? A senior Indian diplomat explained it this way:

> We just don't take these resolutions very seriously. Before the non-aligned meet, various special interest resolutions are drafted within the regional sub-group concerned. The rest of us rarely get a look at the texts until a week or so before the vote. Anyway, we really don't care, since it's all cut and dried and doesn't affect us much. Among the Third World, each region goes along with every other region's agenda. We vote for theirs so they'll vote for ours. That's how we manage to stay a group.

If the Africans and Asians didn't take the Argentine resolution on the Falklands very seriously, neither did the British. When a First World country feels strongly about one of the items and applies bilateral pressure, as the United States has done when resolutions about Puerto Rico have been under consideration, the proposed resolutions are taken more seriously and their implications are considered more carefully. But the British, a Third World ambassador said, "never lobbied us about the Falklands or Gibraltar resolutions when they were before the General Assembly. They seemed to feel they were just a lot of hot air. And we rather felt the same." Unfortunately, the Argentines took them at face value, as a hunting license.

From all this, one might conclude that the principles for which Britain purported to fight in the South Atlantic are bunk, to be trotted out when convenient, then forgotten when not. Every law student knows that for every principle there is a countervailing one. International law is an illusion created by lawyers to gull the naive into serving somebody else's self-interest. Always, in international affairs, ahead of principle comes praxis, which is highly selective, pragmatic, strategic, and indifferent to rules. Well, as T. S. Eliot would say, that is a way of putting it. But let us try another. The Falklands crisis points to a social phenomenon: principles evidently can rally both people and nations, even overcoming countervailing, more conventional, perceptions of self-interest and alliance-politics. This rallying has strategic consequences. There is no doubt that Argentina's diplomatic isolation sapped its will to fight, as well as its ability to secure weapons, replacement parts, and credits.

Besides their capacity to *rally*, principles have another

strategic capability. They can *deter*. Principles which are regularly implemented over a long period of time tend to make certain conduct "unthinkable." The idea that something "just isn't done" is both descriptive and proscriptive. However, once the principle is violated with impunity—the previously unthinkable seizure of an embassy in Teheran, for example—it loses part of its credibility and thus its capacity to deter. It is no longer unthinkable. Restoring its unthinkability is rather like putting toothpaste back in a tube. A government which sees others successfully ignore principles will not give them much weight when calculating its own strategic self-interest. After Goa, West Irian, East Timor, the Western Sahara, Afghanistan, Cambodia, the Iran–Iraq and Mid-East wars, and after the General Assembly's resolutions on the Falklands and Gibraltar, it is hardly surprising that Buenos Aires believed it could invade the Falklands without stirring up a hornet's nest. The principles for which Britain fought in the Falklands had lost their capacity to deter violators, even if they still retained a lingering ability to rally defenders. Unfortunately, a principle with just enough life to rally defenders but not enough to deter violators is not simply another compromise. It is a particular danger to world stability, leading to unpredictability and potentially lethal miscalculations.

The sad truth is that the international community has not very ardently tended even its most basic principles. Yet social scientists tell us that rule-building is a universal social imperative, that a sense of shared, generally obeyed principles gives definition to a society, distinguishing it from a random rabble. The international system does, indeed, maintain many of the trappings of a society: a fixed population (of States), repetitious patterns of interactions, an agreed system of communications, and elaborate, if politically rudimentary, institutions. Yet when it comes to principles, the states in the system remain careless about going consistently to their defense.

Tending principles only once in a while is probably worse then abandoning them altogether. Yet that is precisely what happened in the Falklands. The British military action in the Falkland Islands—costly, prolonged, perhaps Quixotic—was senseless in cost–benefit terms if it was fought merely to reclaim real estate. It is equally indefensible in Benthamite terms, for the relative happiness of the 1800 islanders was purchased by the greater unhappiness of an equal or larger number of battle casualties. The campaign can be justified only as a reinforcement of basic principles crucial to peace. These are surely worth fighting for, if states are thereby persuaded to adhere to them. But a principle asserted occasionally may not be worth defending if only because it is already incapacitated, having lost its power to deter.

In his June 1982 address to the British Parliament, President Reagan emphasized that armed aggression must not be allowed to succeed and that people must participate in the decisions of government under the rule of law. "If there had been firmer support for that principle some 45 years ago," he added, "perhaps our generation wouldn't have suffered the bloodletting of World War II." But so, too, the Argentine invasion of the Falklands and resultant bloodshed would probably have been unthinkable if the international community had defended those principles more vigorously in inconvenient settings like the Middle East, Afghanistan, East Timor, and the Western Sahara. One must assume, perhaps naively, that Britain and all those who supported her at the UN have made a bond in blood which commits them, not to the Kelpers, but to uphold in the future, regardless of pragmatic strategic and geopolitical considerations, the important rules of civilized conduct for which the Falklands War was fought.

Note on Sources: Chapter 3

This essay is primarily based upon the provisional records of meetings of the UN Security Council on the Falklands case from 1 April through 3 June 1982 (pertinent numbers in the series, S/PV. 2345–72). A survey of the *New York Times* for the same period also provided important information.

4

Philosophical and Legal Dimensions of the Use of Force in the Falklands War

ALBERTO R. COLL

I

The great Cambridge historian and student of international relations, Sir Herbert Butterfield, was fond of remarking that most wars throughout history have not been contests between right and wrong, but clashes "between one half-right that was too willful and another half-right that was too proud." Of all the military conflicts since the Second World War, the Falklands War is surely among those to which this Butterfieldian observation is most appropriate. It is difficult to ascribe moral and political responsibility to one side without perceiving also the other party's acts and omissions that contributed to the final military showdown. Both adversaries showed ample reserves of obduracy, pride, nearsightedness, and political willfulness in their relations with one another before and during the war. In spite of these realities which can be found underlying almost all international conflicts—realities which Butterfield categorized under the term of "man's universal sin"—international law during the last seventy years has sought to develop a set of normative standards for curbing the use of force by states.[1]

The animating spirit behind this legal enterprise is seemingly at odds with the Butterfieldian emphasis on the universality of the lust for power and the consequent falsity of making absolute rather than relative judgments on a state's resort to violence. Since the early days of World War I down to the present, international legal scholars, unlike Butterfield, have sought to differentiate aggressors from non-aggressors, states which have breached the peace and set in motion the deadly chain of armed violence from states that, regardless of their other sins, have not committed the ultimate one of resorting to force.

In many ways this differentiation, and the attitudes underlying it, are similar to the efforts of domestic legal systems to define certain acts as crimes which the law will not tolerate and for which it will hold responsible those agents who commit them. Theological and philosophical reflections on the fallen nature of man or the corrupting effects of society on the individual play a very limited role in restricting the ascription of criminal responsibility in most legal orders. With some narrow exceptions such as the venerated McNaghten rule (or "insanity defense"), the kinds of considerations discussed above play a role mostly by redefining the criminal offense to a slightly lower degree (as with "crimes of passion") or as mitigating circumstances suggesting a lighter sentence, but never as justifications for denying the burden of criminal responsibility to the individual who committed the forbidden action.

This refusal of the law to capitulate before the pressures of relativism generated by thoughtful philosophic accounts of the human condition has found support within the Western philosophic tradition itself. Aristotle, whose reflections on equity and prudence in Books V and VI of the *Nicomachean Ethics* correspond with Butterfield's way of thinking, found it necessary for society to have laws and institutions that would punish the agents of particular acts and define these acts with as much precision as possible. The role of equity was to soften the impact of normative standards and adapt them to different conditions, but not to dissolve the standards in a sea of skeptical relativism. St. Augustine, who viewed all political reality *sub specie aeternitatis*, argued that the City of Man needed to define and enforce legal standards of order, even though such standards were admittedly relative and ambiguous by comparison with divine justice and truth. And Fyodor Dostoevsky, who in *The Brothers Karamazov* had Father Zossima exclaim that each of us is responsible in some way for everyone else's sins—a profound insight when applied at certain levels of human relations— throughout his novels also derided much of the intelligentsia of his day for its softness towards criminals and its general inability to draw moral and legal distinctions in its analysis of social problems.

35

Similarly, international law seeks to elaborate norms for the control of armed violence among states. The norms, and the situations to which they apply, are continuously defined with as much precision as possible, even though such precision is extremely difficult and often unattainable. Considerations of equity, prudence, political forgiveness, generosity, and magnanimity are taken into account as the rules are elaborated through the work of diplomacy, that indispensable partner of international law in preventing and settling disputes. But the rules attempt to set certain minimum standards, and offer fairly specific guidelines for the ascription to states of legal responsibility for the outbreak of violence.

II

International law has not always pursued such an ambitious task. During the eighteenth and nineteenth centuries the prevalent view, as stated by William Edward Hall in his *Treatise on International Law*, was that

> However able law might be to declare one or two combatants to have committed a wrong, it would be idle for it to affect to impart the character of a penalty to war, when it is powerless to enforce its decisions ... International law has consequently no alternative but to accept war, independently of the justice of its origin, as a relation which the parties to it may set up if they choose, and to busy itself only in regulating the effects of the relation. Hence both parties to every war are regarded as being in an identical legal position, and consequently as possessed of equal rights.[2]

World War I had a searing effect on the West's consciousness, leading to a reexamination of traditional assumptions about the permissibility of war, and the demand that international law impose far more stringent standards on the resort to force. This change seemed required by three major developments whose pace had accelerated in the opening decades of the twentieth century. First, as historians and sociologists such as Gordon Craig and Raymond Aron have noted, there was a terrifying increase in the destructive capabilities of military weaponry and technology, coupled with a resurgence of the ancient notion that wars were supposed to be total, involving the whole of a nation's capacities in a win-or-die struggle. Second, there was greater economic interdependence among states than ever before, as well as greater complexity and fragility of economic and industrial infrastructures within societies, on which depended the survival and well-being of entire populations. Third, the trend begun during the previous century towards faster population growth and higher urban density proceeded even more quickly. All these seemed to imply that modern civilization was a highly delicate and vulnerable set of arrangements that no longer could tolerate the use of force as allowed by the earlier international law.

It was out of this new awareness that a different view emerged. The Covenant of the League of Nations (1919) restricted a state's freedom to use force by requiring that disputes be first submitted to peaceful methods of settlement, and that a "cooling-off" period of three months be allowed to elapse. Only after these conditions had been met was a state legally permitted to resort to force. None of these restrictions, of course, applied to the use of force in self-defense, in response to a previous act of violence committed against the state.

The new trend marked by the League Covenant was continued by the Kellogg-Briand Pact of 1928, in which the signatories (including the Great Powers at that time: France, Germany, Italy, the United States, Great Britain, and Japan) "condemn[ed] recourse to war for the solution of international controversies, and renounce[d] it as an instrument of national policy in their relations with one another." Since the treaty was concluded outside the League of Nations and is fully consistent with the UN Charter, it theoretically retains its full force today. Although Argentina did not sign it, it represented a growing consensus in the international community on the direction in which international relations should be moving, even though the practice of most of the signatories continued to be at variance with their solemn declaration.

In the Western hemisphere the closest parallel to the Kellogg-Briand Pact was the Inter-American Treaty of 10 October 1933, also known as the Saavedra-Lamas Treaty because of the prominent role played in its proceedings by the Argentine Foreign Minister. Article I states that "the high contracting parties solemnly declare that they condemn wars of aggression in their mutual relations or in those with other states, and that the settlement of disputes or controversies of any kind that may arise among them shall be effected only by the pacific means which have the sanction of international law." The language of this article seemed to limit the obligation to settle disputes peacefully to those controversies arising among the "high contracting parties"; thus, the treaty was not as inclusive as the Kellogg-Briand Pact. Nevertheless, it indicated a significant trend within the Inter-American system to restrict the use of force.

Drafted in view of the bitter experience of World War II, the United Nations Charter (1945) took an even stronger position than that of the League Covenant on the issue of force. In the twenty-six years from 1919 to 1945 the vulnerability of modern civilization had increased considerably; the reasons for the unacceptability of the use of force seemed more compelling than ever. So the Charter took an absolutist position; except for self-defense, the use of force was prohibited as a means of effecting change in international relations.

The Charter's preamble indicates that one of the ends for which the United Nations was established was "to ensure, by the acceptance of principles and institution of methods, that armed force shall not be used, save in the common interest." Article 2 states:

3. All Members shall settle their international disputes by peaceful means in such a manner that international peace and security, and justice, are not endangered.
4. All Members shall refrain in their international relations from the threat or use of force against the territorial integrity or political independence of any state, or in any other manner inconsistent with the purposes of the United Nations.

Even more directly relevant to the Falklands crisis is article 33, which in the first paragraph says that "the parties to any dispute, the continuance of which is likely to endanger the maintenance of international peace and security, shall, first of all, seek a solution by negotiation, inquiry, mediation, conciliation, arbitration, judicial settlement, resort to regional agencies or arrangements, or other peaceful means of their own choice." These provisions are to be read in conjunction with article 37, which specifies that "should the parties to a dispute of the nature referred to in Article 33 fail to settle it by the means indicated in that article, they shall refer it to the Security Council."

The UN Charter's position on the use of force was reflected in the constitutive documents of the Inter-American system adopted shortly after the Charter. The Inter-American Treaty of

Reciprocal Assistance (Rio Treaty) of 1947 stated in its first article: "The High Contracting Parties formally condemn war and pledge themselves in the conduct of their foreign relations not to have recourse to the threat or use of force in any form incompatible with the provisions of the United Nations Charter or of this treaty." Similarly, the OAS Charter (1948) stipulated in article 21 that "the American states pledge themselves in their foreign relations not to use force, except in the case of legitimate self-defense in accordance with treaties in force, and in obedience to such treaties."

III

In the light of these norms of international law, Argentina's forceful seizure of the Falklands on 2 April 1982 was illegal. In response to the specific charge of violation of the legal rules concerning the use of force in international relations, Argentina has made three general arguments. First, British control of the Falklands represented a continuing act of aggression against Argentina and its territorial integrity. Second, Argentina searched for and exhausted peaceful methods of settlement, as recommended by article 33, prior to using force. Third, in signing the UN Charter, Argentina supposedly made reservations concerning the Malvinas, indicating its refusal to accept the legality of the British presence and leaving to itself the freedom to choose in the future whatever means it considered appropriate to enforce its claims.

These legal arguments are difficult to accept. First, there is the 150-year-long peaceful occupation of the Falklands by the British, which does not pose, and has not posed, any threat to Argentina's security. The extent to which the British presence is a threat to Argentina's territorial integrity depends on whether the islands are Argentine territory. The Argentine claim to ownership rests, first, on the argument that by 1833 the islands (regardless of their status during the eighteenth century) were Argentine territory and the forceful British occupation carried out that year cannot be the basis of any legal rights. Second, the islands are part of the South American continental shelf, and since Argentina is the South American nation closest to the islands, they are part of its territory.[3]

This second argument, known as the rule of contiguity, is weak. Not only are the Falklands hardly contiguous, being more than 500 km from the Argentine mainland, but also contiguity is not sufficient to establish territorial sovereignty. As was stated in the well-known Islands of Palmas arbitration of 1928:

> Although states have in certain circumstances maintained that islands relatively close to their shores belonged to them in virtue of their geographical situation, it is impossible to show the existence of a rule of positive international law to the effect that islands situated outside territorial waters should belong to a state from the mere fact that its territory forms the terra firma ... contiguity, understood as a basis of territorial sovereignty, has no foundation in international law.

The first argument supporting Argentina's claim that the Falklands are part of its territory is more plausible, but still highly problematic. Since 1945, when the United Nations Charter placed stringent prohibitions on the use of force, the taking of territory by methods such as those used by the British in 1833 can be considered illegal. Whether the international law of the early nineteenth century took this same position is highly doubtful. Moreover, even if the taking had been initially illegal, a century and a half of continuous, peaceful, unmolested occupation would have given rise to British rights of possession. This is what the international legal doctrine of prescription suggests.[4] According to Hall, for example:

> Title by prescription arises out of a long continued possession, where no original source of proprietary right can be shown to exist, or where possession in the first instance being wrongful, the legitimate proprietor has neglected to assert his right, or has been unable to do so ... The object of prescription as between states is mainly to assist in creating stability of international order which is of more practical advantage than the bare possibility of an ultimate victory of right ... prescription must be understood ... to give title where an immoral act of appropriation, such as that of the Partition of Poland, has been effected, so soon as it has become evident by lapse of time that the appropriation promises to be permanent, in the qualified sense which the word permanent can bear in international matters, and that other states acquiesce in the prospect of such permanence.[5]

In *The Law of Nations*, J. L. Brierly has observed that "many territorial titles and many frontiers are accepted by international law today simply because they have existed *de facto* for a long time; they exemplify the maxim *e facto oritur jus*, which is at the root of prescription in all systems of law."[6] In the development of international law the doctrine of prescription has received the support of other distinguished theorists. Arguing against Vazquez's theory that prescription was inapplicable in international law, Grotius wrote: "Yet, if we admit this, there seems to follow this most unfortunate conclusion, that controversies concerning kingdoms and the boundaries of kingdoms, are never extinguished by any lapse of time; which not only tends to disturb the minds of many and perpetuate wars, but is also repugnant to the common sense of mankind."[7] Vattel, Burke, Phillimore, and Wheaton took a similar position in support of prescription.[8]

Since Argentina's title to the Falklands is not beyond dispute, its assertion that the British presence constituted aggression against its territorial integrity and required Argentina to use force in self-defense is difficult to sustain. One, therefore, has to turn to the second major justification of Argentina's recourse to violence, the claim that Argentina complied with article 33 of the UN Charter and sought a solution to the Malvinas dispute by peaceful means. There are several problems with this claim. The Charter does not say that a party can use force after it has made a good faith effort to settle the dispute by peaceful methods. On the contrary, the obligation to refrain from violence remains absolute, even if the parties have sought and exhausted all forms of peaceful settlement. The fact that the drafters of the UN Charter felt constrained to insert article 51 on self-defense indicates that all other uses of force were understood to be outlawed unless undertaken with UN authorization.

Argentina engaged in negotiations with Great Britain over the islands from 1965 to 1982. The Argentine government, especially since 1982, has described these as barren and futile. This, of course, begs the question. If the islands are assumed to be Argentine, then the British conduct during the negotiations is best described as obdurate and standing in the way of a rightful claimant. If, on the other hand, the underlying assumption is that the legality of both parties' claims is less than firmly established, then the negotiations' slow pace is seen as natural and understandable. In fact, from 1965 to 1982 considerable progress was made in creating many functional links between the Argentine mainland and the islands; travel, communications, and economic contacts increased enormously.[9] While the issue of sovereignty remained intractable, major steps were taken which in the course of time might have led to an equivalent of those "functional solutions" to territorial disputes discussed by David Colson in this book. Far from having run their full course, the negotiations presented many possibilities for a future accommodation, and indeed as late as February of 1982 important negotiations took place in New York.

Argentina did not avail itself of another peaceful method of dispute settlement suggested by the UN Charter: arbitration or recourse to the International Court of Justice. It is not enough to say, as some critics have said, that arbitration and judicial settlement are improper means for resolving disputes such as this one because these legal procedures produce winners and losers instead of balanced compromises. If Argentina's legal rights to the Falklands are as strong as the claims, there would be little to fear from an arbitral or judicial decision. Interestingly, it was Great Britain that offered to submit to the International Court of Justice in 1947 its dispute with Argentina over the Falkland Islands Dependencies (South Georgia and the South Sandwich Islands). Although these are legally distinct from the Falklands themselves, and the claims of both parties to them rest on different grounds than their claims to the Falklands, an ICJ decision on the Dependencies would have required some determination of the status of the Falkland Islands themselves. Perhaps for this reason, or out of political pride, Argentina turned down the British proposal. In 1955, concerned over alleged Argentine encroachments on British sovereignty in the Dependencies, Great Britain applied unilaterally to the ICJ for redress. Argentina, however, declined to submit to the Court's jurisdiction.

Even if Argentina had made full use of some of the peaceful methods outlined in article 33, she was obligated, once it was obvious that an impasse had been reached, to submit the dispute to the UN Security Council, something she did not do. As article 37 states: "Should the parties to a dispute of the nature referred to in Article 33 fail to settle it by the means indicated in that Article, they shall refer it to the Security Council." This article serves to underline the gravity of Argentina's refusal to accept adjudication by the ICJ because its provisions have to be read in the context of the preceding article 36, dealing with the Security Council's role in promoting the pacific settlement of disputes. According to article 36, "in making recommendations under this Article the Security Council should also take into consideration that legal disputes should as a general rule be referred by the parties to the International Court of Justice in accordance with the provisions of the Statute of the Court."

The third major justification offered by Argentina for its recourse to violence is that it made certain reservations with regards to the Malvinas when she adhered to the UN Charter. A perusal of the documents, however, reveals no such reservations. Moreover, had Argentina attempted to make any reservations it is likely that most of the other signatory states would have rejected them, and thus, under no accepted principle of international law would the reservations have been legally valid. It appears that what the Argentine government loosely calls its reservations to the Charter concerning the Malvinas were no more than unilateral statements, made at the time of Argentina's signing of the Charter and addressed primarily to domestic public opinion, which have no legal effects on Argentina's obligations under the Charter.

The key obstacle to all of Argentina's justifications is the absolute character of the Charter's prohibition on the use of force as an instrument of change in international relations. To interpret this Charter norm differently is not only wrong from the standpoint of legal hermeneutics, but also could be politically dangerous. Excluding the Falklands, there are some fifteen active island disputes in the world today, including that between Chile and Argentina over the Beagle Channel islands. There are also eighteen active land boundary disputes, including such dangerous ones as those between the USSR and China, India and China, and Iran and Iraq.[10] There are also, as David Colson has pointed out, over 287 maritime boundary disputes, of which forty-nine are active. In Central and South America alone, as indicated by Srilal Perera in his study of the OAS, numerous territorial and maritime boundary disputes have been the cause of open warfare among states in the past, and could be so again in the future. Finally, in many trouble spots around the world a semblance of peace is tenuously maintained through the acknowledgment of *de facto* boundaries and ceasefire lines that have little *de jure* justification. This is true in much of the Middle East, in Korea, and was true in Europe until West Germany's recognition of the Oder-Neisse frontier with Poland in 1971 and the East–West Helsinki Accords of 1975 that formalized the post-World War II political and territorial arrangements. To admit the permissibility of force in adjusting territorial claims is to introduce a principle of chaos and unlimited destructiveness in an already highly unstable world.

Less needs to be said about Great Britain's use of force which, regardless of whatever moral responsibility (in the Butterfieldian, existential sense of the term) the British may bear for the 1982 war, was allowed by article 51 of the UN Charter:

> Nothing in the present Charter shall impair the inherent right of individual or collective self-defense if an armed attack occurs against a Member of the United Nations, until the Security Council has taken measures necessary to maintain international peace and security. Measures taken by Members in the exercise of this right of self-defense shall be immediately reported to the Security Council and shall not in any way affect the authority and responsibility of the Security Council under the present Charter to take at any time such action as it deems necessary in order to maintain or restore international peace and security.

An interesting legal question is the effect which UN Security Council Resolution 502 had on the inherent right of Great Britain to self-defense. The Resolution, approved on 3 April, noted that two days earlier the President of the Security Council had requested the British and Argentine governments "to refrain from the use or threat of force in the region of the Falkland Islands." It then demanded "an immediate cessation of hostilities ... immediate withdrawal of all Argentine forces from the Falklands Islands," and called on the parties "to seek a diplomatic solution to their differences and to respect fully the purposes and principles of the Charter of the United Nations." The resolution was obligatory, for it was drafted and approved pursuant to article 40, which states:

> In order to prevent an aggravation of the situation, the Security Council may, before making the recommendations or deciding upon the measures provided for in article 39, call upon the parties concerned to comply with such provisional measures as it deems necessary or desirable. Such provisional measures shall be without prejudice to the rights, claims, or position of the parties concerned. The Security Council shall duly take account of failure to comply with such provisional measures.

It would be improper to say that in its use of force, Great Britain was carrying out the provisions of Resolution 502, as if the Security Council had empowered or authorized the British government to carry out enforcement measures on its behalf, which, of course, was not true. What can be said, however, is that, owing to Argentine noncompliance with its terms, Resolution 502 proved ineffectual. To use the analysis suggested by article 51, this was a case in which the Security Council tried but failed to take the "measures necessary to maintain international peace and security." Therefore, Great Britain's inherent right to self-defense was not preempted by any UN actions, and continued to operate in its full scope as long as the Security Council's measures were frustrated by Argentina. Thus, while Great Britain did not act as an agent of the UN, its use of force was legal, resting on a right to self-defense which, as article 51 indicates, antedates the Charter, rests on juridical foundations independent of the Charter, and is sanctioned by the Charter.

Two other legal issues related to the British use of force are, first, the level of violence required to trigger the self-defense provisions of article 51, and second, the level of violence that this article permits an offended state to use in its response to aggression. Although both issues can be highly problematic under many circumstances, they were not so in the Falklands crisis. A full-fledged armed invasion of a territory which has been administered, occupied, and inhabited in its entirety by nationals of a power for 150 years suffices to justify that power's exercise of its right to self-defense.

The second issue can be very difficult, and involves the connection between *ius ad bellum* and *ius in bello*. The extent of one's defensive measures must be proportional to the degree of aggression suffered. Classical just war theorists such as Vitoria and Grotius, for example, insisted that no matter how justified the use of force was, it had to be guided by the principles of proportionate objectives and proportionate means. The legality of one's cause could be tarnished or vitiated if the war's objectives and means were grossly disproportionate to the injury initially suffered. Thus proportionality linked the *ius ad bellum* and *ius in bello*. The same link is acknowledged today by most students of the problem of international violence. Argentina's taking of the Malvinas, for instance, would not have justified massive British bombings of the Argentine mainland (unless, of course, such bombings had been absolutely essential to recovering the islands). As Howard Levie has shown in this book, the British use of force was generally proportional to the degree of aggression initially carried out by Argentina. This proportionality is doubly important in the light of the legal norm outlined by Anthony Arend regarding states' obligation to persue peaceful methods of settlement even during the course of hostilities. Any disproportionate use of force beyond the requirements of self-defense is likely to embitter relations between the adversaries to the point where the reasonableness and moderation required for the functioning of this norm disappear.

IV

To describe the preceding analysis as excessively legalistic and out of touch with the political realities represented by Argentina's burning desire for the Malvinas is to lose sight of larger questions at stake, questions which a realistic understanding of international politics cannot ignore. One such question has to do with the ancient problem of the use of force in international relations, and the degree to which international law should help to regulate and limit recourse to violence. Legal norms are powerless in themselves to transform radically the practice of states. Yet they can exert a subtle, leavening influence on conceptions of international morality, and through these shape notions of prudence within societies and even the conduct of foreign policy itself. Whether or not a legal norm is respected and upheld is, therefore, as Thomas Franck has argued, a question of political and strategic significance.

The Charter's absolute prohibition of force except in strict self-defense is a norm conducive to the establishment and preservation of a reasonably moderate and orderly international system. The value of this norm has been made more imperative than ever by the gradual emergence over the last two decades of a multipolar world in which regional actors have increased in number and grown in independence and power. The ordering influence of the United Nations has decreased considerably during this period as has also that of the Great Powers. As the decade of the 1980s progresses, Hedley Bull's Anarchical Society is becoming more fragmented and chaotic. A general weakening of the principle of the impermissibility of force can only accelerate the dynamism of this trend. Thomas Franck has pointed to several attempts in Latin America and elsewhere to revise frontiers by force in the wake of Argentina's seizure of the Falklands.

Another major question to be considered is that of justice. The criticism is often made that the kind of legal reasoning developed in this essay is best suited to serve the interests of the strong in international relations, at the expense of the weak. Of course, one can argue much more convincingly that in a world where the first use of force is permitted along the lines advocated by Argentina, it is the strong, not the weak, who will profit most over the long run.

Ultimately, however, a legal analysis of the use of force during the Falklands crisis cannot avoid raising a question that is profoundly disturbing to many international legal theorists. To what extent is the Charter's norm true international law, and to what extent is it a moral aspiration clothed in juridical robes? As even the most faithful supporters of the rule of law in international relations will admit, law requires authority as well as control. Without authority, law is tyranny. Without control, it is a fiction which, like the Holy Roman Empire, everyone will pay outward obeisance to but in practical affairs will disregard. The analogy between the Holy Roman Empire and the United Nations is not without instructive parallels. In much of the diplomatic and international legal literature of the fifteenth and sixteenth centuries the Empire was accorded a legal and political significance, and a degree of universal authority, that hardly comported with the realities of state practice. A similar situation may exist today with regard to the UN even though a contemporary scholar has had the courage to suggest that the UN may be "a 'non-system'—a vacuum in imagery, function, and design that invites the substitution of rival models evocative of the Chinese *wei-ch'i* board on which political players are expected to further their independent destinies by dint of intelligence and diplomacy."[11] The behavior of many UN members during the Falklands crisis raises doubts as to how authoritative the Charter norm is, even though in their general rhetoric and in situations where their immediate interests are not adversely affected by an application of the norm these states proclaim their adherence to it. As one observes the practice of states over the past thirty-eight years, one is forced to conclude that the norm is not as authoritative as other international legal norms dealing with issues less critical than the use of force.

The dimension of control presents an even more dismal picture. As revealed by Inis Claude's analysis of the organization's role in the Falklands War, the UN proved incapable of taking even the most modest steps to ensure compliance with the Charter's norm. And as the war progressed, the UN became so divided, confused, and unsure of its identity that it abandoned all pretenses of collective security and called for a mere ceasefire that would have left the aggressor's forces in place and indirectly would have rewarded the first use of force. The Charter's norm was not vindicated by the UN, but by that old representative of power politics distrusted by contemporary international law: self-help, in the form of the Anglo-American entente.

If the Charter norm is far less authoritative than would be suggested by the formal declarations of states in support of it; and if it has no control mechanisms other than those provided by individual states and their allies in accordance with the configuration of the existing balance of power; to what extent is it true law? The arguments advanced here have proceeded on the assumption that it still is, and numerous policy justifications have been offered to support the proposition that it should be law. Yet, should the trends of the last two decades continue with regards to decreasing authority and the lack of control, the time will come when it will be necessary to consider reformulating the norm in the direction of more modest objectives and aspirations, lest the gulf between international law and political realities grow dangerously wide. As Bozeman argued over a decade ago in *The Future of Law in a Multicultural World*:

> Since the modern world is being shaped decisively by war, it is unrealistic to pretend not only that peace is the rule but also that law as the servant of peace can effectively defy force. In this, as in other matters once believed subject to international law, nations would profit, singly and collectively, from a return to the less ambitious Grotian view of the role of international law, in terms of which it was possible to regulate many selected incidents and consequences of war because war as such was accepted as an unfortunate yet common phenomenon of international life. In short, if international law is to have a future in world society, what seems to be called for is a contraction of the domain of law and a de-escalation of legal rhetoric.[12]

Insofar as these reflections run counter to the still widely held belief that international politics is progressively becoming more susceptible to legal regulation, they are not likely to be received with much enthusiasm. Yet the issue cannot be ignored by any sensitive study of the relationship of international law and politics in today's world.

A full return to the pre-1914 permissiveness on the use of force may be unwise as well as unnecessary; given the growing destructiveness of contemporary warfare and military technology, most states are likely to be unwilling to embrace Hall's doctrine again. Nevertheless, some "de-escalation" of the UN Charter's legal rhetoric, a relaxation of the Charter's absolutist stance through some carefully elaborated qualifications, may become imperative. The precise form such qualifications may take is, of course, a broad subject well outside the scope of this essay. But several alternatives, each of them with its share of problems and potential disadvantages, loom on the horizon. One would be to define more broadly the concept of self-defense, as American policymakers and lawyers tried to do during the Cuban missile crisis of 1962. Another would be a partial return to the methodology and analytics of just war theory, as many Third World states and the UN General Assembly itself have been doing since 1967 albeit with a selectivity that is highly undesirable. Yet another possible avenue would be a downplaying of the illegality of first use of force in return for greater development of the norm outlined by Anthony Arend concerning the obligation of states to seek peaceful settlement during the course of hostilities. At some point in the future, the responsibility of statesmen and scholars may be to debate and work out, creatively and thoughtfully, such qualifications in the form of more flexible legal rules, instead of clinging to an absolutist norm that may have lost the inner dynamism and relationship to social realities which Oliver Wendell Holmes and other jurists have considered essential to the life of the law.[13]

Beyond these philosophical considerations, it may be useful to suggest a possible institutional mechanism that in some cases comparable to the Falklands could make it less tempting for states to resort to force. In his report of 7 September 1982, the UN Secretary-General, Javier Perez de Cuellar, commented:

There are many ways in which Governments could actively assist in strengthening the system prescribed in the Charter. More systematic, less last-minute use of the Security Council would be one means. If the Council were to keep an active watch on dangerous situations and, if necessary, initiate discussions with the parties before they reach the point of crisis, it might often be possible to defuse them at an early stage before they degenerate into violence.

In view of the Secretary-General's concerns, this may be an appropriate time to explore the feasibility of setting up a permanent UN commission on territorial and maritime disputes under the direct authority of the Secretary-General and staffed by experienced, competent negotiators. Aside from submitting an annual report to the General Assembly on the general scope of its work, the commission would conduct its proceedings along the lines of quiet, traditional diplomacy.[14] The commission would select a series of disputes where the danger of the use of force is especially acute. Its role would be to persuade parties, quietly and unobtrusively, to use its good offices and mediation. The commission also could try, with the permission of the disputants, to involve third-party states that might provide incentives and guarantees for a settlement. The avoidance of publicity would be essential, in order to avoid the hardening of positions that often takes place when negotiations are conducted in the public eye. Although the Secretary-General did not make as specific a proposal in his report, he suggested the need for and potential usefulness of a mechanism such as this one.

It is illusory to think that mere mechanical tinkering with the UN will increase substantially its capacity to maintain the peace and enforce the norms of the Charter. As long as the bitter, global power struggle between the Soviet and Western blocs persists, the Security Council will be paralyzed, and so will be the UN's capabilities to regulate the use of force by states. There are disputes, however, such as the Falklands, which may be sufficiently removed from the superpowers' rivalry to make it possible for a UN diplomatic commission to provide the necessary incentive to negotiation that can make the difference between peaceful accommodation and resort to war. The proposal would be worth implementing even if all it did was to postpone, or altogether prevent, the outbreak of violence in a few spots in a conflict-torn world.

Notes: Chapter 4

1 Lassa Oppenheim, *International Law*, 7th ed. (Lauterpacht), Vol. 2 (London: Longmans, Green. 1952); Julius Stone, *Legal Controls of International Conflict*,

2d ed. (New York: Rinehart, 1959); C. H. M. Waldock, "The regulation of the use of force by individual states in international law," *Recueil des cours* (Hague Academy of International Law), vol. 81, no. 2 (1952), p. 455; Ian Brownlie, *International Law and the Use of Force by States* (Oxford: Clarendon Press, 1963).

2   W. E. Hall, *A Treatise on International Law*, 8th ed. (Oxford: Clarendon Press, 1924), p. 82.

3   See the speech by Argentina's Foreign Minister, Nicanor Costa Mendez, before the OAS on 5 April 1982, OEA/Ser. G, CP/ACTA 489/82 (Protocolar), 5 April 1982; also the statement by the Representative of Argentina, H.E. Dr. Jose Maria Ruda, before the Subcommittee III of the Special Committee on the Situation with Regard to the Implementation of the Declaration on the Granting of Independence to Colonial Countries and Peoples (New York, 9 September 1964); and *The Argentina Rights over the Malvinas Islands, Georgias del Sur and Sandwich del Sur* (Buenos Aires: Presidencia de la Nacion, Secretaria de Informacion Publica, 1982).

4   W. W. Bishop, Jr., *International Law*, 3d ed. (Boston, Mass: Little, Brown, 1971), pp. 416–17. Note the authorities cited, especially Hyde, *International Law*, 2d ed. (Boston, Mass: Little, Brown, 1945), pp. 386–90; and D. H. N. Johnson, "Acquisitive prescription in international law," *British Yearbook of International Law* (Oxford: Clarendon Press, 1950), p. 332.

5   Hall, *A Treatise on International Law*, pp. 143–4.

6   J. L. Brierly, *The Law of Nations*, 6th ed. (Oxford: Clarendon Press, 1963, p. 167.

7   Grotius, *De Jure Belli ac Pacis*, Lib. II, Cap. IV, section 1.

8   J. B. Moore, *A Digest of International Law*, Vol. 1 (Washington, D.C.: U.S. Printing Office, 1906), section 88, pp. 293–5.

9   See the series of Anglo-Argentine agreements signed and implemented in 1971 and 1972, *Documentos relacionados con la apertura de comunicaciones entre el Territorio Continental Argentino y las Islas Malvinas, en ambas direcciones* (Buenos Aires: Ministerio de Relaciones Exteriores y Culto, Direccion General de Antardida y Malvinas, 1972).

10 See John Norton Moore's discussion in the *American Journal of International Law*, vol. 77, no. 3 (July 1983), pp. 610–15.

11 Adda Bozeman, *The Future of Law in a Multicultural World* (Princeton, N.J.: Princeton University Press, 1971), pp. 185–6.

12 ibid., pp. 184–5.

13 See Oliver Wendell Holmes, *The Common Law* (New York: Little, Brown, 1881); Roscoe Pound, *An Introduction to the Philosophy of Law* (New Haven, Conn.: Yale University Press, 1922).

14 For two highly illuminating discussions of the complex relation of publicity to diplomacy, see Adam Watson, *Diplomacy: The Dialogue among States* (New York: McGraw-Hill, 1982), and Inis L. Claude, Jr., "The impact of public opinion upon foreign policy and diplomacy: open diplomacy revisited", *Publications of the Institute of Social Studies*, Series Minor, Vol. IX (The Hague, 1965).

5

The Falklands War and the Failure of the International Legal Order

ANTHONY C. AREND

The Falklands War confirms two major failures of the contemporary international legal order. First, the crisis illustrates that the method of conflict management envisioned by the founders of the United Nations—a modified form of collective security— does not work; it fails both to deter and to repress aggression. Second, and inextricably linked to the first point, the Falklands War demonstrates that the mechanisms of peaceful change, so vital to the success of even a limited collective security framework, lack legitimacy. These observations are, of course, not new; scholars have repeatedly discussed the shortcomings of the Charter. The step that is often not taken is to determine what these failures mean for the status of contemporary international law. The purpose of this essay is to examine how the Falklands War represents another breach in these fundamental Charter provisions and to explore the ramifications this breach has for the legitimacy of these principles of international law.

Collective Security and the Falklands

The theory behind the collective security mode of conflict management is relatively simple. It is premised on the assumption that the unilateral use of force by a state is never an appropriate means to alter the status quo. Even in the face of a past "injustice" a state cannot use force to augment its territory, alter

52

a boundary, or coerce some other change from another state. Under the United Nations Charter, this unilateral use of force is expressly proscribed by article 2(4), which provides that "all Members shall refrain in their international relations from the threat or use of force against the territorial integrity or political independence of any State, or in any other manner inconsistent with the purposes of the United Nations." The only explicit exception to the prohibition to this unilateral use of force is self-defense, which is described in article 51 of the Charter as an "inherent right." As McDougal and Feliciano explain, the Charter norms proscribe the unilateral use of force for "value extension"—acts forcibly extending the influence of the state beyond its boundaries—but permits force for "value conservation"—protection of the political and territorial integrity of the state.[1]

Under a pure collective security mechanism, if a violation of this basic prohibition against the unilateral use of force does occur, all members of the international community will unite to repress the aggressor. This means that all capable states must take up arms, if necessary, against the recalcitrant state to prevent its aggression from succeeding. In fact, it is hoped that the very willingness of all states to join in the fight against a would-be aggressor would deter any state from undertaking an aggressive act.

This theory of collective security is reflected, in a limited fashion, in the Charter. Chapter VII of the Charter sets forth the framework for preventing aggression. Under article 39, the Security Council is empowered to "determine the existence of any threat to the peace, breach of the peace, or act of aggression" and then to determine what action is necessary to rectify the situation. Article 41 allows the Council to employ a number of different nonmilitary sanctions against the violator. But if these measures fail to resolve the problem, or if they are initially deemed inadequate by the Security Council, the Council "may take such action by air, sea or land forces as may be necessary to maintain or restore international peace and security." Under article 43 all members of the United Nations are obligated to make available to the Security Council "armed forces, assistance, and facilities, including rights of passage, necessary for the purpose of maintaining international peace and security." As long as a member has been allowed to participate in the "decisions of the Security Council concerning the employment of contingents of that Member's armed forces," it must supply troops and other military assistance when ordered by the Council. Indeed, article 43 provides that members must negotiate agreements well in advance of any possible conflict to determine the specific arrangements for troop utilization. Theoretically, if an outright act of aggression—such as the Argentine invasion of the Falklands—were to occur, the Security Council could order member states to initiate an enforcement action against the aggressor.

But even from the adoption of the Charter at San Francisco, it was recognized that the United Nations could be at most only a limited collective security system. Since realistically no collective military action could be taken without the agreement of the major world powers, the Charter enshrined the principle of the veto. Under article 27, no substantive action can be taken by the Security Council without the concurrence, or at least the acquiescence, of the five permanent members of the Council—the United States, the Soviet Union, Great Britain, France and China. It is interesting to note that the only collective military action authorized by the Council to date occurred in 1950 when, due to a Soviet boycott of the Council, the Council was able to recommend that members of the United Nations fight against North Korea. Yet even this action was not an enforcement action proper because the Council did not *order* members to participate in combat, but rather *recommended* that they take part. Aside from this one occasion, the Council has never ordered or recommended collective military action, despite the myriad threats to the peace and outright breaches of the peace that have occurred over the last thirty-three years.[2]

In light of this lack of success that the international community has had with the enforcement of the international law of conflict management, it is no surprise that the United Nations did not militarily come to the aid of Great Britain in her attempt to repel aggression. Instead, the Security Council, in resolution 502, simply determined the existence of a breach of the peace, and called for "an immediate cessation of hostilities" and "an immediate withdrawal of all Argentine forces from the Falkland Islands." The resolution also called upon "the Governments of Argentina and the United Kingdom to seek a diplomatic solution to their differences and to respect fully the purposes and principles of the Charter of the United Nations." In an effort to promote a diplomatic solution to the problem the Secretary-General offered his good offices to the parties. But direct military assistance was not suggested by the Council or any other organ of the UN as a solution, nor would it have been reasonable to expect such a recommendation. In essence, a collective security action was never seriously contemplated as a means of resolving the Falklands crisis.

Peaceful Change and the Falklands

Similarly, the Falklands crisis revealed yet another problem of the international legal order—the illegitimacy of mechanisms of peaceful change. As noted earlier, article 2(4)'s restriction on the unilateral use of force prohibits states from changing the status quo by forcible means. Yet the intention of the framers was not to set the post-World War II status quo in stone. Inasmuch as times and circumstances change, so it is to be expected that states, over the course of time, would have valid reasons to desire some alteration in the existing international order. The purpose of the Charter was not to prevent such a change, but merely to ensure that the change would take place exclusively by peaceful means. Argentina's desire for the Falklands seems to fall into this category.

Even though the Argentines justify their claim to the Falklands in terms of legal title, what they actually seem to want is an alteration to the existing configuration of boundaries. Although, as Professor Rubin has pointed out, Argentina may have had possession stripped from them, the combination of a century and a half of effective occupation by the British and the desire of the "Kelpers" to remain British, sharply brings into question the credibility of an *existing* Argentine legal claim. But this fact does not invalidate the legitimacy of Argentina's desire to *renew* its possession of the islands. What is at stake is not an issue of law, but rather one of policy. As Inis Claude observes, Argentina is requesting not a *legal* determination of ownership but a *legislative* change of the legal status quo.

If understood in terms of a "peaceful change" problem, the Falklands War can be seen in a new light. For years the Argentines sought to work with the United Nations machinery to gain control over the Falklands again. Indeed, as Inis Claude explains elsewhere in this book, the Assembly had seemed to favor the Argentine desire for the Falklands by placing the islands into the category of a "colony whose removal from that status should be negotiated as part of the process of implementing Resolution 1514 (XV), the Assembly's great emancipation proclamation of

1960." The Assembly even adopted Resolution 3160 in 1973 which, as Claude notes, "praises Argentina for its efforts to bring about the decolonization of the territory and presses the parties to make progress in negotiating the end of the colonial situation."

Given this UN support, why did Argentina resort to force to gain the islands? Claude suggests that this support may have been precisely the reason. With the past record of UN approval of "decolonization," Argentina could have perhaps anticipated that the UN would be sympathetic, even if not overtly so, to their action. But under the surface the Argentine action indicates another problem—an utter lack of faith in the legitimacy of the UN system of peaceful change. Under the theory of peaceful change, states give up their right to self-help with the understanding that institutional means will assure them a reasonable way of seeking their desired change. This does not mean that all countries will get what they seek, but rather that the procedure will be workable and relatively impartial. Thus, states will abide by the final result of such a procedure. By attacking the Falklands, Argentina demonstrated that it had no confidence in the ability of the United Nations to provide a just resolution to their claim for the Falklands. Unfortunately, this lack of confidence seems but symptomatic of a general feeling that the United Nations system of peaceful change is ineffective.

International Law Revisited

Given these two shortcomings of international law—the failure of collective security and the little legitimacy of means of peaceful change—international legal scholars are forced to examine the larger question of the current status of international law. If the Falklands War is another confirmation of these two failures, what does this mean for the international law of conflict management?

According to the jurisprudence of Myres McDougal and Harold Lasswell, a legal norm is a rule that is both "authoritative," that is, perceived as legally binding, and to a large extent "controlling" of the actual behavior of states. While some of the Charter provisions dealing with collective security and peaceful change may indeed be viewed as authoritative, it is more difficult to argue that they are to a large degree controlling of state behavior. States did not behave in the Falklands War as though they expected the enforcement provisions of

Chapter VII to be implemented. And the very fact that Argentina resorted to force indicates that her behavior was not consistent with the norms of peaceful change. A realistic assessment suggests that it may no longer be appropriate to call those norms "law," thus leaving a substantial gap in contemporary international law. But what, if anything, is attempting to fill this gap?

(1) The Failure of Collective Security and the Emergence of a New Norm

With respect to the gap caused by the failure of the Chapter VII provisions on collective security, there may be a new norm that is emerging to substitute for collective enforcement measures—the extension of the Charter obligation to pursue the peaceful settlement of international disputes from solely a pre-hostilities obligation to one that continues even once hostilities have begun. Under the Charter, states are obliged to pursue the peaceful settlement of specific disputes. Article 33(1) provides: "The parties to any dispute, the continuance of which is likely to endanger the maintenance of international peace and security, shall, first of all, seek a solution by negotiation, enquiry, mediation, conciliation, arbitration, judicial settlement, resort to regional agencies or arrangements, or other peaceful means of their own choice." Thus, states are to pursue the settlement of disputes that are liable to endanger peace and security. If they are unable to resolve the matter themselves, they are further obliged, under article 37, to refer the matter to the Security Council, which can, of course, intervene "at any stage of the dispute of the nature referred to in Article 33 or of a situation of like nature."

The initial intent of the framers of the Charter seems to have been for this article 33(1) obligation to apply only *prior* to Security Council consideration.[3] Certainly once hostilities had begun, the founders assumed that the Chapter VII provisions would enter into effect. But with the failure of collective enforcement, the international community seems to be trying to extend the article 33(1) obligations throughout the conflict—to the period following Security Council consideration and even after hostilities have begun. This effort by the international community can be seen in certain actions taken during other conflicts, such as the Iran–Iraq War, but it is most recently noticeable in the Falklands War.

As noted earlier, under the United Nations Charter rationale, the blatant violation of article 2(4) by Argentina should have given rise to collective sanctions against Argentina. Instead, Resolution 502, while recognizing the existence of "a breach of the peace" and putting the onus on Argentina to withdraw from the islands and end hostilities, called upon *both* sides "to seek a diplomatic solution" to the conflict. Even though the Resolution placed more responsibility upon one country, the Resolution implied that the Security Council, unwilling to act militarily, expected both sides to fulfill a general responsibility to seek a peaceful solution.

Before the British task force arrived at the islands and succeeded in removing the Argentine forces, a number of efforts were made to achieve a peaceful resolution to the dispute, as Professors Claude and Kinney have pointed out. Among these attempts to bring about a diplomatic solution was the mission led by United States Secretary of State Alexander Haig. Although both sides received Haig at their capitals and discussed the dispute, a compromise became impossible: "Neither side could concede anything on the fundamental principle of sovereignty. Britain demanded a return to the status quo ante; Argentina insisted on recognition of the new status quo."[4] Subsequently, President Belaunde-Terry of Peru and Javier Perez de Cuellar, Secretary-General of the United Nations, attempted to reconcile the parties.

Even though all these efforts failed, they indicate the belief on the part of at least some of the members of the international community that, despite the occurrence of an armed attack, both sides should still try to work out their differences by other means. An example of this belief is revealed in a statement by David C. Gompert, contained elsewhere in this volume. Gompert, who was intimately involved in the Haig mission, seems to acknowledge this mutual obligation to pursue peaceful settlement while arguing that such an obligation cannot nullify the right to self-defense: "Provided they are making a reasonable effort to find a peaceful solution, countries that have been attacked must be spared the onus of refusing to end hostilities." The thrust of his argument is that Argentina cannot simply attack another state, seize its territory, and then contend that the other side has a responsibility to settle and, conceivably, force it to concede the lost territory. But in making this argument, Gompert nevertheless recognized that even the attacked state should make "a reasonable effort to find a peaceful solution." Indeed, it seems to be this assumption that lay beneath both United States and United Nations peacemaking efforts during the Falklands War.

While these responses of the international community do not positively indicate the existence of a new norm of customary international law, they do represent an attempt to fill the void left in international law by the failure of Chapter VII of the United Nations Charter. These efforts do suggest that the obligation to pursue peaceful settlement during hostilities *may* be emerging as a norm of the international law of conflict management. This would be a positive development. Rather than simply tolerating the existing gap in the law, the international community may be attempting to develop a new norm to substitute for collective enforcement.

(2) The Failure of Peaceful Change

The growing illegitimacy of mechanisms for peaceful change poses even more difficulties for the norms of conflict management. Whereas the norm that may be emerging to act as a backup for collective security can be reconciled with the Charter framework, the normative implications of the ineffectiveness of means of peaceful change cannot be so neatly squared with the Charter. Instead of conforming to the Charter prohibitions against the use of force as a means of change, Argentina's actions seem to confirm an unsettling trend toward the legitimization of force based on the "justice" of the cause.[5]

As noted earlier, in 1960 the General Assembly adopted Resolution 1514, which called for an immediate movement toward decolonization. It further stipulated that, contrary to the original desire of the framers of the Trusteeship system, lack of preparation could not be used as a "pretext" for the colonial powers to hinder rapid granting of independence. In the wake of this Resolution, more and more colonies began to gain independence. This decolonization process greatly altered the composition of the United Nations. As newly independent countries became members, they began using the General Assembly as a platform for voicing their demands for international "justice."

These new states' demands for justice took several forms. Of course it was natural that they demanded the continuing of the decolonization process. States under the yoke of colonialism were to be freed expeditiously. But the claims went beyond a simple desire to end colonialism. The former colonies, as less

59

developed countries, began calling for "distributive justice." The new states argued that, in light of the past injustices of the exploitative colonial system, the industrialized countries owed them for gains made at the expense of the colonies. Third World countries began demanding a new world arrangement, a "New International Economic Order" to solve the problem.

This movement toward justice also began to challenge radically the norms of conflict management. Claims for justice began to imply the legitimacy of force to support movements for self-determination. While a right to an indigenous revolution or war of independence is recognized under international law, the new claims implied that external states could forcibly assist the liberation process. When India attacked the Portuguese colony of Goa in 1961, it claimed, among other things, that it was acting in self-defense, since the conquest of Goa in 1510 constituted an act of aggression that continued for 450 years.[6] It also contended that the calls by the General Assembly for rapid decolonization gave India the right to retake the colony. Indeed, the "Definition of Aggression" adopted by the General Assembly in 1974 even suggested that liberation movements may have the right to seek outside assistance. After enumerating a list of actions that should normally be considered aggression, article 7 provides in part that "[n]othing in this Definition ... could in any way prejudice the right of self-determination, freedom and independence, as derived from the Charter, of peoples forcibly deprived of that right ... particularly peoples under colonial and racist regimes or other forms of alien domination; nor *the right of these peoples to struggle to that end and to seek and receive support* in accordance with the principles of the Charter and in conformity with [the Declaration on Friendly Relations]" (emphasis added). Although this right to "seek and receive support" is qualified by reference to the Charter, it, in fact, seems directly to contradict the intent of article 2(4). It implies that liberation movements could receive outside assistance in their struggle against the authority structure of a given state. And, as Inis Claude has noted, the Resolution "is not an isolated bit of United Nations rhetoric, but a passage typical of a long list of resolutions solemnly approved by overwhelming majorities in the United Nations and numerous other international organizations, conferring international legitimacy upon wars of national liberation, wars to achieve national self-determination, wars to end racial oppression, and the like."

In view of these developments, it is not surprising that

Argentina took forceful steps to redress the perceived injustice of British rule over the Falklands. The UN, as noted above, had already labeled the Falklands issue a colonial question. The international community also seemed to be downgrading the importance of peaceful change, by approving resolutions that seemed to make decolonization a legitimate *causa belli*. Given these circumstances, it is no wonder that Argentina did not use international mechanisms that it perceived as ineffective or too slow.

The implications of this trend away from peaceful change are disturbing for the future of international law. With force being used more and more for establishing "justice," there seems to be a retrogression to the pre-League of Nations regime of self-help. If existing modes of pacific change have little legitimacy and if collective enforcement mechanisms are ineffective, the entire normative structure of the international law of conflict management must be carefully examined. If the test that was applied to the Chapter VII enforcement mechanisms is applied to the most basic norm of conflict management, article 2(4), the result is troubling. With the trend toward unilateral use of force continuing, the scholar must question whether article 2(4) is both authoritative and controlling. States often give lip-service to the normative import of this proscription against force, thus lending authority to the provision; but the great discrepancy between the norm and state behavior indicates a lower level of control. In light of this low level of control, it must be asked, as Alberto Coll, Thomas Franck, and others have done, whether this fundamental norm is still "law."

This problem presents a dilemma for students of international law. On the one hand, scholars are obligated by intellectual honesty to provide an accurate assessment of the current state of international law. They must identify those norms that are truly authoritative and controlling. But on the other hand, they must endeavor to promote the maintenance of norms of conflict management that attempt to provide for a more stable, secure, and just world order. Article 2(4) may have lost some authority and much control, but it may still be the best foundation for the international law of conflict management. One does not want to proclaim the norm's demise prematurely, and thereby contribute to its decline.

This quandary is not easily resolved, but perhaps a moderate course can be suggested. First, scholars must acknowledge the shaky condition of article 2(4); they must recognize the trend away from the basic prohibition of the unilateral use of force for change. But, second, they must acknowledge that the norm has not yet passed into oblivion. There is, admittedly, an ever decreasing rate of compliance, but states do feel some sense of obligation and the norm has restrained certain states from using force on occasions when their short-term national goals seemed to demand the use of force. In the Suez crisis, for example, the United States acted against its French and British allies in order to support the article 2(4) prohibition against the forceful takeover of the canal. The United States recognized that the control of force was in the long-term interest of the international community and the United States. One reason Argentina may not have received much physical support from her *compadres* in the OAS who rhetorically supported her is that they sensed the illegitimacy of the Argentine actions. Generally, states still seem to want article 2 (4), even though in a particular setting they may change their minds. Writing in response to Professor Thomas Franck's 1970 article, "Who killed Article 2(4)?," Professor Louis Henkin has commented that " [n]o government, no responsible official of government, has been prepared to pronounce it [article 2 (4)] dead." In sum, article 2 (4) still has a legitimizing and constraining influence that prevents the international environment from disintegrating into something even more anarchical. A pre-League regime of self-help that is legitimized by customary international law would be far worse than the contemporary order, even with all its problems.[7]

Conclusion

From the perspective of international law, the Falklands crisis demonstrates both a positive and a negative trend. With the failure of collective enforcement mechanisms, there is a new norm emerging—the extension of the obligation to pursue peaceful settlement of international disputes. This is positive; it demonstrates the efforts of the international community to compensate for the loss of collective security. But with the perceived illegitimacy and ineffectiveness of means of peaceful change, the normative force of article 2 (4) is being called into question. This negative trend could have grave effects on the Charter structure of conflict management. If, however, as Professor John Norton Moore has pointed out, the international community is constantly engaged in a "struggle for law,"—a struggle to determine what the law will be—then the task for statesmen, scholars, and diplomats should be to encourage the positive development of a new norm, while discouraging a return to the old system of self-help.

Notes: Chapter 5

1 M. McDougal and F. Feliciano, *Law and Minimum World Public Order* (New Haven, Conn.: Yale University Press, 1961), pp. 18–19.
2 T. Franck, "Who killed article 2 (4)? Or: Changing norms governing the use of force by states," *American Journal of International Law*, vol. 64 (1970), p. 809.
3 See L. Goodrich, E. Hambro, and A. Simons, *Charter of the United Nations*, 3d ed. (New York: Columbia University Press, 1969), p. 261.
4 L. Freedman, "The War of the Falkland Islands," *Foreign Affairs*, vol. 61 (1982), p. 146.
5 See I. Claude, "Just wars: doctrines and institutions," *Political Science Quarterly*, vol. 83 (1980), pp. 92–6.
6 Q. Wright, "The Goa incident," *American Journal of International Law*, vol. 56 (1962), p. 622.
7 Quote from L. Henkin, Editorial Comment, "The reports of the death of article 2 (4) are greatly exaggerated," *American Journal of International Law*, vol. 65 (1971), p. 547.

6

The Falklands Crisis and the Laws of War

HOWARD S. LEVIE

One week before the Argentine surrender at Port Stanley, the well-respected British news journal, *The Economist*, published an article captioned "War Laws—Made To Be Broken." After discussing a number of provisions of the laws of war which the writer, obviously not an expert in the field, thought had been violated during the course of the hostilities, he ended up with this alarming conclusion: "These, and no doubt other matters not yet to appear, will be the subject of anguished inquiry, once the fighting ends." Despite such contentions, the laws of war were more widely observed in the Falklands crisis than in any other conflict since World War II. This essay will analyze several law-of-war problems that arose during the hostilities, and will illustrate the degree to which both belligerents succeeded in observing legal norms of combat without any significant military disadvantage.

Maritime Exclusion Zone

The Argentine invasion of the Falkland Islands began on 2 April 1982. Great Britain broke off diplomatic relations that same day; but it was not until 7 April 1982, five days later, that Great Britain took its first real retaliatory step, announcing that as from 12 April 1982 it was establishing a "maritime exclusion zone" 200 miles around the Falkland Islands, and that any Argentine warships and naval auxiliaries thereafter within that zone "will be treated as hostile and are liable to be attacked by British forces." On the following day Argentina responded by establishing a 200-mile defense zone off its coast and around the Falklands.

When the British announcement was made the impression was given, and it was generally understood, that the British nuclear submarine *Superb* was on station in that area and this was undoubtedly the major reason for the failure of the Argentine fleet to emerge from its base at Puerto Belgrano, south of Buenos Aires. There were later complaints that the press, as well as the Argentines, had been intentionally misled when it was discovered that the *Superb* was at its base in Scotland. However, this was a perfectly valid and successful piece of "disinformation" by the British.

Since the 1856 Declaration of Paris it has been a settled rule of maritime warfare that a blockade, in order to be binding, must be effective; that is, the blockading belligerent must be able to enforce its announced blockade. The British declaration was not really a blockade, as merchant ships and neutral vessels were not barred from the exclusion zone; it only applied to enemy naval vessels. It was, therefore, nothing more than a gratuitous warning to the Argentine naval forces. A state of armed conflict certainly existed between Argentina and Great Britain and, hence, the armed forces of each, including naval vessels, were, apart from some limitations not here applicable, subject to attack wherever found. In any event, if, by disinformation, a belligerent can convince the enemy (and neutrals) that there is an effective blockade in existence, then there is an effective blockade.

On 23 April the British informed the Argentine government that "any approach on the part of Argentine warships, submarines, naval auxiliaries or military aircraft which would amount to a threat to interfere with the mission of British forces in the South Atlantic would encounter the appropriate response." At the same time it stated that "all Argentine vessels, including merchant vessels or fishing vessels apparently engaged in surveillance of or intelligence gathering activities against British forces in the South Atlantic, would also be regarded as hostile." Then on 30 April the British extended their maritime exclusion zone to include "any ships and any aircraft" found therein. This was now a true blockade—and, presumably, there were now British submarines on station in the area prepared to enforce the declaration. So far as is known, only one Argentine support ship, the *Formosa*, managed thereafter to reach the Falkland Islands. A number of military cargo aircraft were also successful in reaching their destination before the British carriers arrived in the area. It is interesting to note that sometime after the hostilities had ended a United Press International dispatch from Buenos Aires quoted an Argentine general as saying that the British air and sea blockade "was a success, a total success."

On 2 May the Argentine cruiser, *General Belgrano*, was sunk by a British submarine with a loss of almost 400 lives. The exact location of the *Belgrano* at the time of the attack has not been officially disclosed, but there have been suggestions that it was about 35 miles outside the maritime exclusion zone. Certainly, a cruiser of a belligerent has no right to consider itself immune from enemy attack because it is on the high seas beyond the range of a proclaimed maritime exclusion zone. Great Britain justified its action by pointing out that the cruiser was a threat to its picket ships, frigates, and destroyers, and that it had previously advised the Argentine goverment of the establishment of a defensive zone around units of the British fleet which the *Belgrano* had disregarded. Sympathy for the Argentine loss, and the feeling that the British had somehow been "unfair," were quickly dissipated when, two days later, on 4 May an Exocet missile fired by an Argentine plane hit and sank the British destroyer *Sheffield* with a loss of about twenty lives.

On 7 May the British extended their war zone to 12 miles off the Argentine coast. This blockade was completely effective, made so by the Argentine fear that if its fleet sortied from its base it would be the victim of the British nuclear submarines which were now, beyond any doubt, patrolling the waters off the coast of Argentina outside the twelve-mile limit. However, on 15 May the Soviet Ambassador in London advised the British government that the Soviet Union considered the British blockade to be unlawful because it "arbitrarily proclaim(ed) vast expanses of the high seas closed to ships and craft of other countries," citing the 1958 Convention on the High Seas as the basis for its claim. Of course, a blockade always denies the use of part of the high seas to other countries. While the Soviet Union might have questioned the extent of the blockaded area as excessive, if the blockade was effective (and there seems little doubt that it was), it was a valid blockade under the 1856 Declaration of Paris, to which Russia was one of the original parties.

Fishing Vessels

In 1900 the United States Supreme Court held that by customary international law fishing vessels were exempt from seizure by enemy naval forces in time of war.[1] In 1907 this rule was incorporated into the Hague Convention No. XI. Article 3 (1) of that Convention says, in part, that "[v]essels used exclusively for fishing along the coast . . . are exempt from capture." Paragraph 2 of that same article goes on to qualify that provision by stating that "[t]hey cease to be exempt as soon as they take any part whatsoever in hostilities." As we have already seen, on 23 April 1982 the British government informed the Argentine government that, among other things, "fishing vessels apparently engaged in surveillance or intelligence gathering activities" would be regarded as hostile. This statement was really unnecessary as it was merely another declaration of the British intention to apply existing law.

On 9 May 1982 the Argentine fishing vessel *Narwal* was attacked by British forces and was so severely damaged that she sank on the following day. At the time of the attack she was about 60–70 miles within the British maritime exclusion zone, shadowing British fleet units. According to one report: "She was not armed but she was a spy ship with an Argentine Navy Lieutenant Commander on board sending back information about the [British] fleet's movements."[2] The Argentines have not denied that allegation. That being so, the *Narwal* had lost her immunity and was legally subject to the treatment which she received.

Hospital Ships

Shortly after hostilities in the Falklands began the British government requisitioned the SS *Uganda*, a vessel previously used for education cruises for schoolchildren, converting it into a hospital ship. There were allegations that en route to the South Atlantic the *Uganda* carried combat troops.[3] If such allegations are true, this was a violation of articles 30 (2) and 33 of the Second Geneva Convention of 1949 on the treatment of sick and wounded sailors. While extra medical personnel may be carried on hospital ships, combat troops may not be. The fact that after the combat troops were debarked the vessel was used exclusively for proper purposes does not change the situation.

When a hospital ship is used for improper purposes it ceases permanently to be entitled to the immunity granted to such ships. During both World Wars there were numerous claims of the misuse of hospital ships and rejection of their subsequent entitlement to immunity. It appears that such claims are inevitable and that, all too often, they will be justified.

The Economist (5 June 1982, p. 20) asserted that by bringing the *Uganda* into Falkland Sound at night to pick up wounded and shipwrecked Argentine soldiers the British "may have breached" the provision that hospital ships must "be situated in such a manner that attacks against military objectives cannot imperil their safety." The reporter or editor who wrote that article was obviously not very familiar with the laws of war. He cited the First Geneva Convention of 1949, which is concerned with land warfare, not sea warfare; and the provision he quoted relates to the placement of medical establishments and units on land, not to hospital ships. Article 18 (1) of the Second Convention makes it mandatory that "[a]fter each engagement, Parties to the conflict shall, without delay, take all possible measures to search for and collect the shipwrecked, wounded and sick." This is presumably what the *Uganda* was doing in the Sound, and it is one of the humanitarian functions of every hospital ship.

Incendiary Weapons

Among the Argentine material captured by the British on the Falkland Islands was a large supply of napalm, one of the most effective incendiary weapons in military arsenals. This caused a great deal of critical comment in the British press. Actually, even under the provisions of Protocol III of the still unratified 1980 Conventional Weapons Convention, incendiaries such as napalm are not outlawed, only their mode of use is restricted; and since those restrictions are all directed towards the protection of civilians, it does not appear that they would have been violated by Argentine use against British combat troops.

Protecting Powers

Diplomatic relations between Argentina and Great Britain were broken off on 2 April 1982, immediately after the news of the

Argentine landings on the Falklands reached London. Shortly thereafter Great Britain requested the Swiss government to act as its Protecting Power vis-à-vis Argentina, presumably pursuant to Common Article 8/8/8/9 of the four 1949 Geneva Conventions, while the Argentine government requested Brazil to act in that capacity on its behalf. Even though they performed no major functions in the military area, this is of extreme importance in view of the fact that it was the first clear-cut instance of the use of Protecting Powers since World War II, despite the innumerable international armed conflicts which have occurred in the interim. There were, for example, no Protecting Powers in either Korea or Vietnam, and there do not appear to be any in the Iran–Iraq War.

Civilians

Civilians presented on the whole a physical rather than a legal problem. However, there were a number of rules of the laws of war which came into play. When resistance at Port Stanley ended on 2 April, Governor Rex Hunt (in full ceremonial dress with a white-plumed Napoleon-style hat), his wife, and his family were escorted to an Argentine Air Force plane and flown to Montevideo, Uruguay. The British Antarctic Survey Team's civilian scientists, based at Grytviken, on South Georgia, were also repatriated by the Argentines after a short delay. LADE, the airline which had been operated by the Argentine Air Force between Port Stanley and Commodoro Rivadavia, in South Argentina, continued to fly after the Argentine takeover. While eighty to one hundred British subjects who were living on the islands as civilian employees of the British government elected to avail themselves of this method of departure with their families, only twenty-one "Kelpers" so elected; and when members of the Anglo-Argentine community in Argentina proposed that a neutral ship be sent to the islands to evacuate the 300 children to the mainland, it was the Falkland Islanders, not the Argentine government, who rejected the proposal.

Article 35(1) of the Fourth Geneva convention of 1949 authorizes the departure of protected persons (civilians) from the territory of a party to the conflict. On the basis of the Argentine claim of sovereignty over the Falkland Islands and their dependencies, this article would have been applicable. However, if we adopt the thesis of British sovereignty, then the departure of those who left the islands was an act of grace by Argentina since article 48 of that Convention, relating to occupied territory, only requires the Occupying Power to permit the departure of protected persons who are not nationals of the power whose territory is occupied—and all but thirty of the Falkland Islanders and other residents were British nationals. (The other thirty were Argentines.) One British subject, William Luxton, was deported, probably because he was considered to be a subversive influence; several others were apparently placed in a detention center at Fox Bay. Article 41 (1) of the Fourth Convention states that the only measures of control which the Occupying Power may adopt with respect to protected persons are assigned residence and internment. Deportation is specifically prohibited by article 49 (1) of the Convention but it may be assumed that Mr. Luxton preferred it to internment. Article 42 (1) of the Convention authorizes internment if the security of the Occupying Power makes it necessary—a decision which, of course, is a subjective one made by that power. Accordingly, the action of the Argentines in this respect was within the purview of and in accordance with the provisions of the Convention.

There were estimated to be 17,000 British passport-holders in Argentina when hostilities commenced on 2 April 1982. The Argentine government announced that it would guarantee the safety of these individuals. Nevertheless, on 5 April the British government broadcast a radio message recommending that they leave the country. How many did so is unknown but there is no evidence that the Argentine government made any effort to prevent them from exercising the right granted to them by article 35 of the Fourth Convention, mentioned above, to leave the territory of a party to the conflict.

Argentina claimed in a television broadcast that the British were guilty of "indiscriminate bombing" of Port Stanley as a result of which two civilians were killed and four were wounded. Inasmuch as more than 10,000 members of the Argentine military forces were crowded into the area of that small town (normal population: 1,050), with somewhere between 250 and 600 civilians who had remained in their homes, the civilian casualties appear to have been remarkably light. Certainly, the British bombardment and bombing of the Argentine personnel and positions in Port Stanley cannot be said to have violated any provision of the 1907 Hague Regulations on Land Warfare, 1907 Hague Convention No. IX on Naval Bombardment, or the as-yet inapplicable 1977 Protocol I. The residents of Port Stanley were British nationals and were the persons on whose behalf the British forces had traveled 8,000 miles to fight and there is no reason to believe that the British commanders did not exercise the utmost caution on their behalf. Thus, when, on 13 June 1982, the International Committee of the Red Cross (ICRC) proposed the creation of a "neutral zone" for the protection of the civilians still in Port Stanley, the British immediately agreed. The Argentines did so on the following day and the ICRC announced that it had arranged for such a zone.

Prisoners of War

Article 13 (1) of the Third Geneva Convention of 1949 provides that "[p]risoners of war must at all times be humanely treated." Although there were undoubtedly individual cases in which this provision was violated during the hostilities in the Falkland Islands, on the whole the treatment of prisoners of war, first by the Argentines and later by the British, more closely resembled the Russo-Japanese War of 1904–5 than either World War I, World War II, Korea, or Vietnam. In this respect, as in others, the war was fought as a "gentlemen's war." Thus, although article 118 of the Third Convention merely requires the release and repatriation of prisoners of war "without delay after the cessation of active hostilities," the Royal Marines captured on both the Falkland Islands and on South Georgia were repatriated almost immediately by the Argentines. So also were two Royal Air Force technicians captured at the airfield at Port Stanley, men who were able to provide the British with valuable intelligence information.

When the British began to take prisoners of war, first on South Georgia and then on the Falkland Islands, they followed the pattern established by the Argentines of promptly repatriating them. In fact, the practice was so regular and so prompt that it aroused the ire of the Royal Navy when the entire crew of the Argentine submarine *Santa Fe*, captured by the British at South Georgia, was quickly returned to Argentina. As one report stated, "to give the Argentines back a fully trained crew of submarine specialists seemed the height of folly."[4]

We have seen that article 118 of the Third Convention requires the repatriation of prisoners of war "without delay after the cessation of active hostilities." Despite this clear provision, India held Pakistani prisoners of war for over two years after the

71

complete cessation of active hostilities, from December 1971 to March–April 1974, allegedly because there was no guarantee that hostilities would not break out again, but actually as political hostages in an effort to compel Pakistan to recognize Bangladesh. Contrary to the procedure followed by India, which flagrantly violated the Convention provision, Great Britain began the repatriation of Argentine prisoners of war immediately after the final surrender of the Argentine forces on the Falklands. At first the British sought to obtain a statement from Argentina acknowledging the cessation of active hostilities. Even though such an acknowledgment was not forthcoming, the British quickly repatriated over 10,000 prisoners of war, retaining about 550 officers, including the Argentine commander on the Falklands, General Menendez. Within a month, despite the Argentine government's refusal to admit to a complete cessation of hostilities, the remaining prisoners of war were returned by the British.

There were some instances in which it has been suggested that the provisions of the Third Convention may have been violated. When the Royal Marines at Port Stanley surrendered they were required to lie on the ground, face down, under guard while they were being searched for weapons. Photographs were made of that scene. It has been implied that the taking of those photographs violated article 13(2) of the Convention which requires that prisoners of war be protected against "insults and public curiosity." Inasmuch as hundreds of photographs have been taken and published in every war of the moment of surrender, hands held high in the air, and full-faced, with no complaints by the belligerents, and inasmuch as it is impossible to recognize any particular individual in the Falklands picture, there is at least a reasonable doubt that the photograph violated article 13 (2) of the Convention.

One Argentine naval sub-officer was shot and killed while a prisoner of war, while apparently attempting to sabotage the captured submarine *Santa Fe*. The British immediately informed the Argentine government of the incident through the medium of the International Committee of the Red Cross and instituted a Court of Inquiry, presumably pursuant to article 121 of the Third Convention. The Argentine government was advised of the result reached by that court, which exonerated the British guard, and apparently it was satisfied that justice was done.

As in all modern armed conflicts, land mines were used in the Falklands in great profusion; at the end of hostilities, their removal became a major problem. Article 7 of Protocol II to the as yet unratified 1980 Conventional Weapons Convention contains provisions for the recording of the location of minefields. Apparently, as is not unusual in modern warfare, this was not done in many instances by the Argentines, with the result that the locating and removal of the numerous buried mines became a slow, painstaking, and dangerous procedure.

After World War II large numbers of captured German soldiers were retained in France for the purpose of removing mines, and a substantial number were killed or injured in the process. As a result, article 52(1) of the Third Convention specifically provides that only prisoners of war who volunteer for the task may be employed on labor which is of a dangerous nature, and the third paragraph of that article provides that the removal of "mines and similar devices" is to be considered dangerous. It has been asserted that captured Argentine soldiers were "ordered" to clear minefields near Goose Green. If this was so, it constituted a clear violation of the provisions of the Convention. If they were volunteers, it did not.

Article 117 of the Third Convention provides that "[n]o repatriated person may be employed on active military service." While the meaning of this phrase is subject to numerous interpretations there can be no doubt that it precludes the use of repatriated personnel in actual combat. There are charges that some Royal Marines, captured by the Argentines on South Georgia and repatriated to Great Britain, were subsequently included in the British Task Force. If this was so, it was a violation of the provisions of the Convention.

One interesting episode occurred with respect to prisoners of war. When Captain Alfredo Astiz, the commander of the Argentine forces on South Georgia, surrendered to the British forces on 22 April 1982, he and the commander of the *Santa Fe*, the Argentine submarine which had been captured that morning, were entertained at dinner by the British officers. Subsequently, it was alleged that Captain Astiz was the infamous "Captain Death," one of the most sadistic of the government's interrogators during the suppression of the guerrilla movement in Argentina some years before. Sweden wanted to question him concerning eyewitness reports that he had shot a young Swedish girl. France wanted to question him concerning the disappearance of two French nuns. This raised an interesting question of law. The offenses were alleged to have occurred in Argentina long before the beginning of the hostilities between

Argentina and Great Britain. Assuming that they constituted violations of article 3 of the Fourth Convention, dealing with non-international armed conflicts, can a Detaining Power in a subsequent international armed conflict turn over a prisoner of war to a third state, a party to the Conventions, for possible trial and punishment? The British answered that question in the negative, rejecting the Swedish and French requests. Whether that decision was correct remains an open question. After being taken to Great Britain, where he was subjected to what has been described as a "token" interrogation, Captain Astiz was repatriated.

Mercenaries

One of the most difficult problems which confronted the Diplomatic Conference drafting the 1977 Protocol I involved proposals seeking to eliminate the use of mercenaries. Under the definition now contained in article 47 of that instrument, one of the requirements for categorizing an individual as a mercenary is that he "is motivated to take part in the hostilities essentially by the desire for private gain and, in fact, is promised by or on behalf of a Party to the conflict, material compensation substantially in excess of that promised or paid to combatants of similar ranks and functions in the armed forces of that Party".

The Gurkha Rifles have been part of the British Army for well over 100 years. They are recruited from an ethnic group which lives in what is now Nepal. During World War II there were 100 battalions of Gurkhas in the British Army; today there are five such battalions. When it became known that the 7th Gurkha Rifles was being sent to the Falklands, Argentina protested to Nepal. Whether that protest was based on the allegation that the Gurkhas were serving the British as mercenaries, or was made merely because they were Nepalese citizens, is not known. The Gurkhas are certainly motivated by the desire for private gain. They serve the required number of years, and then retire in Nepal as relatively prosperous citizens. However, inasmuch as they receive a considerably smaller pay than do British soldiers, it is doubtful that they come within the definition of mercenaries.

Neutrals and Neutrality

Prior to World War II, during hostilities there was a dichotomy under which all states in the world community were either belligerents or neutrals, with well-established rules applicable to each status. At various times in the course of World War II, Italy and Spain, and perhaps others, announced that they were "non-belligerents." That term can be defined best by saying: "I hope that you win, and I will do everything I can to help you, except fight." During the Anglo-Argentine hostilities in the Falkland Islands, the United States did not officially use the term "non-belligerent," but that was undoubtedly its status. After Secretary Haig failed in his peacemaking efforts, the United States announced its support of Great Britain which included a willingness to supply any military aid short of direct involvement of American combat forces. On 29 April 1982 the United States Senate adopted a resolution in which it declared that "the United States cannot stand neutral." Five days later, on 4 May, the United States House of Representatives adopted a similar resolution in which it expressed "full diplomatic support of Great Britain in its efforts to uphold the rule of law." In the course of the war the United States furnished the British with a secure method of communication with its nuclear submarines in the war zone, weather information, aviation fuel, use of the airfield on Ascension Island, ammunition and missiles, and KC-135 tanker planes.[5] A request for AWACS was refused because it would have involved American airmen in the hostilities. Whether the United States acted in accordance with the rules of neutrality which existed prior to World War II is, at the very least, questionable.

There was speculation that, despite the strong anti-communist stance of the Argentine junta, it was receiving aid of various kinds from the Soviet Union. It can be assumed that if the Soviet Union considered the granting of such aid to be in its own interests, it would not have found it impossible to overlook the ideological differences. The USSR abstained on, but did not veto, United Nations Resolution 502, calling for Argentina to withdraw its forces from the Falkland Islands. The Soviets also employed surface vessels and planes from Angola and Cuba for surveillance of the British Task Force as it sailed towards the South Atlantic. This, however, may have been routine since Soviet ships and planes do this with respect to all naval movements of Western powers; there is no hard evidence that the USSR passed the information so obtained to the Argentines. In fact, it has been suggested, with a good deal of reason, that had the Soviet Union been doing so the *Narwal* would never have been sent on the suicidal spy mission in which it was engaged when it was sunk by the British.

Implications for the Laws of War

In some important respects, the Falklands crisis offers much hope for the continued viability of the laws of war. Despite the intense nationalistic rivalries underlying it, the conflict illustrates that states can wage conventional warfare in compliance with the laws of war without thereby giving adversaries a substantial military advantage. But, on the other hand, one must be mindful of the peculiar qualities of the Falklands War that made it possible for the laws of war to exert their restraining influence. First, this was a limited war, fought for limited ends with limited means. For both parties the end was quite specific—control of a particular territory. This was not an abstract, hazy goal, but rather a concrete, easily recognizable objective. The means, too, were limited. The adversaries restricted their operations to the disputed territory, and refrained from military actions against the enemy's homeland; had it not been conducted otherwise, the war would have been much more violent and destructive and could have released the kind of political frenzy and hatred that weaken the observance of the laws of war. Second, the adversaries, despite obvious differences in political regimes, saw themselves as members of the same civilization, and shared many cultural affinities and bonds—some stretching over centuries. This helps to explain why the war was in many respects a "gentlemen's war." Third, the conflict was brief. It is difficult to predict how well the laws of war would have been observed had this been a protracted struggle, filled with the usual weariness and mounting frustration against the enemy. It is an open question whether further conflicts that lack all these special characteristics will have as encouraging a record on the observance of the laws of war as did the Falklands War of 1982.

Notes: Chapter 6

The facts presented in this essay were drawn primarily from Christopher Dobson, *The Falklands Conflict* (1982), and from press reports contained in such publications as *The Economist*, *U.S. News & World Report*, *Time*, the *New York Times*, and others for the period of 1 April to 1 July 1982.

1 The Paquete Habana, 175 U.S. 677 (1900).
2 Christopher Dobson, *The Falklands Conflict* (London: Hodder & Stoughton, 1982), p. 104.
3 The *Uganda* may have been confused with the *Canberra* (*New York Times*, 28 May 1982, p. A8:4). In a letter dated 8 October 1982 Captain L. W. L. Chelton, R.N. Chief Naval Judge Advocate of the Royal Navy, advised the author that no British hospital ship carried combat troops to the South Atlantic; and that members of the International Committee of the Red Cross, carried thereon, could verify this.
4 Dobson, *The Falklands Conflict*, pp. 156–7.
5 The British were legally entitled to use the Ascension airfield under an agreement, "Use of Wideawake Airfield in Ascension Island by United Kingdom Military Aircraft," signed at Washington, 29 August 1962 (13 UST 1917, TIAS 5148, 449 UNTS 177).

PART TWO

The Challenges to Diplomacy

7

Anglo-Argentine Diplomacy and the Falklands Crisis

DOUGLAS KINNEY

Argentina raised the question of the Malvinas Islands in the Subcommittee on Small Territories of the UN Special Committee on Decolonization (the C-24) in 1964. Both Britain and the United States were then members of the C-24. The British position was that sovereignty was not negotiable but that questions of the welfare of the islanders and contacts with Argentina should indeed be discussed. The report of the Special Committee resulted in General Assembly Resolution 2065 of 16 December 1965, citing the Falklands as an instance of "colonialism." The Resolution called for bilateral negotiations toward a peaceful settlement of the territorial dispute and referred to both the UN Charter and the 1960 General Assembly Resolution 1514 (XV) on decolonization.

In January 1966, Foreign Secretary Michael Stewart discussed the Falklands with authorities in Buenos Aires and six months later a bilateral meeting was held in London. The British hoped to lessen friction and limit the scale of the dispute. But Argentina sought the return of its sovereignty over the islands. They saw the 1966 talks as too formal and without any serious results. The Argentines made a four-page statement. In response, the British unofficially, and under the cover of public disclaimers to the contrary, suggested that the United Kingdom had no strategic, political, or economic interests to pursue in the Falklands, that the islands were almost self-sufficient, that they would eventually become Argentine territory, and the main question was the timing and method of Argentina's recovery of sovereignty.

81

Unofficial incidents raised Argentine public consciousness about the Falklands as much as official policy. In September 1964 a light plane landed at Port Stanley, planted an Argentine flag, and took off without being stopped. In September 1966 twenty Argentines hijacked an Argentine Airline's DC-4 and forced it to land at Port Stanley. The Argentine government denied responsibility for or association with both incidents. The first of these incidents led to the establishment of the contingent of Royal Marines on East Falklands, and the second one to that contingent being raised to platoon strength.

In November 1966 Britain proposed a thirty-year freeze on the question of sovereignty. During the freeze no actions regarding normalization of relations, trade, and other contacts would be taken as affecting either party's position. At the end of the freeze, the Falklanders would choose between British and Argentine sovereignty. Argentina rejected the freeze proposal.

In March 1967 the British informed Argentina that under certain conditions the United Kingdom would cede sovereignty of the Falkland Islands to Argentina. The primary condition was that the wishes of the islanders were to be a determining factor. It was made clear in parliamentary and public statements that the United Kingdom would not cede sovereignty without the express consent of the Kelpers.[1] As the parties began to negotiate a preliminary understanding, the islanders objected to what they perceived as a movement toward Argentine sovereignty. They began lobbying Parliament and the British public through the Falkland Islands Emergency Committee against any discussion of sovereignty transfer. Soon the British government publicly stated that there would be no such transfer without the consent of the islanders.

Discussion of the wishes of the islanders, however, was a less difficult issue than safeguarding their interests in the event of a sovereignty transfer. In August 1968 the United Kingdom agreed to language recognizing future Argentine sovereignty following a settlement of how the "interests of the islanders would be secured by the safeguards and guarantees to be offered by the Argentine government." In a unilateral statement to be published in parallel the British government would state that the transfer of sovereignty would have to be acceptable to the people on the islands. This was the high water mark of concrete discussions of the transfer of sovereignty but it was turned back by the reaction of the Kelpers, Parliament, and the British press. The Argentine government stated that it could accept neither the contingency on the wishes of the islanders nor the United Kingdom's unilateral statement on the subject being linked to the memorandum of understanding. The British Cabinet then decided to abandon the attempt to reach a settlement on the basis of transfer of sovereignty as sketched out in the memorandum.

From December 1968 the principal course of British policy on negotiations was set. They would negotiate with Argentina, yet make it clear that the transfer of sovereignty without the Kelpers' consent was not negotiable. The wishes of the islanders (self-determination) were enshrined as the basis of British negotiation policy.

Strangely, Argentina was willing to reopen talks in June 1970. Sovereignty was not on the agenda. Improved communications and transport were successfully negotiated and, in 1971, air and sea services arrangements between the Falkland Islands and Argentina were agreed upon. Argentina offered the Kelpers a travel document allowing them freedom of movement in Argentina and a package of economic inducements, including reciprocity on taxes, exemption from Argentine military service, scholarships and domestic-rate mail service, telegram and telephone service. Within five years the agreements led to the Treaty of Communications, which included the abolition of passports and the Argentine construction of an airstrip. Argentina undertook to supply fuel and air transport for the Falklands. Argentina perceived that with the communications agreement it had made major concessions; it had abandoned years of consistency on subjects such as rejecting postal and passport arrangements and, in its view, had received no reciprocal concessions from the United Kingdom.

The British government in January 1974 began to assess the possibility of a condominium rather than an outright transfer of sovereignty. After consultations with the islands' executive council, the new Wilson government raised with the Argentines the possibility of a condominium without the approval or participation of the islanders. By August 1974 it was clear that the Kelpers were balking and the United Kingdom informed the Argentine government that the discussions would not be practical.

Taking a cue from the apparent Argentine willingness to pursue the mutual benefit approach, the United Kingdom proposed in July 1975 discussions of joint development of the southwest Atlantic. Argentine Foreign Minister Vignes accepted the possibility and linked it to a transfer of sovereignty with a lease-back for a fixed term. The Argentine proposal included immediate occupancy of South Georgia and the South Sandwich Islands.

The hardening of the Argentine position, under way for some two years already, was cemented by the announcement in October 1975 of the Shackleton survey to assess the long-term economic possibilities for the development of the Falkland Islands and its dependencies. Argentina noted that the Shackleton team arrived in the islands on the anniversary of the 1833 occupation, and increased its strong rhetoric implying the possibility of an invasion. Argentina also rejected Prime Minister Callaghan's offer of 2 January 1976 to send a senior British official for confidential discussions.

In February 1976 the Argentine destroyer *Storni* fired on and attempted to board a British vessel, coincidentally called the *Shackleton*, 78 miles south of Port Stanley. Interestingly enough, this action took place under a civilian government. The military, though apparently not the Argentine government, had been planning the action since before the first of the year with the apparent intention of avoiding casualties and, not incidentally, reinforcing the Argentine claim to a 200-mile territorial sea which included the continental shelf and encircled the Falklands as well.

In July and August 1976 private talks began with the military government which had taken power in the coup of 23 March. The Callaghan government had reviewed its policy and decided in March that a fresh dialogue on the full range of issues in the dispute, including future constitutional relationships (sovereignty), was in order.

It is interesting to note that the first instinct of President Videla's military government was to turn not to the force of arms but to bilateral talks and then to the United Nations. Argentina secured in Resolution 31/49 approval of the view of the C-24 that Argentina had made continuous efforts to facilitate decolonization and to promote the well-being of the Kelpers. The military were also pursuing a parallel track along the lines of the earlier *Shackleton* incident. The patrol helicopter of HMS *Endurance*, the icebreaker on station each Antarctic summer, discovered an Argentine military presence on the South Sandwich island of Southern Thule. The Argentines apparently had gone ahead with a unilateral occupation. The British Foreign Minister requested a military response.

A formal British protest on 19 January called the establishment of the station a violation of British sovereignty in the South Sandwich Islands. The United Kingdom presented no ultimatum, however, simply expressing the hope that Britain would soon learn that the program had been terminated. This left the Argentines the opportunity either to retain their presence or gracefully retreat, confident that the effort and the precedent were worthwhile for their cause. The British made no public announcement and the existence of the station remained a closely held secret for almost five months. During that period the station was reinforced. Indeed, the intention had been to reinforce it to considerable size until mid- or late March when weather would prevent British ships from entering South Atlantic waters.

If any one factor would make succeeding Argentine decision-makers doubt the political will or military capability of the British government, it was their continuing, militarily unchallenged presence on Southern Thule. Distinct, minor, and token as that presence might be, the United Kingdom had labeled it a violation of its sovereignty, as it clearly was. The fact that it was tolerated from 1977 to 1982 spoke well for British restraint in the Falklands negotiations but augured poorly as a demonstration of British will to the Argentines.

In November 1977 the British government secretly dispatched a hunter-killer submarine and supporting surface ships to the Falklands in response to both the earlier firing on HMS *Shackleton* and the Argentine landing on Southern Thule. The diplomatic climate was bad. The Argentine press was rife with invasion rumors and the Argentines had interrupted the fuel supply to the Falklands. New York talks were scheduled for December with Ted Rowlands leading the British delegation. But Argentine press and public opinion saw these as unlikely to be productive. Invasion was again the watchword in Argentina's lively political culture. The British colony of Belize also bordered on crisis, reinforcing the general feeling that Argentina might try force in the Falklands.

The level of bilateral tension decreased, as the New York talks were smooth, if not highly productive. The parties set up subcommissions to discuss sovereignty and the parallel economic/social conditions and programs. The submarine and its escorts remained on station during December as these negotiations proceeded in New York. The British Cabinet decided that the dispatch of the submarine should be kept secret lest it prompt the Argentines to invade. Since Argentina was not informed of the submarine's presence in the area, it was neither militarily deterred nor made aware of the potential cost of an invasion. The attack on a British vessel and the other hostile measures were not met with any known British response other than a return to the negotiating table.

The high water mark of the lease-back concept came in the winter of 1979–80. Under this proposal formal sovereignty would be transferred to Argentina but administration of the islands would remain with Great Britain for a limited period (to be negotiated, likely to be somewhere between twenty and fifty years). Lease-back as a concept antedated the Tory government of 1979 but, while it was favored by those concerned with relations with Argentina and Latin America in general, it was vitriolically opposed by the Falklands lobby and its supporters in Parliament.

Minister Ridley of the Foreign Office nonetheless pursued what he saw as the only rational, viable policy alternative for settling the Falklands crisis. Lord Carrington saw its policy merits but also its domestic political liabilities. Mrs. Thatcher opposed any concessions to the Argentines. The Overseas and Defence Committee of the British Cabinet passed the idea to the Cabinet itself which gave Ridley little or no support. He was instructed to put a range of options to the islanders in consultations, which predictably resulted in their choosing the status quo.

In February 1981 another round of the New York talks began. Ridley had no realistic negotiating strategy given the political constraints on British diplomacy concerning the Falklands. Nor did this leave him even clever means of delay. The British had little to offer or discuss on sovereignty. As reported later by *The Economist* (19 June 1982, p. 37) the British were considering a ninety-nine year lease, and the settlement that was to commence the lease was to be finalized somewhere between the years 2000 and 2081.

In the subsequent negotiations of February 1982 the Argentines were fully aware of the extensive discussion within the British government of the lease-back option and may indeed have decided that it was their own best alternative. Costa Mendez's instructions to the Argentine delegation in New York were to obtain a regular schedule of meetings, inclusion of sovereignty in the list of negotiable items, and a firm commitment to reach agreement within the calendar year. The compromise reached on 26 February 1982 met the Argentine demands to a large extent. A negotiating commission would meet with an open agenda and aim for settlement in 1982. Each side would seek political agreement as rapidly as possible. The closing communiqué was positive.

On the morning of 3 March, however, the Argentine junta stated its total dissatisfaction with the outcome of the February New York talks and implied that it would no longer feel bound to pursue its national interests by peaceful means. Argentina's stated goals had been for the discussions to continue and progress to be made. The junta's unstated agenda, however, was sovereignty by the year's end. The appropriate national means was to be Argentine Marines. The only question now was when. The invasion's architects were junta member Admiral Anaya and Foreign Minister Costa Mendez; the latter indicated that a nonviolent invasion would provoke little or no reaction from the United Kingdom or elsewhere.

While rumors and press speculation on the invasion reached a crescendo, they were not based on any substance until 19 March when the scrap metal crew landed on South Georgia and raised the Argentine flag. In response to British diplomatic protests Costa Mendez assured the British that he would have the party removed. The *Endurance* embarked twenty-one Marines and moved to the area from Port Stanley. She was drawn away with half the Marine force, hundreds of miles from the real drama for which the South Georgia incident was a cause or pretext: an Argentine invasion of the Falklands.

Argentina seized the moment. The absence of a British naval presence, a reduced Marine garrison, the onset of Antarctic winter, the diplomatic cover of recent "unsuccessful negotiations", and finally the British "menace" to Argentines in South Georgia determined the timing. They were proximate and permissive factors, not causes. The Argentine grievance was centuries old, the motivations as deep as culture, the reasons of convenience many. At its heart, however, the invasion was a diplomatic inevitability. It had loomed several times over several decades. Seventeen years of British diplomacy unsupported by either military force or the political leeway to settle a territorial question definitively had inevitably failed.

The Mediation Attempts

There were major diplomatic efforts to mediate the Falklands dispute by American Secretary of State Alexander Haig, President Belaunde-Terry of Peru, and UN Secretary-General Javier Perez de Cuellar. Their approaches and working methods were radically different. They worked by shuttle flight, telephone, and alternating sessions with the parties. Their efforts spanned the stages of military crisis from standoff to full-scale war.

The proposals by the three mediators had several elements in common, stemming from the combination of the military and territorial nature of the crisis. Each proposal sought a military disengagement, an arrangement for interim administration of the territory, and provision for continuing negotiations to solve the underlying sovereignty dispute. Military disengagement involved the end of military hostilities by mutual withdrawal of armed forces, and a commitment not to reintroduce those forces. Arrangements were to be made and verified by a third party, but each side wanted to be in a position to act unilaterally if it considered it necessary. Interim administration of the islands also would involve a third party, national, multinational, or international. Proposed third-party administrators were to be essentially independent of, although in cases assisted by, the traditional organs of local self-government. Local autonomy was balanced in most proposals by the possibility of increased Argentine access to the Falkland Islands (and their dependencies) during the period of interim administration.

During those mediation efforts the United Kingdom had six basic objectives. First, it sought a cease-fire and permanent withdrawal of Argentine forces. Second, it wanted the restoration of British authority, either in whole or in part. Third, it desired a guarantee of local rights and institutions. Fourth, it wanted third-party assistance in the implementation of the settlement. Fifth, it sought to reestablish Argentine access to and communication with the islands at preconflict levels, as governed by the 1971 bilateral agreements. Finally, the United Kingdom wanted an interim agreement which would not prejudge the final outcome of sovereignty negotiations.

Argentina had at least eight major goals. First, they desired the continuation of negotiations, leading to Argentine sovereignty in the near term. Second, they wanted the interruption of British rule. Third, they sought effective Argentine control of interim administration of the islands. Fourth, they wanted freedom of access to the islands. Fifth, they desired a settlement formula which would result in Argentine sovereignty at a near (fixed) future date. Sixth, they wanted involvement of third parties principally to limit British use of force and help secure Argentine gains. Seventh, they wanted immediate military withdrawal to home bases, preserving Argentina's geopolitical advantage and ability to use force again with minimum warning time. Eighth, they sought widened recognition that this was a decolonization issue and that the controlling norm was territorial integrity.

Since the civilian landings of March 19 in South Georgia, Argentina had reasserted its claim that Britain had illegally seized the Falkland Islands in 1832. On 30 March (three days before the invasion) Britain had stated that "the unauthorized presence of Argentine citizens" on South Georgia was unacceptable and that, "if it comes to the point, it would be our duty to defend and support the Falkland islanders to the best of our ability." An armed British ice-patrol vessel was standing by, and the hunter-killer submarine *Superb* had reportedly been dispatched from Gibraltar on 25 March.

On 2 April the British UN delegate charged Argentina with aggression and asked the Security Council to demand that the Argentine forces withdraw from the islands immediately. The Argentine delegate denied the charge, stating that Argentina had "recovered for its sovereignty islands that properly belonged to it." Argentina, he said, would negotiate any issue with Britain "except for sovereignty." The Argentines stated that "if the Argentine people are attacked by military, naval, land or air means, the Argentine nation in arms, with all means at its disposal, will present battle." The Argentine Navy was on alert, and it was reported that two of its three submarines left for the islands on 3 April. Military supplies were arriving hourly by plane at Port Stanley. A naval transport ship had brought dozens of heavily armored amphibious vehicles to the harbor there. Such was the diplomatic climate in which the United States volunteered to mediate. That climate would affect the mediation before the mediation could begin to affect relations between the parties.

According to the British Ambassador to Washington, Sir Nicholas Henderson, Secretary of State Haig operated from two premises. Haig believed that Argentina was guilty of aggression and should not be allowed to get away with it lest they set an example with dire consequences for world peace; and, second, that a military solution would harm not only both parties but also the United States.[2]

Henderson has characterized Haig's approach as one of taking sides while giving the impression of complete impartiality. This neutral posture, maintained until the end of April, "was difficult for people to understand on the other side of the Atlantic" since the British saw themselves as an ally who had been the victim of aggression. Haig was worried that any tilt toward Britain prepared fertile ground for the Soviets in Argentina and in Latin America at large. Although Haig assured the Ambassador several times that there would be "no repeat of Suez," Henderson insightfully has captured some of the American doubts about the Falklands case which made the Suez analogy very applicable: "a recessive feeling about colonialism, concern that the United States would eventually expect Britain to pick up the check, worry about the Russians and the fear that what Britain was doing would rally other countries in the area against Western interests."

The United States was, as Haig assured the ambassador, "not at heart impartial." It was partial in two directions; strong currents of support were running for both the British and Argentine causes. The traditional United States neutrality on territorial disputes had tacitly favored the status quo and thus Great Britain. Neutrality now favored the Argentine status quo in occupation of the Falklands. Haig met separately with the Argentine and British ambassadors to Washington on 6 April. The two adversaries represented competing U.S. interests in that the United States wanted to maintain a full range of constructive bilateral relationships with each.

Britain's new Foreign Secretary, Francis Pym, instructed his ambassador in Washington to inform the Reagan administration on 6 April that the British goal was Argentine withdrawal and the return of British administration to the Falkland Islands. Pym's message to Haig also made clear the British view that the American role would be crucial.

Secretary of State Haig's response to the British *démarche* was that he had indeed been thinking of an American mediation of the crisis aimed at possibly securing a mixed or multilateral administration of the Falklands.[3] The British ambassador clarified to Haig that the British government could not enter negotiations about the future of the Falklands until Argentine troops were withdrawn. Further he said that it was improper to think in terms of multilateral administration. He stressed that Argentine withdrawal and the reimposition of British administration were preconditions for negotiations and that the United Kingdom was not concerned with Galtieri's future; he indicated that the political climate in Great Britain was analogous to America's attitude in 1980 to its fifty-two hostages in Iran. Accepting the British precondition of Argentine withdrawal, Haig suggested a mixed commission to mediate and function as an interim administration, or the possibility of involving the Organization of American States. The British ambassador expressed doubt that either would be constructive and spoke against further involving the United Nations, describing Resolution 502 as a sound basis for action.

The British view throughout the diplomatic efforts was that, with the British Task Force under way, unsuccessful diplomacy would lead to use of force by the British. The British impression was, nonetheless, that Argentina did not believe that the United Kingdom was prepared to use force to retake the Falklands. The British also believed that this might become a self-fulfilling prophecy due to the Antarctic winter, the length of the supply line, and the expenditure of fuel and other scarce resources. Argentina probably also hoped to discourage the United Kingdom militarily with the semblance of offensive preparations and a gradual acceptance by international opinion of its occupation.

There was no major Argentine preparation to defend the recovered islands, no second half of the Malvinas plan. If the old war game for invasion relied on U.S. or UN intervention leading to resumed bilateral negotiations, the ad hoc plan seemed to rely on a series of third-party mediations. Argentine diplomacy held little room for concessions, taking rather an all-or-nothing approach. Holding out for guaranteed sovereignty by a certain date, Argentina abandoned the most creative aspect of the traditional "just war" plan: the return to the bargaining table without absolute insistence on the fruits of military victory. Such insistence led to diplomatic and then military failure.

President Reagan directed Haig actively to sound out the United Kingdom and Argentina on ways of avoiding a military confrontation. Haig began that process on 8 April in London by meeting with the senior British officials, including Prime Minister Thatcher.

The British were prepared to back up with force their insistence on Argentine withdrawal, British sovereignty and administration, and self-determination for the islanders. The War Cabinet, for example, had declared a total exclusion zone of 200 miles around the Falklands while Haig was en route from Washington. Since the legal validity of such blockades rests on one's ability to enforce them, the implication was that British submarines would be on station when the TEZ came into effect on 12 April. Diplomacy was preferable, but not in any absolute sense; force could and would be used. The Thatcher government pictured itself in a political corner in which national honor would not permit either appeasing "a dictator" or appeasing invasion, much less the two combined.

Haig was caught between this British posture and an Argentine administration which demanded either a time-specific negotiated solution yielding Argentine sovereignty, or a system of interim administration which would give Argentina a dominant role in the interim period leading inevitably to sovereignty. Haig was firm to the British government. He did not pretend to proceed from identical interests, only parallel ones. His tactic was to emphasize to the British that Argentina needed a way to withdraw with its national honor intact. He expressed his concern about the risk of an enhanced Soviet presence or role. He emphasized the great hazards to the British of a military landing, and realistically pointed out that a solution other than a negotiated one would have public opinion costs, especially in the United States. He urged Britain to be less unequivocal in asserting sovereignty and suggested an international or multinational solution as he had originally speculated about with Henderson in Washington.

The British Cabinet and Foreign Office were of the opinion that Haig did not understand their position. Many of his themes were old material to Falklands experts, and seemed to amount to a plan, a plan they found overtaken by events. Its balance seemed to them to ignore the new element in an old equation: aggression. At the Foreign Office and in 10 Downing Street the British government became disillusioned. Haig's emphasis on giving something to the Argentines and on avoiding war seemed to the United Kingdom to limit both its options and the legitimacy of its cause. Hence, the Prime Minister and later her Cabinet seemed in their response more stern and purposeful than even they intended.

Next, Haig met in Buenos Aires with Argentine Foreign Minister Costa Mendez for four hours and held two short meetings with President Leopoldo Galtieri. The principal opening question was: in the event that Argentine withdrawal and a halting of the British Task Force could be arranged, on what basis, and by whom, would the islands be governed *ad interim*? The United States suggested a joint interim government with participation by Britain, Argentina, and a third party, possibly the United States. The Argentine government rejected this proposal as not guaranteeing Argentine sovereignty as the outcome of negotiation. They felt that, at a minimum, the Argentine flag must fly until its sovereignty was formalized by negotiations. Argentina's public position was that it did not "reconquer" the Falkland Islands simply to return to the *status quo ante*.

On Monday, 12 April, Haig returned to London as the British blockade took effect and President Belaunde-Terry of Peru proposed a seventy-two-hour truce. Argentina immediately accepted the Peruvian proposal and stated that it would await a British response, but Argentine officials tacitly acknowledged that cease-fires and negotiations benefited Argentina given its occupation of the Falklands. Peru had created the first of the overlaps and conflicts which would characterize the mediating process.

On the same day, 12 April, Haig's mission almost collapsed when Argentine officials reneged on an understanding with Haig about the possible terms of settlement. The change involved a new junta proposal which would have the effect of prejudicing in favor of full Argentine sovereignty and setting the date in advance. (Haig had thought their agenda to be ratification of interim administration.)

Thatcher said publicly that she had made it plain to Secretary Haig that Argentine troop withdrawal was a precondition for negotiations and that the wishes of the Falklanders would govern British positions in any negotiations. Raising the political-military temperature slightly, she not only warned against any Argentine testing of the total exclusion zone, but said that any such challenge would be taken as evidence that diplomacy had been abandoned in favor of force. Before the junta proposal, the United Kingdom had shown some flexibility on Monday. The British had suggested that it might be possible to consider joint administration while discussing sovereignty.

On Tuesday, 13 April, the Prime Minister conceded only that the interests of the islanders might be considered as well as their wishes and that the islands' administration must at least be "recognizably British." Upon leaving London, Haig said that he had received "some new ideas" which indicated British willingness to pay some diplomatic price to avoid the necessity of using force.

The mediation then stalled. As the Secretary returned to the United States, British officials were openly confident about American backing and pessimistic about a diplomatic solution before the arrival of the British Task Force. Haig returned to Washington to brief the President, describing the situation as increasingly dangerous since neither side showed flexibility. They decided to sharpen the point to be made to Argentina. On 14 April Reagan urged Galtieri to show flexibility and to exercise restraint. On the same day Prime Minister Margaret Thatcher, in a speech before the House of Commons, stated that a prerequisite for settlement was the withdrawal of Argentine troops from the islands. She further insisted that "the sovereignty of the islands is not affected by the act of invasion and that, when it comes to future negotiations, what matters most is what the Falkland islanders themselves wish." Britain had set her political goal: self-determination, which was also the status quo desired by the Kelper majority. Thatcher reaffirmed Britain's desire for a peaceful solution, but warned that if the 200-mile blockade zone around the islands was tested, the British would conclude that the Argentines had abandoned the search for a peaceful solution in favor of force. Britain had reached the limit of its preference for diplomacy over force; Argentina was not to consolidate what it held.

The Argentines, for their part, stated that the British fleet must halt before Argentine forces would withdraw. The Argentine government staked out its minimum political condition: that the Argentines retain some element of sovereignty, for instance, the continued presence of the Argentine flag over the islands, during discussions on the area's future.

Haig followed with talks in Buenos Aires from 15 April to 19 April, impressing on the Argentines the long-standing nature of American obligations to the United Kingdom. He warned that when the first major armed clash took place the United States would have to stand at the side of the United Kingdom. During this second round of talks in Buenos Aires, the British fleet was nearing Ascension Island, about a week's sailing time from the Falklands. The junta began to focus on holding what they now saw as a possible military threat at Ascension. Haig advanced a preliminary plan calling for Argentine withdrawal, diversion of the British fleet, the establishment of provisional administration under Argentine-U.K.-U.S. supervision (until December 1982), and then negotiations over the final status of the islands to begin in December 1982.

Argentina rejected the proposal indirectly. Argentine officials were clear, at least in public, on their position at this point: there was not going to be a peaceful settlement unless Britain conceded the sovereignty issue. Admiral Anaya's navy was prepared, they believed, to defend the islands. Air Force chief General Lami Dozo was hesitant about war, but his service decided to commit themselves. Galtieri led the fifty-four army generals toward war. The three services were "unanimous."

Realizing that his "Five Points" were not selling, Haig reworked Costa Mendez's proposal and conveyed it to the British telegraphically at 9:00 P.M. on the evening of Monday, 19 April. The Argentine proposal specified joint administration with U.S. supervision; Argentine representation on the Council; and United Nations resolution of the sovereignty question.

The British had considerable reservations about the Argentine peace proposals which Haig had conveyed earlier. The insistence on guaranteed Argentine sovereignty was unacceptable. The essential elements of settlement in the British view were a return to British authority in the islands, including the return of the Governor-General, as well as self-determination for the Kelpers. In their view the aggression must be completely undone and the prewar situation restored.

The British would not confirm reports that the Argentine proposals, as reworked by Haig, included referring the sovereignty issue to the United Nations. On the basis of previous General Assembly resolutions, Great Britain perceived that the UN favored Argentine sovereignty. The British also feared that the Security Council, despite Resolution 502, had become reluctant to support them.

As Haig left Buenos Aires on Monday, 19 April, the Argentine government was still adamant about the guarantee of Argentine sovereignty. There was also an equally firm British stance that open-ended negotiations would be the only negotiations upon which the United Kingdom would enter. Argentina thus began pursuing other channels. It was already in the process of requesting a meeting of the Organ of Consultation of the Rio Treaty and was notifying foreign offices and diplomatic missions that Argentina fully intended to invoke the "attack on one, an attack on all" clause in the 1947 document.

Argentina offered to withdraw its troops in favor of joint administration and full Argentine sovereignty by the end of 1982. There seemed to be no way around Argentine insistence on guaranteed sovereignty. There was hope until the end that Galtieri might settle for "territorial integrity" rather than "sovereignty" as the end of the proposed talks. Costa Mendez not only could not deliver that but he also brought to the Buenos

Aires airport, as Haig prepared to depart, news of an OAS initiative and a new demand. In the end, Haig's efforts failed. The British tacitly rejected the Argentine offer, as the Argentines had Haig's. Haig, however, still told the Argentines as he left that the last Argentine text should be considered the basis for a settlement.

Argentina went on the offensive and the junta pursued a Rio Treaty meeting. The OAS decided on 21 April that it would convene on the 26th as the Organ of Consultation of the Rio Treaty. Galtieri flew to the Falklands, where he stated that Argentina would continue to insist on a guarantee of its sovereignty. He restated the junta's rejection of the British proposal for compromise, but dispatched his Foreign Minister to Washington to meet again with Haig.

Great Britain responded with equal force to the Argentine escalation. On 24 April Pym termed the latest Argentine proposals unacceptable and returned to London. The next day, British forces recaptured South Georgia. The Argentine Foreign Minister announced, somewhat belatedly, that Argentina and the United Kingdom were at war. He arrived in Washington on 25 April. In view of the British retaking of South Georgia, Costa Mendez postponed his meeting with Secretary Haig. He indignantly cited the attack on South Georgia as having led the Argentine government to believe that "negotiations with Britain had terminated." But the United States would not agree that the U.S. mediation effort was ended. Haig told the OAS that UN Security Council Resolution 502 was the proper basis for a peaceful settlement. He said that the Rio Treaty did not provide such a basis and was not an appropriate or effective way to solve the Falklands crisis.

The United States made an urgent appeal to the parties to accept a proposal as the basis for settlement to avoid major military engagement. Haig did indeed resume talks with Costa Mendez, who informed him that Argentina had not rejected the US proposals. Costa Mendez seemed to imply that the impending hostilities were leading to some flexibility in the junta and some preference for diplomatic over military solutions. Chief among these areas for flexibility would have been the removal of Argentine troops in exchange for the lifting of the British threat, but Argentine thinking at its most *posibilista* was still focused on a brief period of British administration, to be followed by a formula such as joint rule of the islands. Argentine sovereignty was still assumed as the outcome.

Major elements of the detailed U.S. proposed memorandum of agreement were cessation of hostilities; a fifty-percent reduction of forces within several days; total Argentine withdrawal within fifteen days; the end of economic and financial sanctions; a tripartite U.S.-U.K.-Argentine special interim authority, each party to be staffed by not more than ten persons and accompanied by his flag; the presence of at least one Argentine on each island council; restoration of movement, travel, and transport; and negotiations on removal of the Falklands question from the UN's List of Non-Self-Governing Territories by 31 December 1982. Had the parties been unable to reach agreement by the end of the year, the United States would have undertaken a six-month mediation.

The United Kingdom increased the political-military pressure on 28 April by extending its 200-mile sea and air blockade around the Falklands to apply to all traffic of all nations beginning on 30 April. Both sides were in the process of official consideration of the Haig plan, but the plan was widely noted to contain neither of the party's stated preconditions; it had no guarantee of ultimate Argentine sovereignty, nor did it make a firm commitment to self-determination of the Kelpers as sought by Great Britain. British commandos were known to be ashore in the Falklands and attention turned to the possibility of full-scale amphibious landings. Prime Minister Thatcher told the Commons in emergency session that the issue of war and peace was up to Argentina. She had concluded, she said, that *diplomacy was not going to produce Argentine withdrawal*. She discounted the usefulness of UN or ICJ intervention, but was not yet willing to reject the Haig proposals.

In retaliation to the British action, Argentina declared its own blockade of 200 miles around the Falklands as a free-fire zone, effective immediately. Elements of the British fleet were known to be within the 200-mile zone and the declaration seemed directly aimed at them.

Secretary Haig told the House of Representatives Committee on Foreign Affairs that it was unlikely that war could still be avoided. He stated that the United States agreed with Great Britain that aggression should not be rewarded, and believed that his diplomatic shuttle had apparently failed to produce a solution to the crisis.

In retrospect, it is clear that the Argentines interpreted Haig's consultation process with the British as a successful upgrading by the United Kingdom of their special relationship with the

United States. Unconsciously grouping the Anglo-Saxons, and misreading a partnership which comes as close to sovereign equality as any in the modern world, the Argentines clung to their hope that the United States would wish to restrain the United Kingdom and would be able to do so, both militarily and politically. With the Suez analogy in mind, they ignored the new realities of the Trident partnership and the influence, in the mainstream politico-legal culture, of the principle of non-resort to force, a principle which is especially against the interests of major states.

Galtieri's reaction to Haig's approach was critical all along. Two elements of the U.S. approach were particularly objectionable to the Argentines. The first was the insistence on Argentine withdrawal as the key element of what the Argentines saw as the larger and ongoing problem. Founded on UN Resolution 502, this American position was nonetheless seen by the Argentines as the enforcement of British interests as opposed to equity. The second major irritant was the increasingly clear fact that not only did Argentina have to get out, but that if it did not, the United States would help the United Kingdom. These two perceptions led to hardened Argentine positions, including the insistence on the 31 December deadline for the transfer of Argentine sovereignty, and poisoned both the American and Peruvian peace initiatives. They also led to thinking along the lines of "even if we lose, we can still obtain the original objective of getting the United Kingdom to bargain seriously."

Foreign Minister Costa Mendez thought that the greatest stumbling block in the Haig proposals was British insistence on consulting the islanders. He interpreted the proposed return to British administration without a fixed date for ending the negotiations as *status quo ante*, since the population would clearly not choose Argentine sovereignty. He harbored equally grave doubts about the U.S.-U.K. majority vote in interim administration.

Argentina also failed to adjust its conduct militarily and diplomatically. It was preparing for siege warfare in both these fields. Amphibious warfare doctrine attributes such strength to dug-in defenders that overwhelming superiority (six-to-one) in troops is needed for an amphibious attack. Thus the uncoordinated Argentine planning to hold the Falklands did not pay attention to the brevity of the thirteen-month Argentine conscription period (only recently begun for the bulk of the troops on the Falkland Islands), nor to the lack of combat experience for the few hundred career officers and noncommissioned officers, whose services had not fought a war since the Chaco War with Paraguay in 1876, but on the simple preparation of trenches and lightly fortified positions for a seemingly adequate number of defenders.

Argentine diplomacy had the advantage but also the constraint of being singleminded; the goal of sovereignty had been embedded for 150 years in the national consciousness. The Argentine position was widely known, and known to be firmly held. No Argentine diplomat needed to wonder about overarching goals, or government support in pursuit of them. Yet this also limited the creativity of Argentine diplomacy. Argentine diplomacy in the pre-invasion years had been a relentless but creative pursuit of one goal through such diverse means as naval gunfire, the establishment of weather stations, and the agreement to supply oil and education for the islanders. In the crisis stage it became cautious, inflexible, and a prisoner to its own consistency. First abandoned in favor of force, diplomacy was then called on to prevent counterforce, an inconsistent and self-defeating use of the instrument.

Although it was more flexible and creative, British diplomacy was hampered by political considerations, principally the unyielding requirement that the Kelpers approve any solution which could be negotiated. In addition, national honor demanded that British administration, dislodged by force, be reimposed by negotiation if possible, by force if necessary. As in the years of bilateral negotiations, Britain found itself with little to offer in bargaining. Concessions could not be made on those issues which national honor determined were questions of principle: self-determination and non-resort to force.

Tactical military developments and prospects seemed to determine to an unreasonable degree the negotiating postures of the parties to the Falklands dispute, yet larger strategic developments were ignored by one side as they gave firmness to the other. The British declaration of the 200-mile exclusion zone around the Falklands should, for example, have pointed out to Argentine authorities how limited their options were. Resupply by air was inefficient and expensive. It limited the defenders of the islands to a low volume of military material and, as the Antarctic winter approached, food, fuel, and other supplies. The aging Argentine fleet, while it might use the ship and air-launched Exocets as well as the air arm to inflict deadly harm on the British, would certainly not itself survive such attacks. The sinking of the *Belgrano* made this all too clear to the Argentine Navy which played no further major role in the Falklands conflict. The navy took the islands, then left attack to the air force and defense of the islands to the army and marines. What compelled Argentina to pursue the military rather than diplomatic course at this juncture? Certainly, the air bridge was an encouragement. C-130 transports were able to continue supply and personnel changes through early May to the main airport at Stanley. And there were also the illusions generated by that critical high-technology weapon, the Exocet missile.

On 30 April President Reagan announced full U.S. support for the United Kingdom, framing Argentina's taking of the islands as "armed aggression," ordering partial economic and arms sanctions against Argentina, and offering materiel support to the United Kingdom in any armed conflict. Former Argentine Ambassador to the United Kingdom, Ortiz de Rosas, believes that the U.K. request to the United States to take sides was fatal to peace and even to the United Kingdom's own interests. He argues that the United Kingdom knew that U.S. military support would be available if needed and ought to have recognized that U.S. good offices (in other words, neutrality) should have been maintained and the United States kept in reserve as an ongoing intermediary.

President Belaunde-Terry's initiative on 2 May was a peace plan based on Security Council Resolution 502. The text suggested by Peru to Argentina and the United Kingdom called for a cease-fire, a troop withdrawal, a commitment not to introduce troops again, an interim administration by a contact group, consultation with the islanders on a definitive settlement, acknowledgment of the conflicting claims of the two parties, and consideration of both the *aspirations* and the *interests* of the Kelpers, with an effort to bring the British and Argentines to a definitive agreement before 30 April 1983. A contact group of Peru, the United States, Brazil, and the FRG was to be established for purposes of arbitration, supervision, and *ad interim* administration.

At the time, British forces were not yet militarily engaged in large-scale hostilities. South Georgia had been recovered and East Falkland bombed, but neither Argentine military credibility nor survival of forces were yet major factors. Even following the occupation of the islands by Argentina, the dispatch of the British Task Force, and the failure of the American mediation, the Peruvian initiative seemed to offer a last chance for peace.

The principal Argentine objections to the 2 May proposal were the presence of the United States among the four guarantors and the continuing British insistence on both the interests and wishes of the islanders being reflected in the settlement. Costa Mendez proposed the substitution of the "views of the islanders concerning their interests" early in the morning of 2 May. Also during the morning of 2 May Argentina conceded the U.S. participation in the interim government. At 11:00 A.M. Buenos Aires time on 2 May Belaunde-Terry called and said the United Kingdom had agreed to consider his plan.

At 2:15 P.M. Buenos Aires time Belaunde checked with Galtieri to confirm that his Foreign Minister was empowered to propose and agree upon language. Galtieri confirmed that Costa Mendez was so empowered. He said, however, that he, as President, must still ratify it with his "senate." Belaunde pressed for an answer and was promised that at a scheduled, 7:00 P.M. meeting the junta would consider the proposal favorably, and that Belaunde would have firm Argentine agreement by 8:00 P.M. Buenos Aires time, or 6:00 P.M. in Washington or Lima. Belaunde scheduled a 6:00 P.M. Lima press conference to announce peace in the South Atlantic.

At 3:00 P.M. Washington time the nuclear hunter-killer submarine HMS *Conqueror* put two torpedoes into the Argentine cruiser ARA *General Belgrano,* sending her to the bottom. In the political calculus of the junta, the sinking of the *Belgrano* made compromise at that moment unacceptable for Argentine national honor. Within hours of the sinking of the *Belgrano,* Galtieri informed Belaunde that the deal was off. It is still to be established that it was ever on.

The British view of the state of negotiations on 1 and 2 May was conditioned by the military situation. Pym had returned to Washington stating that he was there to visit an ally instead of a mediator. Port Stanley had been bombed and other attacks had been made on the Falkland Islands themselves. South Georgia had been retaken on 25 April. Around midday 2 May the War Cabinet met at the Chequers country residence of the Prime Minister and decided to authorize the sinking of the Argentine cruiser *Belgrano* by the nuclear submarine *Conqueror.* At 8:00 P.M. London time (3:00 P.M. Washington time) the order was carried out.

Pym had met with Haig for two hours on the morning of 2 May in Washington. Signals to the British were mixed: while conveying President Reagan's conviction that U.K. forces were

101

"doing the work of the free world," Haig also pleaded that large-scale hostilities were unnecessary. He outlined the Peruvian initiative in general form. Haig noted that the ideas were similar to his own of the previous month, but thought they would be more acceptable to Buenos Aires having been presented by another South American government. Henderson's view is that they could not possibly have been described as proposals.

Pym replied that while he was, of course, ready to consider new ideas, the Peruvian plan was not all that different from the Haig proposals Argentina had tacitly rejected. Pym said that he would need to discuss any new ideas with the Cabinet on his return to London. Haig agreed that both more time and work were needed. They met later for lunch at the British Embassy and spoke again by phone before Pym's departure for New York. Henderson's account is that it was only at this point in the afternoon that it was possible for Pym to telegraph a report to London. The telegram was dispatched at 5:15 P.M. Washington time, that is, 10:15 P.M. in London, or two hours and fifteen minutes after the captain of the *Conqueror* carried out his instructions to torpedo the *Belgrano*. The British view is that the lack of a sense of urgency concerning the Peruvian initiative was justified by the fact that "nothing had happened in Washington to suggest that any new peace initiative was afoot, or that anything more significant was likely than the numerous proposals that had been made in previous weeks, to which the Argentines had always responded negatively."[4]

From the British perspective in early May, Argentine air and submarine forces were real and immediate threats. Argentina was still supplying the Falklands by sea. The British Task Force lacked early warning, reconnaissance, and air defense capabilities. The British Task Force was, in its own estimation, highly vulnerable.

What specific threat, though, did the Argentine surface fleet represent? The British view was that the task force of the *Belgrano* was itself a threat, and that the two escorting destroyers, at least, were equipped with Exocet missiles. Whatever the *Belgrano's* position or course at the time of the attack, she was thought to be searching for and providing guidance for air attacks on the British Task Force, if not herself executing the order to seek and destroy Royal Navy surface units.[5]

The diplomatic loop, from the British point of view, was

closed. The Peruvian plan was discouraged, if not rejected, because of its vagueness and its similarity to previously rejected suggestions. There seems to have been no firm or specific communication to the United States, much less to Great Britain, or an Argentine willingness to consider the Peruvian effort. Therefore, there was no urgent communication with London, Northwood, or Chequers.

The Peruvian effort was criticized as not being original and fresh, that is, it was seen as emanating from earlier efforts by the United States; as not being serious since it did not involve a convening of the parties; as biased, involving a Latin American with strong sympathies for Argentina in the Falklands crisis. But it also seems to have been criticized because of its ad hoc and straightforward effort. Yet its very simplicity and the ease of conveying its points by telephone were what almost made it work.

Belaunde-Terry made a second try on 5 May after Argentina's vengeance on the *Sheffield*, but the spirit of compromise seemed to have been lost. Argentina was already in the process of considering the good offices of the UN Secretary-General, and probably estimated that it could maximize its gains in the politically hospitable forum of the United Nations. The British government, however, expressed its willingness to negotiate the possibility of diluted British sovereignty as in the Peruvian proposal. Whether or not the Thatcher government could have steered the Peruvian plan through the Parliament is an interesting but academic question. It made the political commitment to the United States and Peru to negotiate on the basis of the Peruvian proposal, demonstrating considerable political courage.[6] On 5 May Great Britain responded favorably to the Peruvian mediation. But, crucially, the United Kingdom raised the stakes: their reply added the unacceptable element of reimposition of British sovereignty. By now, however, the similarities of Belaunde's proposals to those of Haig were dominating the discussions in Buenos Aires. Exocet reloads seemed in the offing, and as Thatcher began to prefer Peru to the UN, Argentina decided the opposite. Exocet sadly made terms unobtainable in the era of bilateral negotiations seem undesirable now. Costa Mendez indicated that Argentina had already accepted the mediation of UN Secretary-General Perez de Cuellar. The Peruvian efforts ended in tragic and unnecessary failure.

The United Nations Secretary-General, Javier Perez de Cuellar, had maintained close contact with Argentina and the United Kingdom from the beginning of the Falklands crisis. At the outset, he quietly began preparation for UN Secretariat involvement. On 5 May the Secretary-General began a formal mediation. In the exercise of his good offices he made specific proposals for interim arrangements which might serve as the basis for a settlement.

Perez de Cuellar began his series of separate meetings with each side. He was to hold over thirty such sessions at which he explored the parties' positions. He introduced his own ideas to guide both toward possible common ground. In response to the *Sheffield*, the United Kingdom yielded on the question of pure self-determination but insisted on an Argentine surrender of a guarantee of sovereignty. The junta pondered from 6 May to 11 May, then accepted. It was an historic leap of diplomatic imagination. The two sides edged closer. The British in turn added the idea of interim UN administration rather than the return of British administration (somewhat implied already by the entering of this mediation process). By 13–14 May a settlement was emerging: UN supervision of withdrawal, administration, and negotiations that would conclude within the year. The British Ambassador to the UN, Sir Anthony Parsons, decided to take the emerging deal to London to explore its advantages and disadvantages with his government.

It was not accepted in London, but was judged a start. In the week since the landing force had been dispatched from Ascension the Cabinet had accustomed itself to the possible costs of a military solution. These costs, however, were clearly growing daily and apparently this was the basis of Argentina's bargaining strategy, not only in New York but for any resulting negotiating period. Although Argentina did not gain sovereignty firmly, Britain certainly surrendered in its proposal the prospects of continued effective British administration.

Parsons took an amended proposal back to New York. At that stage it is likely that Argentina could have secured three-quarters of its interests in the Falklands in the following approximate form: United Nations administration, with both the British and Argentine flags flying along with that of the United Nations. There would have been no return to traditional British administrative or military presence in the islands. The inevitability of full Argentine sovereignty would have been established. It would have been most difficult for the United Kingdom to reestablish any political or diplomatic momentum for a return to the status quo. Indeed it can be argued that

Britain had no desire, except insofar as the Kelpers were not convinced, to return to the prewar insecurity.

Argentina balked. Concentrating on procedure and drafting instead of substance, Argentina found the drafting of the British version unacceptable. The Argentine decision to reject the British proposal does not appear to have been well-reasoned. It is clear that Argentine decision-making by this juncture in the crisis was confused, awkward, and imprecise. The image that many held of an autocratic government, with the presumed attendant advantages of centralized power enhancing the clarity and speed of decision-making, was inaccurate. An imaginative diplomatic solution at this point would have consolidated Argentina's territorial, diplomatic, and military gains by dislodging British forces. Far more than the miscalculations resulting in the decision to invade, the decision not to accept UN administration on 18 May was at the root of Argentina's tragedy in the Falklands. If not its last, it was its best chance.

On 20 May, the Secretary-General informed the President of the Security Council that his efforts did not offer the prospect of success. The following day, he so informed the Security Council. On 21 May the British Task Force established its beachhead at San Carlos Bay on East Falkland Island and the British campaign to regain the Falkland Islands militarily was under way. International diplomatic mediation and negotiation had failed their most crucial test, to prevent war.

Notes: Chapter 7

1 House of Commons *Official Report*, 26 and 28 March 1968.
2 Sir Nicholas Henderson, "America and the Falklands: case study in the behaviour of an ally," *The Economist*, 12 November 1983.
3 ibid., p. 32
4 ibid., p. 35
5 Admiral Lombardo, Argentina's operations commander in the South Atlantic at the time, later publicly confirmed the Belgrano's orders: search out and sink.
6 See the House of Commons minutes of the proceedings of the Foreign Affairs Committee, session 1982–3 (London: HMSO), 11 May 1983, Draft, Chairman's report on a policy for the Falkland Islands, section 3, para. 11.

8

American Diplomacy and the Haig Mission: An Insider's Perspective

DAVID. C GOMPERT

The Falklands War holds great fascination for military and political analysts. Militarily, it had a bit of everything: air, naval, and ground operations in every conceivable combination; staggering logistical difficulties; decisive tactical judgments; and widely varying behavior of troops under extreme conditions. Moreover, these military phenomena occurred under laboratory-like circumstances: we know why some weapons systems worked well and others not, why some soldiers fought well and others not; we can work our way through the campaign with great precision, and we can see clearly the logic of the result.

The war is just as compelling a subject for students and practitioners of diplomacy and law, providing them, too, with a little bit of everything: a major peacemaking effort was undertaken by the United States; both the United Nations and a regional organization became involved; and certain key principles of international conduct were tested. Furthermore, neither the underlying dispute nor the conflict itself was so entangled in the East—West strategic and ideological competition that one's conclusions about it are skewed by prejudices about those larger questions. Finally, there is little confusion or room for debate about what happened. Negotiations had proved barren for seventeen years, and there was no reason to foresee progress. Argentina was clearly the first to use force. The British right of self-defense was beyond reasonable challenge. Even taking into account that the territory was in dispute—which has been and remains the view of the United States—the inhabitants and their administration were unmistakably British.

Despite these seemingly ideal conditions for assessing the conflict, it is important to realize that this peculiar episode was an aberrant blip on the radar scope of world affairs. Future historians may find the significance of the conflict as mystifying as its origins. For example, lest one assume that there are clear lessons to be learned about the norms and patterns of decolonization, one should recall that decolonization never was the real issue. The Argentines went to war not because the Falklands are governed from London but because they are not ruled from Buenos Aires. Independence for the islands is as objectionable to the Argentines as is British rule. The underlying problem virtually defied solution through compromise, another reason to avoid drawing exceedingly broad lessons from the war. Argentina was unable to entertain any solution short of a guarantee of eventual sovereignty over the Malvinas, while London excluded solutions that would not have the support of the islanders themselves. For their part, the islanders remain inalterably opposed to Argentine sovereignty.

Those of us involved in the Haig negotiating mission knew from the outset that the logic and force of each side's position would not only make a settlement depend on a high degree of compromise, but would make such compromise extremely difficult. The first round of talks in London and in Buenos Aires—when we heard the sides' positions point-blank—left us even more pessimistic than when the mission began. And by the time the U.S. effort had run aground and the UN effort was under way, we who had tried and failed knew better than anyone—save perhaps the British—that there would be a fight to the finish.

Yet if the politics and passions of the situation reduced the hope for peace, the clarity with which the military outcome could have been foreseen should have facilitated a political solution. Once the British decided to use force—and with Thatcher this was never in doubt—the real choice for the Argentines was not between their goal of sovereignty and the solution offered by the United States, namely, some improvement over the *status quo ante* but short of sovereignty. Instead, the choice was the U.S. proposals or defeat. Nevertheless, the Argentine junta had great difficulty realizing this, and insofar as it did, it consistently failed to take this reality into account in its decisions. Much of our time in the negotiations was spent trying to convince the Argentines that what did happen would happen.

It is difficult to derive clear-cut lessons about diplomacy and law on the basis of an episode that inherently defied negotiated solution and in which one of the two governments had trouble appreciating reality. But some tentative conclusions can be drawn. It may be helpful at this point to explain how the conflict was seen from three different vantage points: Buenos Aires, London, and Washington.

No goal has had greater salience in Argentine foreign policy over the years than the establishment of Argentine rule over the Malvinas. There is a genuine national feeling that the country will remain less than whole—and not just in the geographic sense—until the Malvinas are returned. Far from dissipating when economic and political conditions on the mainland worsened, the passion for the Malvinas only intensified. The proximity of the islands, and the image of a tiny British garrison hanging onto real estate of such great value to Argentina and seemingly little interest to London, made the British presence all the more repulsive, heightening the Argentine sense of frustration.

For seventeen years negotiations had led nowhere. The British seemed to hold all the cards. Every time a solution was conceived—such as a lease arrangement, with the Argentines gaining sovereignty—it was aborted by what the Argentines viewed as a handful of Tory M.P.s acting on behalf of the Falkland Islands Company under the banner of self-determination. Moreover, from the Argentine perspective, the British used a web of discriminatory restrictions to make it impossible for the Argentines to compete through trade, investment, and immigration. This was Catch-22: the islanders were to determine the islands' future, but the islanders would always be exclusively of British stock.

One of the most striking revelations for us when we first arrived in Buenos Aires was that the rage among the professional diplomats in the Foreign Ministry was if anything more intense, though of course less frenzied, than the rage in the streets. This was more than a bungled decision by a handful of officers who whipped up and then had to answer to the crowd outside the Casa Rosada. It took extraordinarily poor judgment to invade the Falklands, and it is unlikely to happen again. But the fury in Argentina will not go away.

The Argentines had lost hope that they could obtain their

central foreign policy goal through peaceful means. Moreover, they did not see themselves committing a crime, at least not one with a victim. They recalled Goa and other territories that have shifted hands without great harm done. They did not think there would be a war, as evidenced by the fact that they made no real preparations for one. They meant no harm to the Falklanders; they had every intention of compensating those who wanted to leave and accepting those who wanted to stay.

It has been argued that the goodwill shown by the Reagan administration toward Argentina led the junta to conclude that Washington would prevent a major fuss. Undoubtedly, the Argentines misread Washington almost as badly as they did London. Yet there is no reason to believe that continued bad relations between the United States and Argentina would have given Galtieri pause. And it is absurd to argue, as some have, that the Reagan administration should have had the foresight to refrain from improving relations with Argentina lest the junta be emboldened to invade the Falklands. Indeed, we were thankful in the negotiations that we had at least some influence, though it proved inadequate.

If frustration and miscalculation caused the war, rigidity assured that it would run its logical military course. At times during the course of the American mediation effort it appeared to us that the Argentines might accept something less than a guarantee of sovereignty. They seemed willing to discuss a peaceful outcome involving a severance of direct rule from London, partial relief from the restrictions on contacts between the islands and the mainland, and a timetable and sympathetic, though not prejudicial, terms of reference for negotiations on sovereignty. But in the end, the obsession with sovereignty made compromise impossible. The occasional flicker of progress in the talks was only enough to keep us going, not enough to create any momentum.

In contrast to the Argentine perspective, the British prior to April 1982 never had viewed the Falklands as an issue of the first order. It did not occur to London that one of the very last, and very least, remnants of history was so combustible. The British have managed to shed scores of colonies efficiently and gracefully. (Indeed, as one member of Thatcher's Cabinet pointed out to us, the British Empire may be the only one in history to have been dismantled without leading to the death of the metropole.) The British underestimated Argentine frustration and will to use force. With greater attention and awareness of the risks, as well as a little ingenuity, the British could have found a way to solve this problem over the years, consistent with their (our) principles. Once the Argentines struck, however, several powerful forces impelled the British toward military action.

First, the Thatcher government could not allow the use of force to go uncontested. Many in Great Britain, though not including the Prime Minister, wanted above all to punish the Argentines. Mrs. Thatcher's policy was to restore British authority and remove the Argentine forces by whatever means were required: negotiations, military pressure, or the use of force. Her first message to us in the talks was that she was prepared to fight but not determined to fight. She felt compelled by both British interests and legal principle to show in one way or another that the Argentines could not gain by force what they could not gain by peaceful means.

Second, and quite apart from the question of who struck first, the cause of the islanders' self-determination came to be seen in Great Britain as the cause of democracy threatened by dictatorship. Only at some risk could English politicians take the position that this was a cause not worth fighting for, especially since the victims were Her Majesty's subjects.

Third, the British considered the Argentine attack one more humiliation, having been battered over the years by a series of reverses and predicaments from Suez and Northern Ireland to their more recent economic problems. A success was needed to revive the British spirit. Mrs. Thatcher would have done what she did even in the absence of this mood, but the mood ensured public support and therefore bolstered the chance for military success.

Not surprisingly, the outbreak of hostilities dramatically transformed the stakes for the British. The Argentines failed to understand that the British, once attacked, would fight for that which, by objective standards, might not have been considered a vital national interest.

The initial American reaction combined concern about the consequences of being caught between two friends, with determination that the resort to force not go unchecked. Important American interests were on a collision course with one another: on the one hand, the Anglo-American special partnership and the principle of non-aggression, on the other, our Latin American relationships and our ability to maintain peace and tranquility in this hemisphere.

The United States faced a number of early tactical questions. Since the dangers to its interests existed whether or not it made a diplomatic effort to avoid war, it had to weigh the costs of trying such an effort and failing, against the costs of failing to try. Since we were hesitant to conclude that a political solution was utterly impossible, the case for trying was compelling. Critics have argued that the Reagan administration failed to follow the dictum that the smart player saves his strongest card until the end of the game, in other words, that the Haig mission was too soon and too senior. Yet the Secretary realized that unless the United States was involved centrally in a negotiating effort, it would be expected to—and, indeed, should—support the British, and that, once having supported the British, it would lose its credibility in Buenos Aires and thus its effectiveness as mediator. Such considerations made it necessary to launch a negotiating effort without delay, postponing active support for the British until that effort ran its course. Haig also feared that, as their forces drew closer together, the parties to the conflict could become less flexible, an additional reason for the urgency of American mediation.

The question of level of effort was also resolved quite easily. Since the antagonists held diametrically opposed positions, the United States knew that one or both of them would have to modify their positions drastically in less time than it would take the British fleet to reach the Falklands. We kept maps with us on the London–Buenos Aires shuttle with the progress of the British fleet depicted in terms of how many days we had left before our diplomacy would be overtaken by hostilities. At 12 knots, the fleet was much swifter than we. It was also clear that any political solution that would permit the survival of one of the two governments would likely bring down the other. No one short of the Secretary of State could have produced the sort of rapid and major movement that was needed. The U.S. aim was not simply to avert bloodshed, though the immediate human consequences weighed heavily on our minds. Rather, our aim was to produce an interim political solution that met two basic criteria: first, that Argentina would not be granted control over the islands as a reward for the first use of force; second, that the solution would provide a solid, albeit unbiased, basis for subsequent negotiations on the final disposition of the islands.

While the United States wanted to prevent loss of life, it was willing to allow the British to recover the islands by force. At no point were the British asked to alter their military plans to give more time for diplomacy. Had the Argentines thought that negotiations could be used to delay military action until the British suffered either logistical or political collapse, they would have had little incentive to negotiate. Paradoxically, the clock was our enemy but we dared not tamper with it.

In the course of the Haig mission we made several pivotal decisions. We decided to urge London to accept an arrangement more advantageous to the Argentines than was the *status quo ante*. General Galtieri could not contemplate a withdrawal with nothing to show for it. Although we realized that such a proposed solution might be interpreted as rewarding the use of force, we thought that Argentina might accept minor gains well short of sovereignty as the prospect of defeat became nearer and clearer. While we tried to persuade the Argentines to leave the islands peacefully, our inducements were never so substantial as to run the risk of encouraging others around the world to contemplate aggression.

When it became evident that the negotiating positions of the two sides were drawing closer together far more slowly than their forces, the Haig mission came forward with its own proposal on 27 April. Our purpose was to convince the Argentines that, irrespective of the British attitude, we were not prepared to support a settlement that guaranteed Argentine sovereignty. Haig told his Argentine counterpart, Costa Mendez, that time was running out and that the U.S. offer was the most Argentina could hope to obtain. We felt that if the Argentines came to realize that this proposal was their historic opportunity they might settle for interim arrangements that would improve their position without assuring sovereignty.

Had Argentina accepted the U.S. proposal of 27 April, it would have been difficult for the Thatcher government to reject it in favor of hostilities, since the U.S. plan safeguarded the principle of self-determination. When the Argentines rejected the American plan, hopes of a peaceful solution all but evaporated, notwithstanding the continued—and noble—efforts by the President of Peru and the UN Secretary-General. At that point, the United States decided to break off its mediation effort and support the United Kingdom. While obviously not helpful to current U.S. interests in Latin America, American support for the British reflected the view in Washington that successful seizure of disputed territory would have been the worst outcome of all. Throughout the crisis we were absolutely candid with the Argentine government, warning them not only that the British would fight but that unless Argentina displayed flexibility we would end our negotiating effort and support the British. We were careful, of course, not to tell the Argentines that we knew the British would *win*, for that would have offended them and damaged what influence we had. But it was my distinct impression that the Argentines did not have to be told what the result of hostilities would be.

The tentative lessons to be learned from this conflict—its origins, its course, and its outcome—extend into the spheres of national diplomacy and decision-making, international order, and organization. The first is that it is essential to be clear about the principles on which one's foreign policy is based. There is a natural tendency to express national policy goals and limits in terms of interests instead of principles. Of course, states are far more disposed to act to protect their interests than their principles. Yet the two are obviously related, in the sense that our principles are the offspring of a marriage between our interests and our values. Failure to act in defense of principles can lead others to conclude that aggression can be safe and successful provided it is not directed against the interests of any state strong enough to frustrate it. And if we are prepared to act in defense of principles, it is important, for the sake of avoiding miscalculation, to make sure that others know this. British policy during the Falklands War was a vivid reminder of the legitimacy, indeed the morality, of the use of force under such circumstances.

Furthermore, the fact that the British negotiated in good faith, and that the United States made a major peacemaking effort before backing the British, underscore the importance of exhausting all available peaceful means. The Soviets sometimes are puzzled by American reactions to Soviet moves that do not imperil U.S. interests. Perhaps, they will learn the lesson that the United States is quite capable of acting in support of the rule of law, even when our immediate interests might suffer.

A second lesson is that world public opinion can have the wrong effect on international politics, even when undergirded by noble intentions. It is a perfectly normal, indeed admirable, human impulse to want to stop a conflict before it gets worse, especially given justifiable fears about escalation in the nuclear age. The problem is that wars often begin with an act of aggression, and aggressors are usually better prepared at least to start a war than their victims. So they tend to get the upper hand early. Then, as world political pressures to stop the war mount, well-intentioned people begin to think that if only the fighting were stopped the adversaries could sort things out and achieve a just settlement.

The problem, however, is that those who initiate wars can too easily find support for a ceasefire without a return to the *status quo ante*, while the defender comes to be seen as resisting world demands for peace. When an institution like the United Nations becomes a vehicle for such pressure, it is difficult for it to play a constructive role. It is ironic that the British were put in the position of needing to minimize United Nations involvement in the later stages of the conflict for fear of coming under pressure to compromise their right of self-defense. Overcoming this curious problem requires resolve, discipline, and emphatic clarity about the right of self-defense. Provided they are making a reasonable effort to find a peaceful solution, countries that have been attacked must be spared the onus of refusing to end hostilities.

A third lesson is that one cannot assume that democracies are at a disadvantage in a war because of the difficulty of holding public support. The perseverance of a free people obviously depends on their attitudes about the merits of the conflict: the Falklands and Vietnam were vastly different. But the point is, support for Mrs. Thatcher actually increased after the casualty lists started coming in. Of course, it is also clear that once the public is enraged an elected government may have less room for compromise. Democracies can be formidable adversaries.

There are also lessons to be learned about the effectiveness of international organization. The main shortcomings of the United Nations were the failure to require compliance with a Security Council Resolution, and the tendency to exert political pressures to stop the fighting without first ensuring withdrawal of the invasion force. We can hardly count on internationally legislated solutions to crises, especially without strong sanctions for noncompliance.

Neither was the Falklands War a moment of glory for Western hemispheric security mechanisms, which have had and will continue to have American support. Indeed, the United States traditionally has viewed the Rio Treaty and the Organization of American States as providing a more effective framework for dealing with hemispheric problems than the United Nations. Regional bodies, however, cannot act at odds with the purposes and principles of the UN Charter, and are expected to help discharge UN Security Council decisions. In supporting the Argentine position, the Rio Treaty's Foreign Ministers did not support either Great Britain's right of self-defense or the Security Council's call for Argentine withdrawal. Unfortunately, at a moment when the world should have affirmed the basic rule of law with one voice, irrespective of relations with the disputants and differences over the merits of the dispute, condemnations were reversed and the law became muddled. While it would be unwise to conclude that the OAS and Rio Treaty mechanisms cannot be constructive and effective, it is important to realize that they are best equipped to deal with situations not involving aggression against an extra-hemispheric state.

One can learn not only from the crisis itself, but from the seventeen years of futile negotiations that preceded it. The best way to ensure that disputes are not settled violently is to settle them nonviolently. Every dispute that festers is not only a crisis waiting to happen but also a failure of international order in its own right. In this case the Argentines, at least momentarily, gave up on peaceful means because, from their perspective, these means had failed.

The scores of outstanding disputes, including the Falklands dispute itself, raise questions about national diplomacy as well as multinational cooperation. Should the United States depart more frequently from its traditional position of not taking sides on territorial disputes? Would the expression of strong American views on the merits help to drive disputes toward resolution before they turn violent? They might, or they might not, depending on whether the U.S. views have powerful political or moral weight with the parties. There is also the question of whether the United States should play a *de facto* judicial role, that is, whether the United States could strengthen international order by exerting pressure on the direction a settlement should take, as opposed to pressure on both parties to settle through compromise and the use of available machinery. Naturally, the political costs to the United States of taking sides would have to be considered.

The durability of territorial disputes is the result of a lack of community pressure, will, and spirit of compromise, not lack of machinery. The International Court of Justice could be used far more than it is, but states often lack confidence in the Court and in their own legal positions. There is also the Hague Permanent Court of Arbitration and a network of extant regional agreements on arbitration and conciliation. Much of this

115

machinery is rarely used. (Every machinist knows that the best thing for machinery is use.) Moreover, binding third-party decisions are sometimes reopened, as we have seen in several cases. Sadly, domestic politics in many states rewards the maintenance of claims more than the settlement of disputes.

What is needed may seem fairly obvious. First, compulsory jurisdiction of international judicial machinery should be expanded. But that would require the consent of states. Second, binding settlements should be reopened only under extraordinary circumstances. Yet how, short of sanctions, can compliance with third-party decisions be enforced? Third, it makes far more sense to revitalize and use existing mechanisms than to create new ones. There may be some value in blowing the dust off some of the older agreements, updating them, and promoting their use in the course of a systematic, case-by-case review of oustanding disputes, at least in the Western hemisphere.

Better international dispute-settlement machinery would not necessarily have resolved the Falklands issue before it exploded, nor can it resolve it now. And it is difficult to prove that had the United States taken a position on the merits of the dispute it would not have flared into war. But the Falklands tragedy does serve to remind us of the importance of settling differences whether or not conflict has occurred or seems imminent. While the prospect of conflict inevitably stimulates efforts to settle disputes, one must be careful not to allow the threat of violence to be used advantageously in settling disputes, lest one reward the threat of force, which is scarcely more consistent with the rule of law than rewarding the use of force.

The subject of law and order in a decentralized and highly diverse international society is filled with paradoxes and quandaries. The ultimate determinant is politics. And politics need not be the enemy of compromise, fairness, or principle. There may be little basis for optimism if one looks only at the mechanics of peacemaking. But what will surely matter far more over the long run is whether politics, international and domestic alike, will exert a normative pressure which will reward compromise without abandoning justice.

The UN Secretary-General correctly placed the Falklands on his recent list of UN failures. In fact, one could safely list the Falklands on the list of failures of the entire postwar international order. True, the resort to force did not pay, which is, of course, an important lesson. But this was the result of relative military capabilities. One can hardly count on the targets of aggression to have superior military forces. It is difficult to be an optimist about the rule of law. But this should only strengthen our own commitment to principle.

9

UN Efforts at Settlement
of the Falkland Islands
Crisis

INIS L. CLAUDE, JR.

The long-standing dispute between the United Kingdom and
Argentina over the Falkland Islands has been in some sense
before the United Nations since 1965, when the General
Assembly passed a Resolution dealing with the matter. That
body passed similar Resolutions in 1973 and 1976. The acute
crisis in relations between the claimants was brought to the
Security Council on 1 April 1982, just before Argentina's
military move, and received the close attention of the Council
and the Secretary-General throughout the period of impending
and actual military conflict. We know how it all turned out.
What remains is to see what we can learn about the United
Nations from an examination of what happened and what did
not happen in this case.

The observation that seems naturally to come first is that the
United Nations failed to achieve a peaceful settlement of the
dispute and thereby to prevent war. A case can be made for the
proposition that the organization hoped and tried to produce
that result: the Security Council, by consensus procedure,
backed its president on April 1 in urging Argentina to refrain
from sending troops to the islands, and the Secretary-General,
who had made a similar appeal on 1 April, worked valiantly first
to head off and then to persuade the parties to call off the war,
acting first without and later with a formal mandate from the
Security Council. Why did these efforts fail?

A notable feature of the case was its old-fashioned slow-moving quality. From the first, the United Kingdom made clear its intention to respond militarily to Argentina's military initiative, but it moved to do so at the pace of the steamship rather than the jet plane. Nearly a month went by before significant encounters began, and nearly two months before large-scale British landings turned the confrontation into real war. The occurrence of this interval makes it all the more striking that the peacemakers failed; shortage of time was clearly not one of their handicaps.

The Secretary-General deferred to the government of the United States and then to that of Peru as they undertook mediatory efforts. He entered actively into the picture only after those efforts had failed, at about the beginning of May, although he had carried on careful preparations during the period of Secretary Haig's shuttle diplomacy and had passed the word that the United Nations would provide whatever assistance might be needed in implementing a settlement. Although it might have been better if the April mediator had been Perez de Cuellar rather than Haig, we can never know. It appears that Haig had better credentials for the task, for both the British and the Argentines regarded the United States as a friendly country, while Britain appeared to have some misgivings about the Secretary-General's capacity to transcend his Latin American origins and about the capacity of the United Nations to set aside its anticolonial bias. Not for the first time, the United States seemed more neutral than the United Nations. In any case, it is not evident that it was a mistake for the Secretary-General to await his turn, or that the delay in his moving to center stage doomed his efforts.

If there was an error in the timing of the UN's peaceful settlement efforts, it can be argued that it occurred before, not after, Argentine forces moved into the Falklands on 2 April. Before that date, there was a dispute in the settlement of which the assistance of third parties might have been valuable. After that date, there was a conflict to which the theory of collective security might well have been regarded as more pertinent than the theory of pacific settlement. Indeed, the first action of the Security Council supported that view of the matter: it passed, as Resolution 502, a draft submitted by the United Kingdom that treated the Argentine invasion as a breach of the peace and demanded withdrawal. Moreover, Britain asserted without challenge that the Council was acting under article 40 of the Charter—that is, under the enforcement provisions of Chapter

VII rather than under the pacific settlement provisions of Chapter VI. One might argue that, after the Council had passed such a Resolution, the United Nations ought to have pressed Argentina to comply with the order for withdrawal rather than shifting to a mediatory role; in short, there should have been a continuation under Chapter VII instead of a reversion to Chapter VI. According to this viewpoint, Argentina had started a war, even if Britain had not yet fought back, and the possibility of pacific settlement had been superseded by the necessity for enforcement action.

On the theoretical plane, there are numerous unsolved problems in the relationship between the pacific settlement and the collective security functions of international organizations. Both the League of Nations and the United Nations have been constitutionally assigned both types of function. It seems logical to assume that, whenever possible, the search for peaceful solutions is to be made first, and that collective security measures are to be treated as a last resort. But what are the characteristics that mark a situation as appropriate for the one or the other approach? At what point should pacific settlement efforts give way to the sterner measures of enforcement? What problems stem from the conflicting requirements imposed by the two approaches upon international organizations or individuals serving as their agents—pacific settlement's requirement of scrupulous neutrality and avoidance of normative judgment of the positions of conflicting parties, as against collective security's demand for condemnation of the offending party and mobilization of support for the victim? The awkwardness of the normative switch required by the turn from the former to the latter approach was illustrated in this case by the charge made several times in the Security Council against the United States, that its taking the side of Britain after negotiations had failed was proof that the United States had been dishonest in purporting to serve as an impartial mediator in the earlier stage of the crisis. It is unlikely that those who insisted that the United States had been pro-British all along, and had strung out the negotiations to give the British time for military preparations, would have been mollified by the explanation that the switch from impartiality to partisanship is required by the transition from pacific settlement to collective security. A United Nations that sometimes takes sides can hardly avoid compromising its reputation for the kind of neutrality that is essential to some of its most important functions. In short, the notion that mediatory and enforcement roles can be combined without difficulty in an international organization requires more careful consideration than scholars or statesmen have yet given it; it may be acceptable as a conclusion, but not as an assumption. We have been spared major difficulty about this combination only by the failure of the League and the UN to take the assignment of the collective security function seriously. In the absence of its second half, the combination poses no problem.

In any case, the Security Council's approval of Resolution 502 would have been a fitting introduction to the operation of a collective security system, if such a system had existed. It was far less appropriate as a preliminary to efforts to promote agreement on a settlement, although I cannot see that it actually hampered the Secretary-General in the negotiations that he conducted, on his own initiative, after other mediators had failed. Perez de Cuellar is generally acknowledged to have performed with admirable professionalism, and he evidently commanded the respect and confidence of both sides, overcoming the doubts said to have been initially harbored by the British. The incongruity between the Council's original approach to the case and the subsequent actions of the Secretary-General and the Council does, however, offer us a clue to the collective indecisiveness of the members of the UN and the conflicts of purpose among them that affected the organization's handling of the Falklands crisis. The failure of the UN's peacemaking efforts cannot be ascribed to lack of time, mistaken technique, or inadequate facilities. We must look for something more fundamental.

It may be that the first step toward understanding is to emancipate ourselves from the assumption that the central objective of the United Nations in this case was to achieve a peaceful solution. Peace has universal appeal only as an abstraction; in the concrete case, commitment to peace is rarely unqualified. The prominence of other values inspires attention to the terms on which peace is to be welcomed or accepted. In the UN, as in the world outside, states recognize that the commandment "Do not fight" must frequently be translated "Accept the status quo," and their devotion to peace varies with their satisfaction with things as they are. For most participants in the UN proceedings concerning the Falklands affair, the urge to maintain the peace was secondary to some other consideration. If this was least clearly true of the Secretary-General, whose motivations surely included the improvement of the organization's reputation for effectiveness as a peacemaker, it was most

121

conspicuously true of the parties to the dispute. They switched places on the scale of enthusiasm for peace after the Argentine landing on 2 April. Before that event, peace meant victory for Britain in the quarrel over the islands; afterwards, until the ouster of Argentine forces, peace meant victory for Argentina. The UN was not simply used, unsuccessfully, to promote a peaceful resolution of the conflict. It was also used by the parties and their sympathizers for purposes less related to settling than to winning the dispute, and the insistence of the parties on using it in this way was undoubtedly the fundamental cause of the Secretary-General's failure in the use that he sought to make of the organization. Our consideration of the UN as peace conference must now give way to consideration of the UN as battlefield.

Both parties attempted to exploit the organization's value as a dispenser of collective legitimacy, which is to say that each undertook to secure the blessing of the UN for its own cause and to call down a UN curse upon that of the opponent. They were less concerned about what the UN might do, as a mediator, for both of them, than about what it might do, as a partisan, for one of them and to the other. Neither, I think, seriously expected the UN, as an organization, to "do anything" in the furtherance of its cause, in the sense of military activity, but both clearly attached considerable importance to the UN's distribution of praise and blame, symbolic support and opposition.

Argentina came off rather badly in this battle for the support of the UN, or, more precisely, the battle in the UN for the support of other states. For the relatively dispassionate observer of the case this was something of a surprise, and may be taken as hopeful evidence that the ideological predictability of the organization, the knee-jerk inexorability of its moral reflexes, is less perfect than we have sometimes supposed. For Argentina, it was a bitter pill. Argentina, quite legitimately, felt double-crossed by the UN. It had expected, and had ample reason to expect, that the organization's overwhelming majority would consider this a case of necessary and proper military initiative to achieve decolonization. Argentine spokesmen invoked the analogy of Goa, which India had liberated from Portuguese colonial rule in 1961, and elaborated the theme in much the same way as India had done: the UN has outlawed colonialism; the retention of colonies is an act of continuous aggression; their liberation is therefore a defensive reaction to aggression and a service to the community, worthy of praise and support. In the case at hand, Argentina was freeing a portion of its national domain that Britain had illegally occupied in 1833 and now illegally persisted in occupying. Since a state cannot be said to invade its own territory, Argentina's forces were to be described as liberators, not as invaders. The UN's condemnation, the act of judgment that is the essence of the collective legitimization function and would serve as the trigger for the operation of a collective security system if there were one, should fall upon the United Kingdom, guilty of *l'agression de tous les jours*.

Everything that the General Assembly had officially said in the past about the Falklands encouraged the expectation that this Argentine position would be endorsed by the United Nations. In Resolution 2065 (XX) of 1965, ninety-four members of the Assembly had voted for, and none had voted against, the classification of these islands as a colony whose removal from that status should be negotiated as part of the process of implementing Resolution 1514 (XV), the Assembly's great emancipation proclamation of 1960. In 1973 the Assembly had adopted, by a vote of 116 to 0, with fourteen abstentions and five absences, a text recommended by the Special Committee charged with overseeing the implementation of Resolution 1514. This Resolution 3160 (XXVIII) expressly praises Argentina for its efforts to bring about the decolonization of the territory and presses the parties to make progress in negotiating the end of that colonial situation. A substantially similar document, which invoked the authority of declarations emanating from the conferences of the Non-Aligned Countries at Lima in 1975 and Colombo in 1976, had been approved by the Assembly in 1976, as Resolution 31/49. The Argentine position was also formally endorsed in that year by the Inter-American Juridical Committee. In summary, most of the states of the world had repeatedly gone on record, in the United Nations and in other multilateral forums, as supporting Argentina's contention that the removal of British rule from the Falklands was in keeping with the sacred mission of decolonization.

Why, then, was Argentina unable to rally the UN to its side in the spring of 1982? Was it, perhaps, because Argentina shifted from negotiation to the use of military forces, thereby creating the risk, later turned into reality, of war? It is true that the General Assembly had not endorsed the use of force to oust the British. It had called for negotiations, and its Resolutions were themselves intended to serve as instruments of diplomatic pressure to be wielded by Argentina against the United

Kingdom, but they called for the political surrender of the colonial power, not its military defeat. Nevertheless, Argentina anticipated general acquiescence in, if not overt approval of, its resort to military action to take the islands. Its spokesmen seemed to rely heavily upon the Goan precedent, in which India's use of force had elicited no formal condemnation and had in fact been widely regarded as a blow for freedom. They undoubtedly relied as well upon the record of steadily increasing multilateral support, in the UN and elsewhere, for the activities of entities that are billed as liberation movements—the various groups that succeeded in turning Rhodesia into Zimbabwe, the PLO, SWAPO, Sandinistas, and the like. Their expectation must have been nourished by the proliferation of texts adopted by organs of the UN, including the Assembly's 1974 definition of aggression (Resolution 3314 [XXIX]), affirming that the use of force for decolonization is excluded from the disapprobation generally conferred upon violence. For some twenty years, the trend in the UN had been for anticolonialism to override anti-aggression—for aggression in the anticolonial cause to be regarded as justified and therefore not to be called aggression. Given that history, the Argentine expectation of friendly reaction in the UN to the military seizure of the islands seemed reasonable.

It turned out, of course, that Argentina had guessed wrong. Resolution 502, proposed by Britain, deplored Argentina's occupation and called for withdrawal of its forces. Only Panama fully endorsed Argentina's case and voted against the Resolution. The most striking feature of the Security Council's action was the defection from Argentina of Third World states, the custodians of anticolonialism; Guyana, Jordan, Togo, Uganda, and Zaïre constituted half of the majority that passed the Resolution. These states supported Argentina's claim to the islands but rejected the resort to military measures, and insisted that this was the position of the Non-Aligned Movement. Argentina won on the merits, but lost on the method.

Why was the Argentine military initiative deemed unacceptable by most members of the Council, and most particularly by Third World states? Some of the opposition can be attributed to a general conviction that violence is too dangerous a thing to unleash in today's world. Argentina was especially culpable because it had acted in defiance of urgent appeals by the Council and the Secretary-General; it could not say that it had not been warned. This explanation will not suffice, however, for most members of the United Nations have a record of excusing or even extolling violence when it appears to be used in support of what they consider just causes. The argument that the UN abhors violence, unconditionally, will not wash. The crucial fact, then, was that the Argentine cause was not regarded as good enough to justify resort to military action; the anticolonial aspect of the case was considered weak. This is the point on which Argentina felt itself betrayed. For years, the General Assembly had declared the Falklands a colony that ought to be emancipated. Now, the Security Council took the position that the islands' colonial character was not sufficiently clear to give legitimacy to their seizure. More precisely, the Third World abandoned Argentina. Its earlier call for decolonization of the Falklands was now hedged by the proviso that force must not be used. This access of squeamishness was occasioned by second thoughts about the validity of the anticolonial aspect of the case.

The heart of the matter was that the ethnic combination was wrong. Decolonization justifies violence only when it is a matter of freeing non-Europeans from European rule, so as to satisfy their presumed demand either for independence or for union with their non-European neighbors. The Goan case, for instance, was a proper one: India evicted the Portuguese so that its kinsmen in Goa could join India. This case was altogether too much an intra-European affair. The Argentines, an essentially European people, undertook to establish their rule over a British population that clearly preferred to remain under British rule. This could hardly be represented as emancipation; it was a peculiar brand of decolonization that violated, rather than implemented, the principle of self-determination. It threatened to establish, rather than promised to remove, alien dominance over the Falklanders. According to the Third World's doctrine, British rule over a British people could hardly qualify as colonialism—certainly not as the kind of colonialism that is wicked enough to justify violence for its extirpation. Argentine rule over a British people *might* qualify.

British and Australian representatives used the phrase "Argentine colonialism" in the Security Council, but it remained for the delegate from Kenya, in the meeting of 24 May, to offer a devastating rebuttal of Argentina's claim that its military initiative deserved praise, as an act of decolonization, rather than blame, as an act of aggression. He accused Argentina of treating the people of the islands like chattels, as it sought to establish colonial rule over them. Moreover, he denied Argentina's anticolonial credentials, reminding his audience that Argentines, unlike Africans, had not lived for the last century under colonial rule. Finally, he repudiated the interpretation of Argentina's claim against British possession of the islands as a colonial question; it was, he said, "a pure territorial claim against the United Kingdom based on history, in total disregard of the people who now live on the Falkland Islands." Note the importance of this characterization. He was saying that it was not the kind of claim that African states feel bound to support—a demand for the defeat of colonialism, so as to permit the exercise of self-determination. Rather, it was precisely the kind of claim that African states generally regard as most dangerous to their security and tranquility—a demand for redrawing of boundaries, justified on historical grounds, without regard for the will of the affected people. Kenya was telling Africa that Argentina's action was not a continuation of the crusade against colonialism but a precedent that might produce chaos in Africa. A more dramatic demonstration of Third World defection from Argentina's cause would be hard to imagine.

In short, when push came to shove—when diplomatic pressure was succeeded by military seizure, and rhetorical consideration by the General Assembly gave way to efforts at crisis management by the Security Council—the Third World discovered that it had previously overstated its commitment to Argentina's campaign to wrest the Falklands from Britain. If it had believed as deeply as it had purported to believe in the colonial character of the case, it would not have been as troubled as it was by Argentina's resort to force. In the moment of truth, the Falklands did not appear to be a full-fledged colony, nor did Argentina's liberationist credentials seem clearly valid. This episode may confirm the notion that the Latin American states, or at least the ones exhibiting most conspicuously the evidence of their European origins, are acknowledged only as supporters, not as real members, of the Third World—having a status somewhat analogous to that of white participants in the American civil rights movement. The action that Argentina had expected to be hailed as a blow for decolonization was regarded instead as an effort to round out its territory, in disregard of the principle of national self-determination.

The United Kingdom had greater success in the United Nations than Argentina. As we have noted, the Council's

Resolution 502 was an endorsement of the British position that Argentina's invasion of the islands was an improper and unacceptable act. In effect, Britain succeeded in having its adversary characterized as an aggressor and itself as the victim of aggression. As we have also noted, this might have been the first stage of a collective security procedure, but in fact there was no serious expectation on the part of anyone that the UN would do anything more than deplore and urge Argentina to reverse its military intrusion. The case confirms the world's frequently noted, but never quite admitted, abandonment of the ideal of collective security. A few months later, in the introduction to the first Annual Report that he had submitted as Secretary-General, Perez de Cuellar vaguely revived that ideal, but I have found no evidence that either he or anyone else displayed the slightest interest in the notion that the Security Council might organize the enforcement of its demand for removal of Argentine troops from the Falklands. For better or for worse, that conception of the role of the UN had long since evaporated, and it was evident that collective legitimization was to be considered a substitute for, rather than a preliminary to, collective security operations. Britain got more than it ought to have expected from the UN: an official characterization of the situation that at least put Argentina in the wrong and at most could be construed as authorizing Britain and its sympathizers to respond militarily to the Argentine challenge.

Having gained in the Security Council an implicit license to mobilize pressure against its adversary, Britain, without neglecting conspicuous preparations for the ultimate contingency of military action, turned to its allies. The European Community imposed economic sanctions upon Argentina early in April, and, with two defections from its ranks, renewed them on 25 May. The United States, frustrated in its efforts to mediate the dispute, joined the British side at the end of April, and resorted to sanctions. The NATO Defense Ministers declared their support for Britain early in May. On the other side, Argentina's case was endorsed by the Organization of American States in a Resolution approved on 28 April, which also deplored the EC's sanctions; the OAS reiterated its support for Argentina on 29 May. The Soviet bloc stuck resolutely to the view that the West was compounding the sin of unrepentant imperialism by resorting to economic aggression—and planning military aggression—against Argentina, in retaliation for its eminently proper liberationist initiative. All this demonstrates with dramatic clarity that the Security Council's act of declaring the community's will that force not be used to press demands for change, however meritorious they may be, had been an aberration. The community, concerned about the general order, was a passing fancy; what remained in the UN was a congeries of competing alliances, concerned about victory and defeat.

A significant qualification needs to be added, however, to this comment about the persistence of the habit of choosing sides. Although it is true that European and Latin American states played their predictable favorites, it is also true that both sets of allies displayed an ambivalence, as did the UN as a whole, that seems to me explainable primarily by reference to the phenomenon of quasi-pacifism, an ill-defined but powerful aversion to violence.

Argentina, as we have seen, was the first victim. Numerous states that supported its claim were alienated by its military action. Argentina was disappointed in the strength of the support given by the OAS, which was purely verbal; at no point did Argentina's hemispheric brethren seem inclined to do more than denounce Britain and its supporters. They were not quite comfortable about Argentina's initial use of force, and, although they sharply disapproved of Britain's violent riposte, they were unwilling to consider participation in the fray.

The quasi-pacifist reaction affected the British position in an even more striking way. Although the Security Council's initial disapproval of Argentina's occupation could logically be construed as implying approval of British military action to oust the invaders, if other means should fail, it does not appear that this is an accurate interpretation of the attitude of those who supported Resolution 502. Britain's partners in the EC became notably less enthusiastic about involvement in economic sanctions as it became apparent that the issue was moving toward a military dénouement, and two of them, Ireland and Italy, dropped out when the sanctions were renewed. The Europeans seemed to draw a nice distinction between deploring and resisting Argentina's action; they confined their participation, and perhaps even their approval, to the former. Other states, less identifiable as partisans of the British cause, were even less sympathetic to Britain's insistence upon taking the islands back by force if necessary. In Security Council debates and elsewhere, British recourse to coercion to oust the Argentines was widely regarded as aggression. In some measure, this is attributable to Britain's willingness to delay response to the Argentine invasion and to seek a nonmilitary solution; the longer the interval between attack and resistance, the greater is the risk that the defender will seem to be starting the fight.

Britain's success in the UN was substantially confined to the passage of Resolution 502, just after the Argentine invasion. What was to happen after the event? In the British view, Argentina was to be pressed to withdraw, in accordance with that Resolution, and could properly be forced to do so, if persuasion and economic sanctions failed. The prevailing attitude in the UN was quite different: Britain and Argentina were to negotiate a settlement, which means that an arrangement for handing the islands over to Argentina was to be worked out, and new violence was to be avoided. Support for Britain in the UN was inversely related to the proximity of British forces to the Falklands. As those forces began to arrive in the South Atlantic, and clashes with the Argentine forces began, it became clear that fighting back was little more popular in the UN than picking a fight. In short, the collective-security slogan "Thou shalt not commit aggression, but shalt resist it" gave way to the quasi-pacifistic slogan "Thou shalt neither commit nor resist aggression."

After serious fighting began—that is to say, after Britain launched its effort to force the Argentine withdrawal for which Resolution 502 had called—support for the British cause steadily declined in the UN. *Ceasefire*, always an appealing notion with its implication of movement from war to peace, became in effect an anti-British slogan; it meant that Britain should not challenge the new status quo that Argentina had created by seizing the islands. Britain countered with *withdrawal*, which meant that the preinvasion status quo should be reestablished. On 26 May the Council unanimously approved a new formulation, Resolution 505, which was a compromise between these positions. It called for negotiations under the auspices of the Secretary-General to achieve a ceasefire, rather than demanding that Britain desist, and it referred approvingly but vaguely to Resolution 502, rather than reiterating, or talking of enforcing, the demand that Argentina withdraw. This Resolution, which produced no results, was significant mainly as an indicator of the shift of opinion that was occurring in the UN; if Argentina had been the villain in Resolution 502, Britain was at least equally culpable in Resolution 505.

In the next stage of the Security Council's action, Britain was treated even more clearly as the defendant in the case. Beginning on 2 June, the Council considered a Draft Resolution submitted by Panama, Argentina's most avid supporter in the Council, along with Spain. This draft would have had the Council order a ceasefire, abandoning the earlier motif of urging the parties to negotiate such an arrangement. Britain took this as an effort to have the Council insist that Argentina be permitted to retain the islands, and declared that it would accept a ceasefire only if it were linked to a definite plan for the immediate withdrawal of Argentine forces. The draft was amended so as to imply that withdrawal was to follow the cessation of hostilities, but Britain was unconvinced that the amendment genuinely altered the original "Britain must surrender the islands to Argentina" thrust of the Resolution. Hence, when it came to a vote on 4 June Britain, along with the United States, voted against the Resolution. Nine states voted for it, and four abstained. This meant that the British and American negatives were vetoes. In view of the fact that Ambassador Kirkpatrick subsequently announced that American policy called for abstention rather than use of the veto, it appears that Britain really stood alone in opposing a Council majority.

This impression is somewhat diluted by the fact that four of the states voting for the draft—Ireland, Japan, Uganda, and Zaïre—asserted that they shared the British view that a ceasefire should be tied to withdrawal and believed that the amended draft satisfactorily made that connection. Hence, even though they disagreed with the British reading of the document, they did not oppose the British position. In fact, however, the British interpretation seemed to be confirmed by the Argentine representative, speaking after the vote. He, quite accurately, treated the episode as a victory for his country, and he gave no intimation that Argentina considered the vetoed resolution as anything other than a call for peace in the sense of Britain's abandonment of its effort to force Argentina to give up the islands. No member of the Council other than Britain had clearly opposed that Resolution.

When Argentina used force to take the Falklands, the Security Council objected. When Britain used force to retake the Falklands, the Security Council objected. In these matters, I believe that the members of the Council were reasonably representative of the full organization. This may be taken to mean that members of the UN are deeply devoted to peace, or, what comes to the same thing, that they are mortally afraid of the spread of international violence. It may also be thought to mean that positions stated in the name of the UN are frequently not to be taken seriously—that members set forth symbolic positions, for the record only, unaccompanied by any serious interest in their effectuation. The UN supported decolonization of the Falklands, until Argentina sent in its troops, whereupon the UN became less interested in decolonization than in preventing aggression. In keeping with its commitment against aggression, the UN demanded the withdrawal of Argentine troops, until Britain sent its forces to compel that withdrawal, whereupon the UN became less interested in resisting aggression than in keeping the peace.

These two interpretations of the Council's vacillations in the case at hand are not antithetical, but can be combined. One can draw from this story the conclusion that spokesmen for states, gathered in international organizations, can neither resist the urge to endorse high principles nor muster the resolve to uphold them, particularly when the upholding entails the risk of violence. The commitment to peace, like other commitments, is hedged in this way; peace is to be sought, but not at the price of accepting positive responsibility for suppressing its violation.

A Note on Sources

This essay is based primarily upon the provisional records of meetings of the UN Security Council on the Falklands case from 1 April through 3 June 1982 (pertinent numbers in the series, S/PV. 2345–72). A survey of the *New York Times* for the same period also provided important information. Reference is also made to the Introduction to the Report of the Secretary-General on the Work of the Organization submitted to the thirty-seventh session of the General Assembly, which appeared in preliminary form as UN Document A/37/1, 7 September 1982.

10

The OAS and the
Inter-American System:
History, Law, and Diplomacy

SRILAL PERERA

In its numerous attempts throughout its history to ensure peace and stability in the Western hemisphere, the Organization of American States has had to deal with two types of conflicts: first, extracontinental ones involving the threat or use of force between a member of the OAS and a nonmember state outside the American continent, and, second, intracontinental conflicts in which all the participants are member states of the OAS. The Falklands War fell into the former category, and it illustrated a series of ambiguities and challenges which the OAS is constitutionally and structurally ill-equipped to handle.

In order to provide a better understanding of the OAS and its limitations in extracontinental conflicts such as the Falklands, this essay will survey the evolution and history of hemispheric security arrangements that culminated in the Inter-American Treaty of Reciprocal Assistance of 1947 and the OAS Charter of 1948. These treaties will then be examined to determine the degree to which they have been effectively applied, and the extent to which some of their provisions may conflict with the UN Charter. The essay will probe also the different positions taken by member states prior to and during the crisis, and the underlying causes for these differences, and will conclude by offering some tentative guidelines through which the OAS could become a smoother and more effective organization for promoting regional and international order.

The Early Phase: Meeting Security Threats from Europe

The first two decades of the nineteenth century witnessed the formation of a number of newly independent states on the American continent. In July 1811 Venezuela declared its independence from Spain. Simon Bolivar led this struggle for independence in the northern sector of South America, and successfully routed the Spanish Army at Boyaca in New Granada. Following the independence of Venezuela and then Ecuador, the colossal new state of Colombia, comprised of New Granada, Venezuela, and Ecuador, was created. In the south, José de San Martin carried out the struggle for independence and defeated the Spanish in decisive battles that won independence for Uruguay, Peru, and Chile. Brazil's transition into independence was peaceful. It came in December 1822, when Pedro, the son of King Joao, formally proclaimed himself constitutional Emperor of Brazil. A serious concern to safeguard this newly won independence in South America motivated Bolivar to call for the establishment of an inter-American organization that would "serve as a council in great conflict, as a point of contact in common dangers, and as a faithful interpreter of public treaties where difficulties occur, as a conciliator, in short, of our differences." The new states feared that Spain, with the assistance of the Holy Alliance, to which it was a party, might try to recover its lost colonies.

These and other security concerns were articulated at the Congress of Inter-American States which met in Panama and drafted a treaty in 1826. The Panama Treaty, which never came into effect, was but one of several legal instruments proposed at the conference which incorporated the ideas of collective defense and peaceful settlement of disputes. The parties to the treaty would have bound themselves to settle all disputes peacefully and where there was potential for conflict, to bring all disputes before the assembly of the confederation. The treaty also stipulated that any state could be excluded from the confederation if it substantially changed its form of government. Once excluded, such members could rejoin only with the unanimous consent of all other members. The reason for this stipulation was to prevent monarchical elements from gaining power in a Latin American state and subjecting it to the hegemony of Spain or the Holy Alliance. In essence, a major objective of the treaty was to thwart any Eurocentric extracontinental threats, even when they might be posed by a regime in the area serving as a surrogate for a European power.[1]

By this time, Great Britain was already the world's mightiest naval power. Throughout the eighteenth century, the British had developed an intricate network of strategic military and commercial outposts connecting their colonies in North America, Africa, and Asia. Spanish America, where British influence was negligible, gained increasing attraction for the advocates of a more extensive British Empire, a development which coincided with the gradual, but undeniable, retreat of Spain from its former position as a first-class world power. The British incursion into the Falklands in 1766 was but one of a series of forays into Central and South America that culminated in the colonization of several territories, including many of the Caribbean islands. The efforts of Great Britain to conquer and control new markets for its widely expanding commerce and industry were also illustrated by such military enterprises as the Anglo-French blockade of the River Plate from 1806 to 1807.

But despite the Spanish, British, and French threats to the region, Bolivar's efforts to build a confederation that would provide security against European powers failed. A number of internal factors help to explain why the Panama Treaty of 1826 was not ratified. First, there was the growing sense of national separateness, which divided South and Central America into a large number of states, each jealous of its newly won sovereignty. Also, nearly all Latin American states had unsolved boundary problems with each other, which caused friction among them. Hence, publicly expressed sentiments of solidarity and brotherhood were undercut by private suspicion and jealousy.

The immediate post-independence period in South and Central America was marked by numerous frontier disputes. To reconcile these disputes, the new states agreed to use the Roman Law principle of *uti possidetis* with the critical date of 1810. This principle meant that for purposes of setting the boundaries for these states, the administrative divisions used by Spain in 1810 to govern her colonies would become the borders for the new states. Hence, *uti possidetis* could only apply to boundary disputes *among* former Spanish colonies. The problem was that many of the old Spanish boundaries which were to serve as the source of the new frontiers had been drawn arbitrarily, often on the basis of faulty maps that indicated Spanish possession even of uncharted and unexplored territory. Thus,

by the late nineteenth century, most of the disputes over territorial issues were intracontinental rather than extracontinental
conflicts. But it was this series of latent intracontinental security
threats, in the form of simmering boundary disputes, that
played the most critical role in wrecking the Panama Treaty's
efforts to address the extracontinental threats facing the new
republics. During the last century and a half, this curious relationship between intra- and extracontinental security problems
has remained essentially unaltered. Intracontinental conflicts
have been the greatest bar to united action on extracontinental
challenges to the region's security. One can safely assume that
only when Latin America succeeds in developing institutions for
effectively regulating its intracontinental disputes will it be able
to speak and act in concert on extracontinental issues.

During the nineteenth century, the tension among Latin
American states continued. The lack of a mechanism to ensure
peaceful settlement of regional disputes was demonstrated by
the protracted and costly Paraguayan War (1864–70), involving
Bolivia's claim to the Chaco Boreal on the west bank of the
Paraguay River, and the War of the Pacific (1879–83), in which
Bolivia lost control over its outlet to the Pacific and became a
land-locked state. Where vital interests were not involved,
better prospects for peaceful settlement were visible, as in the
Argentine Paraguayan Boundary Arbitration, where a stronger
state yielded to a weaker claimant. In 1882 James G. Blaine,
Secretary of State of the United States, called for the convening
of a Congress of All American Republics. Since the United
States was already a strong power, fully capable of thwarting
any European threats to the hemisphere, its interests in the
cause of regional cooperation and unity had shades of political
and economic hegemony. South and Central America were by
this time renowned for their natural resources, and American
investments in the region were growing. Blaine's proposed
conference, which never took place, included on its agenda a
scheme for establishing arbitration as a mode of securing international order and the development of closer economic relations
between the United States and Latin America. The most
significant attempt to devise a major system of arbitration came
in 1899 when, with the exception of Costa Rica and Honduras,
the rest of the Latin American countries became parties to the
First Hague Convention, which included purely obligatory
provisions for investigation and arbitration of disputes. In
subsequent years, Mexico and Venezuela were the only two

countries which submitted their disputes for arbitration before the Permanent Court of Arbitration at the Hague.

While most intracontinental disputes during the nineteenth century were based on territorial issues, confrontation with Western powers and the United States revolved around financial problems. Outstanding debts to foreign states and nationals and the lack of compensation for expropriated property resulted, for instance, in the blockading of the ports of Venezuela by Germany, Great Britain, and Italy to demand remedies. In 1902 Argentina's Foreign Minister, Louis Drago, proclaimed what is now known as the Drago Doctrine—that states should abstain from the use of force to collect outstanding debts. The United States agreed with this proposition so long as the disputing parties submitted their causes to arbitration. Although a version of the Drago Doctrine had been included in one of the Hague Conventions of 1899, this Convention was ratified only by Mexico and a few Caribbean states. The same proposal was agreed to at the Second International Conference of American States held in Mexico in late 1902, but the treaty, though ratified, was on no occasion referred to or followed. It effectively lost its validity as an enforceable instrument.

The Intermediate Phase: Intervention from Within

With a position of unquestioned leadership in the Western hemisphere, the United States saw no necessity during the early part of the twentieth century to forge any mutual defense arrangements with other Latin American countries. The latter, however, became increasingly apprehensive about U.S. power and its exercise in several military interventions in South and Central America. The Spanish-American War and the consequent occupation of Cuba; the annexation of the Philippines and Puerto Rico; the occupation of Vera Cruz and Pershing's invasion of Mexico in pursuit of Villa; and the control exercised at different times over the Dominican Republic, Haiti, and Nicaragua provided ample grounds for Latin American suspicions of U.S. imperial ambitions. On all these occasions the United States justified intervention through a broad interpretation of the Monroe Doctrine formulated by President Theodore Roosevelt, against the strong opposition of a number of Latin American jurists and statesmen. Because no single American republic could challenge the United States by force, it gradually became clear that a collective defense system would be necessary, among other things, to prevent American intervention in the region.

At the Havana Conference of 1928, Latin American jurists strongly advocated certain principles. They argued that no state has the right to intervene in the internal affairs of another. States were, in fact, juridically equal. International disputes were to be resolved by peaceful means; the use of force to settle disputes was to be proscribed; aliens were to be treated by the law on an equal basis with citizens; and states were to be committed to democracy and social justice. The United States strongly defended intervention in regional affairs using general principles of international law. Charles Evans Hughes, who headed the U.S. delegation, stated that intervention was necessary purely on grounds of self-defense, to safeguard American rights. He claimed that in most of the countries where the United States had intervened, the governments had no *de facto* control; law and order had ceased to function; there were serious constitutional violations; property, including that of U.S. nationals, had been expropriated without compensation, and the lives of U.S. citizens had been in danger. Nevertheless, the Havana Conference helped to make clear to the United States that continued intervention in the hemisphere would only further strain inter-American relations and would jeopardize any prospects for productive regional associations. The Washington Treaty, drawn shortly after the Havana Conference, made provision for the compulsory arbitration of disputes. But the treaty was accepted with so many reservations that its objectives were nullified, and it was therefore never used.[2]

The Good Neighbor Policy enunciated by Franklin D. Roosevelt in 1933 signaled a major shift in U.S. behavior toward Latin America, bolstering hopes for the establishment of a genuine regional security system rooted in the principles of the equality of states and peaceful procedures for the settlement of disputes. At the heart of the Good Neighbor Policy was the principle of non-intervention. While dispensing with unilateral intervention, the United States also took other deliberate steps to diffuse the growing tensions between itself and its neighbors. As Drier explains:

In the field of doctrine and policy, the United States, in the Clark memorandum of 1928, formally abandoned the

Roosevelt corollary to the Monroe Doctrine. The military interventions in the Dominican Republic, Haiti, and Nicaragua were liquidated as rapidly as circumstances permitted. The Platt Amendment under which the United States was given the right to intervene in Cuba, was abrogated in 1934. A new treaty regarding the Canal was negotiated with Panama in 1936, eliminating some of the more objectionable aspects of the original agreement.[3]

Constructive proposals for nonintervention and the settlement of disputes through pacific means were included in articles 8 and 10 of the Convention on the Rights and Duties of States agreed to at the Seventh International Conference of American States at Montevideo in December 1933 with the United States as a signatory. Article 8 reads: "No state has the right to intervene in the internal and external affairs of another." Article 10 states that "The primary interest of states is the conservation of peace. Differences of any nature which arise between them should be settled by recognized pacific methods." But although the Convention's provisions were motivated by good intentions, words such as "intervention" and "pacific methods" were never defined. The United States defined "intervention" as the use of military forces, whereas the Latin American countries understood the term to include even diplomatic representations for the protection of persons or property of nationals of the intervening state. There was also no agreement on the means and methods adopted for applying peaceful procedures for the settlement of disputes. Like its predecessors, the Convention lacked real support. Notwithstanding the Montevideo Conference, the Chaco War between Bolivia and Paraguay continued. Without hemispheric solidarity, even U.S. efforts lacked the strength to produce an effective security system. Only much later, after the end of World War II, did the fear of "international communism" succeed in producing the kind of bold initiatives necessary to formulate regional law for hemispheric security.[4]

The Tertiary Phase: Emergence of Basic Instruments

The outbreak of the Second World War and complications arising out of subversive activities by Nazi and Fascist sympathizers heightened the need for hemispheric solidarity against external threats. During the course of the war the Foreign Ministers of the American republics met three times. At Panama (1939) they adopted a common policy of neutrality. The second meeting convened in Havana (1940) made concrete suggestions for the adoption of a regional security system. Resolution 14 of the Declaration of the meeting stated that "any attempt on the part of a non-American state against the integrity or inviolability of the territory, and sovereignty or the political independence of an American state shall be considered an act of aggression against the states which sign this declaration." The Resolution only mentioned non-American states. It also stated that in the event of such aggression or threat of aggression, Latin American states would "consult among themselves in order to agree upon the measures it may be advisable to take." Subsequently, when the OAS Charter incorporated a similar provision, the term "non-American states" was dropped from its text.

Following the Japanese attack on Pearl Harbor, there was a more determined attempt to formalize the many proposals that had been made in the past, to incorporate them into a legal framework for regional security. The Third Consultative meeting at Rio de Janeiro (1942) restated the idea that an attack against an American state was an attack against all, as did the Act of Chapultepec adopted at the Inter-American Conference on the Problems of War and Peace (1945).

These meetings led to the Treaty of Rio de Janeiro in 1947, the first instrument adopted that had prospects for effective application. Although the drafters of the UN Charter had acceded to strong pressure from Latin America to incorporate regional efforts into the UN's system, certain contradictions remained; the major problem was the issue of which international organization has precedence in regional conflicts, the UN or an inter-American body. The Rio Treaty, formally known as the Inter-American Treaty of Reciprocal Assistance, imposed upon its members obligations based on principles that had developed within the hemisphere for nearly a century. The treaty's major focus was on collective defense. Article 6 indicated the circumstances and conditions under which principles of collective defense ought to be applied. It provided for consultation among the American states whenever the inviolability, integrity, sovereignty, or political independence of any state was affected by an act of aggression, an armed attack, an extracontinental or intracontinental conflict, or any other fact or situation that might endanger the peace of the Americas.

The language of the treaty left room for broad interpretation, and some key phrases were not defined. A mere threat was sufficient cause for consultation among member states to examine the feasibility of applying regional defense measures. The precise nature of these measures, however, was never indicated in the treaty. Although article 6 called for consultation even in the case of intracontinental conflicts, a different standard was to be applied in the resolution of such conflicts. Article 7 stressed the need for peaceful settlement of disputes, and required the parties to suspend hostilities and "restore matters to the status quo ante." The parties were to take necessary measures to reestablish inter-American peace and security and to seek a peaceful resolution to the underlying conflict. An interesting corollary to article 7 was the statement that "the rejection of the pacifying action will be considered in the determination of the aggressor and in the application of measures which the consultative meeting may decide to adopt." Hence, article 7 gave considerable latitude to the Consultative meeting to pass judgment and to enforce collective security measures. But a similar provision in the OAS Charter eliminated any such process for the determination of an aggressor.

Since the OAS Charter had direct implications during the Falklands crisis it is necessary to examine several articles that relate to conflict management. During the 1945 Chapultepec Conference, the delegations instructed one of the earliest institutions of the Pan American system, the Inter-American Juridical Committee (IAJC), to prepare a draft of an "Inter-American Peace System which would coordinate existing agreements in such a way that gradual and progressive application of these agreements will perforce lead to the desired end." The OAS Charter is primarily the product of IAJC work. For the most part, the Rio Treaty was incorporated into the Charter. Articles 15 through 19 of the OAS Charter address the issue of nonintervention; article 16 states:

> No state may use or encourage the use of coercive measures of an economic or political character in order to force the sovereign will of another state and obtain from it advantages of any kind.

Article 17 states:

> The territory of a state is inviolable; it may not be the object even temporarily, of military occupation or of other measures

140

of force taken by another state, directly or indirectly on any ground whatever. No territorial acquisition or special advantage obtained either by force or by other means of coercion shall be recognized.

These articles along with articles 15 and 19 were subject to article 18 that gave a party to a dispute the right of self-defense.

The articles dealing with pacific settlement of disputes are important in any analysis of the OAS Charter. Article 20 states (emphasis added) that "all *international disputes* that may arise among American states shall be submitted to the peaceful procedures set forth in the OAS Charter *before* being referred to the Security Council of the United Nations." Article 21 delineates peaceful procedures such as direct negotiations, good offices, mediation, investigation and conciliation, judicial settlement, arbitration, and those which the parties agree to. A key issue is whether all the provisions dealing with pacific settlement of disputes restrict themselves to intracontinental conflicts or whether these articles, particularly when read in conjunction with others, allow an interpretation that might lead to the application of the Rio Treaty to extracontinental conflicts.

Chapter V of the OAS Charter applies directly to extracontinental threats and deals specifically with collective defense. It is important to note its implications because of its direct relevance to the Falklands crisis. Article 24 declares that:

every act of aggression by a state against the territorial integrity or the inviolability of the territory or against the sovereignty or political independence of an American state shall be considered an act of aggression against the other American states.

Article 25 states that:

should there be such violations, the American states in furtherance of the principles of continental solidarity or collective self-defense shall apply the measures and procedures *established in the special treaties on the subject.* (Emphasis added)

It is not clear what the special treaties on the subject are, because of the number of instances in which the term "special treaty" is used in the Charter. One of the special treaties referred to in the OAS Charter is the Bogota Pact (the American Treaty of Pacific

Settlement). The Pact was negotiated and approved in 1948, and states that it was concluded in fulfillment of the requirements of article 23 of the Charter. Provisions incorporated in the Pact included the following procedures:

(1) The establishment of a commission of conciliation and rules for the cooperation of disputing parties with the commission in its attempts to resolve the dispute.
(2) Submission of the dispute to the ICJ in the event that a settlement could not be achieved.
(3) Reference of the dispute to arbitration in the event that the ICJ decided that the dispute was "non-justiciable."

The stringent requirements contained in the Pact are both its weakness and strength. If applied without reservation, the process would have ensured peaceful settlement of all disputes. Yet provisions relating to compulsory jurisdiction of the ICJ and arbitration required sacrifice of sovereignty from the signatories. Nevertheless, the United States was willing to accede to the compulsory jurisdiction of the ICJ with the reservation that "submission on the part of this government of any controversy to arbitration, as distinguished from judicial settlement, shall be dependent upon the conclusion of a special agreement between the parties to the case."

The Pact of Bogota has been rarely, if ever used. It was made directly applicable only in the border dispute between Nicaragua and Honduras in 1957. In this case the Council of the OAS with great difficulty persuaded Nicaragua and Honduras as signatories to the treaty to refer the dispute to the ICJ.

According to article 102 of the OAS Charter, none of the provisions of the OAS Charter should be construed as impairing the rights and obligations of the member states under the Charter of the United Nations. And article 7 says that every American state has the duty to respect the rights enjoyed by every other state in accordance with international law.

One can identify several problems with the major legal instruments at the foundation of the inter-American system:

(a) There are no clear linkages between the Rio Pact, the OAS Charter, and the Pact of Bogota. It is difficult to identify the instrument, as well as the specific provisions, that are applicable to a given situation.
(b) There is insufficient clarity with reference to the special

treaties. These special treaties should have been named in the OAS' Charter and appended thereto for operational purposes.

(c) There is some confusion on the distinction between extra-continental and intracontinental conflicts. It is also unclear whether the articles on peaceful settlement of disputes and collective security apply to both types of conflicts in the same way.

(d) Despite article 102, the question of whether regional procedures should take precedence over UN procedures or vice versa is not answered with the necessary clarity. This is a major procedural and legal problem.

All these problems emerged during the Falklands crisis and had to be dealt with by the OAS. The manner in which the OAS confronted them, and the different interpretations which member states offered of their legal obligations, are of great interest, especially when viewed within the context of the internal problems of each member state and their relations with one another.

Relevant Antecedents to State Behavior during the Falklands War

Outstanding intracontinental frontier disputes have been a major source of divisions within the OAS. Besides its conflict with Great Britain over the Falklands, Argentina's relations with Chile have been strained over ownership of three small islands at the mouth of the Beagle Channel at the tip of South America. This dispute has recently been exacerbated by Argentina's unilateral rejection of the unfavorable arbitral award. Chile has further territorial claims against Argentina in the north, and is embroiled in territorial disputes with Peru and Bolivia dating back to Chile's victory in the Pacific War of 1879–83.

Another important actor in intracontinental disputes is Venezuela. Its major dispute began on an extracontinental level, involving Guyana which was a former British colony. Venezuela claims that a cartographer employed by the British in 1840–3 improperly drew Guyana's boundary far into eastern Venezuela in order to facilitate the work of British gold prospectors. Largely through the good offices of the United States, an international tribunal was set up to examine the issues. In its finding the tribunal decided in favor of the British. Venezuela, however, reopened the case, citing a memorandum from a U.S. tribunal member alluding to a secret deal between the British and Soviet tribunal members. In 1970 Venezuela and Guyana agreed to set aside the dispute for twelve years. With the lapse of this period in 1982, Venezuela refused to renew the protocol. Next to the Falklands, this dispute has had the greatest potential for outbreak into violence; large oil deposits are believed to exist in the disputed territory and Venezuela has a clear military advantage.

Venezuela is also involved in a dispute with Colombia over sea rights in the Gulf of Venezuela, the entry-way from the Caribbean to Venezuela's petroleum fields in Lake Maracaibo. All attempts at third-party mediation have failed. Bilateral talks between the two countries from 1968 to 1980 were equally unsuccessful. Although Colombia agreed to a treaty in October 1980, Venezuela refused to accede. Two armed incidents occurred between the two countries immediately after the Falklands War. Colombia itself has had troubled relations with Nicaragua over ownership of the islands of San Andres, Providencia, and three adjoining keys. In 1979 the Sandinistas repudiated a 1928 treaty in which Nicaragua had ceded to Colombia its historic claims to these islands.

Guatemala claims that the British seized what is today Belize (formerly British Honduras) from Spanish-held territory. Guatemala has threatened to invade Belize repeatedly, but has been deterred by a British garrison of 1,600 troops and a squadron of Harrier jet fighters. British troops have remained in Belize, even though the country was granted independence in September 1981. The regime of General Rios Mont reiterated Guatemala's historic claims to Belize, as has also its successor.

Ecuador and Peru clashed in 1981 over territorial claims to a region near the headwaters of the Amazon known as the Cordillera del Condor. The claims date back to the fifteenth century. Sporadic attempts at arbitration have failed. The Rio protocol of 1942 recognized Peru's *de facto* control of the upper Amazon basin. Although Ecuador has challenged the legal authority of the protocol, the Peruvians have insisted upon its validity on the grounds of Ecuador's ratification of it. This dispute has been brought before the OAS at every one of its meetings since its inception.

In addition to the conflicts cited above, literally every state in Central and South America is involved in territorial disputes:

Chile and Argentina (frontier dispute); Panama and the United States (rights over the Panama Canal); Brazil and Paraguay (Brazil's control over Guaira Falls which recently have shown potential as an unlimited source of hydro-electric energy); Guyana and Surinam (boundary dispute); Costa Rica and Nicaragua (frontier dispute); Honduras and Nicaragua (territorial dispute); Mexico and the United States (area of land between El Paso and Ciudad); Haiti and Dominican Republic (boundary dispute); and many more, numbering nearly fifty.[5] Except in a few instances where open conflict has occurred, most of these disputes have never been brought before the OAS. But their continued existence has colored inter-American relations, and during the Falklands War they affected the position which some states took towards Argentina's seizure of the islands.

The Falklands Crisis: Conflict of Laws

Because extracontinental parties have no jurisdiction before the OAS, a conflict between such a state and an OAS member presents serious constitutional difficulties for the organization. This is especially true when the member state insists that the OAS take up the matter, even though the extracontinental party cannot appear before the OAS to present its version of the case. For this reason, Argentina traditionally has been hesitant to use the OAS to settle the Malvinas problem, preferring instead the United Nations.

Although there is evidence that Argentina brought to the notice of the OAS its rights over the Malvinas during the Rio Convention of 1947, it was only in 1976 that the dispute was formally considered by the Inter-American Juridical Committee (IAJC). In a Declaration dated 16 January 1976 the IAJC, after referring to Argentina's just title to sovereignty over the Malvinas, stated that "the Republic of Argentina has an undeniable right of sovereignty over the Malvinas Islands, for which reason the basic question to be resolved is that of the procedure to be followed for restoring its territory to it." The IAJC did not point out or recommend any procedures that could have been unilaterally or collectively applied to restore the Falklands to Argentina. This was probably not within its jurisdiction, although article 108 of the Charter gives it "the broadest possible technical autonomy." For all practical purposes, therefore, the declaration had little usefulness except as evidence of Argentina's efforts to resolve the dispute peacefully through the OAS. As an instrument of Argentina's title to the Malvinas, however, the IAJC's declaration probably had little validity under international law, a point which was strongly emphasized by the representative of Trinidad and Tobago during subsequent OAS meetings.

The occupation of the Falklands by Argentine troops in April 1982 prompted Great Britain to request a meeting of the United Nations Security Council. In its Resolution 502 the Council demanded an immediate withdrawal of Argentine forces from the islands, and called upon the parties to seek a diplomatic solution to their problems. The United States voted in favor, while Panama, the only Latin American country on the Security Council at the time, voted against it. The fact that Resolution 502 preceded any formal attempts by the OAS to resolve the crisis is of great importance. Without complying with Resolution 502, Argentina next attempted to bring its case before the OAS permanent council. At Argentina's request, the OAS agreed to raise the issue at its 12 April meeting. It is significant to note that during this meeting the OAS failed to agree on a resolution on the crisis. An impasse was reached when several of the English-speaking Caribbean nations (all former British colonies) refused to support a Latin American Resolution that did not condemn Argentina's use of force. The OAS finally passed an innocuous Resolution expressing its deep concern over the crisis and offering its cooperation to reach a peaceful solution.

Faced with the vehement opposition of the Caribbean member states (many of whom have been helped by Great Britain to gain special economic advantages in the European Economic Community), Argentina made the important move to invoke the Rio Treaty. Since only the original members of the Rio Treaty have rights of participation in proceedings related to it, Argentina's move was calculated to leave out of the decision-making process the pro-British former Caribbean colonies which had joined the OAS in the 1960s and 1970s. Eighteen of the twenty-one original members voted to convene a meeting under the Rio Treaty. The United States, Colombia, and Trinidad and Tobago abstained. The 20th meeting of Consultation of Foreign Ministers was convened on 26 April, and its first session lasted until 28 April. The Argentines received the support they sought, though it was qualified. In their Resolution the Foreign Ministers recognized Argentina's right to sovereignty over the Falklands, and the government of the United Kingdom of Great Britain was urged "immediately to stop the hostilities it is carrying out within the security region defined by Article 4 of the Inter-American Treaty of Reciprocal Assistance, and also to refrain from any act that may affect Inter-American peace and security." Interestingly, the Resolution was preceded by a preamble which stated: "*Having Seen*: Resolution 502 (1982) of the UNSC, *all of whose terms must be complied with* ... Resolves ..." Whether this was a direct recommendation to the antagonists or a purely ceremonial bow to Resolution 502 is uncertain. In any event, the Resolution did not instruct the British to withdraw their fleet, and Argentina was asked to "refrain from taking any action that may exacerbate the situation." It seems that the Foreign Ministers paid some attention to UNSC Resolution 502, for article 6 of their Resolution stated that it deplored the adoption of coercive measures of an economic and political nature by the EEC, indicating that they "constitute a serious precedent inasmuch as they are not covered by Resolution 502 of the UNSC." Did this mean that all other conditions in Resolution 502, mentioned in the preamble, had to be met? This was left unclear. The conference also agreed to keep the meeting open "especially to oversee faithful compliance with this Resolution." The Resolution was carried by seventeen votes with four abstentions: the United States, Chile, Colombia, and Trinidad and Tobago. But the quick pace of events soon consigned these early OAS maneuverings to little more than irrelevance; the fighting escalated; the Haig mission failed; and the mediating efforts of the President of Peru and the Secretary-General of the United Nations foundered.

On 27 May the Foreign Ministers of the OAS reconvened to consider Argentina's claims of British aggression. It was at this meeting that the divisiveness among OAS members came out into the open. After several warnings, the United States informed the OAS that it had no alternative but to support Great Britain. Secretary of State Haig reiterated the U.S. position as stated by the U.S. Senate's Resolution of 27 April 1982 regarding U.S. policy in the Falkland Islands. The Senate had declared that since the UNSC Resolution 502 had been passed in response to a breach of peace, it was binding under international law. While there was no treaty obligation (including the Inter-American Treaty of Reciprocal Assistance) requiring or implying U.S. support of, or neutrality toward, an act of international aggression, the United States could not stand neutral with regard to the enforcement of Resolution 502. The Senate added that the U.S. government should prepare, through consultations with the Congress, "to use all appropriate means to assist the British government in achieving in the Falkland islands full withdrawal of Argentine forces and full implementation of the principle of self-determination." This Senate Resolution thus became a handy justification for the Reagan administration to wield before its frustrated Latin American neighbours.

With the United States deviating from neutrality and supporting the principles of adherence to Resolution 502 and self-determination, any hope for inter-American solidarity disappeared. Argentina and its friends resented the U.S. position that since Argentina had been the first to use force in invading the Falklands, and therefore was the *causus belli*, there was no basis for taking collective action under the terms of the Rio Treaty. But the Argentines also had difficulty in obtaining the full support of several other influential powers in the region. Remembering the involvement of other OAS members in similar frontier disputes, Brazil (for reasons of hemispheric hegemonial aspirations) and Mexico argued that the Rio Treaty should not be invoked in support of Argentina, for the proper forum to resolve the conflict was the United Nations. While supporting Argentina's rights to the Malvinas, the Foreign Minister of Mexico, Rafael de la Colina, stated that "the parties to the conflict must comply loyally and fully with the Secretary-General of the United Nations," who was entrusted by Resolution 505 with carrying out a ceasefire, not disregarding the terms of Resolution 502.

Ecuador, faced with the almost identical situation of Great Britain in its confrontation with Peru, supported Argentina with the reservation that Ecuador wished to reaffirm its permanent disregard for territories obtained through threats or the use of force, and that the occupation of territories did not validate the title to such territories with the passing of time. Ecuador's representative, Sr. Falconi, further reiterated the importance of the use of peaceful means to settle international controversies.

Chile and Colombia also were placed in the same position as Ecuador. Like Mexico, they alluded to Resolution 502 and informed the OAS that it could not evade the fulfillment of its requirements. Chile officially declared its neutrality during the Malvinas crisis and stated that the Rio Treaty could not be invoked because all of its provisions had not been strictly adhered to. Colombia, fearful that Nicaragua's Sandinista regime might be encouraged to seize the San Andres archipelago, declined to support Argentina, arguing that it did not recognize any legitimacy in the principle of seizing disputed territories by force.

One of the most articulate protests against Argentina and its allies came from the delegation of Trinidad and Tobago. As the Foreign Minister, Mr. Ince, remarked during the OAS session of 27 April 1982,

> my delegation *is unable to agree* that the OAS or any of its agencies, including the Inter-American Juridical Committee, possess any competence to confer sovereignty on any territory or land claimed. The OAS is not a court of justice and cannot therefore usurp the functions of the Hague Court. One of the elemental rules of justice includes the question of hearing the other party to a dispute, and this in my delegation's view has gone unsolved. My delegation has made reference to the fact of the adjudication by the Inter-American Juridical Committee in a dispute without calling up the other party to the dispute. My delegation regards this action as contrary to the principles of natural justice.

The Foreign Minister then alluded to articles 52 and 53 of the UN Charter, and to article 103 of the same Charter which states that obligations of member states under the United Nations Charter must prevail over obligations under any other regional arrangements. Thus, Trinidad and Tobago stressed the preeminence of UN arrangements over regional treaties, a position which it reiterated at the 27 May meeting by emphasizing that a settlement should be reached only through the application of Resolution 502.

The proponents of the Argentine cause were equally articulate about the propriety of a regional settlement for the Malvinas issue, the legality of Argentina's claims over the islands, and the validity of Argentina's interpretation of the terms "aggression" and "self-determination." Argentina based the legality of its claims to the Malvinas on the grounds that it had inherited title to them from the rights enjoyed by Spain; she argued that Captain Vernet, an Argentine, had established and maintained an Argentine settlement between 1828 and 1833 when the islands had reverted to a status of *terra nullius*; and geophysically the islands were a natural extension of the Argentine continental shelf. In addition, Argentina deplored the neo-colonial status of the islands and Great Britain's inflexibility.

Argentina's allies never doubted the validity or applicability of the Rio Treaty in the Falklands War. They argued that to stretch the precedence of UN efforts over and above any possible regional efforts, as suggested by the Ambassador from Trinidad and Tobago, was to nullify the whole concept of regional arrangements acknowledged by the UN itself. While the efforts of the UN via Resolutions 502 and 505 were never at any point dismissed even by Argentina, there was a deliberate attempt to focus on regional measures by countries like Venezuela, which proclaimed that the bellicose actions undertaken by Great Britain provided a direct threat to the solidarity of the Americas. More specifically, Venezuela, in a speech by its Foreign Minister on 28 May, claimed that by escalating its aggression Great Britain had disturbed the peace and security of the Americas and manifested its intentions to defy the collective security pact embodied in the Rio Treaty. (The term collective security was perhaps loosely used by the Foreign Minister because the collective security option under the Rio Treaty was never invoked.) Others, like Nicaragua and Peru, went further and charged the United States with violating the Rio Treaty. The Peruvian Foreign Minister indicated that the United States, by materially supporting Britain in its measures against Argentina, had violated its obligations as a member of the inter-American system, of the OAS, and as a signatory of the Rio Treaty.

At no time, however, was there any serious consideration of applying collective defense measures against Britain. The OAS adopted on 29 May a Resolution in which, recalling its earlier Resolution of 29 April, it agreed to "condemn most vigorously the unjustified and disproportionate armed attack perpetuated by the United Kingdom affecting the security of the entire American hemisphere." Further, it urged "the government of the United States of America to order the immediate lifting of coercive measures applied against the Argentine Republic and to refrain from providing material assistance to the United Kingdom, in observance of the principle of hemispheric solidarity recognized in the Inter-American Treaty of Reciprocal Assistance." It also requested parties of the Rio Treaty to give the Argentine Republic the necessary assistance that each judged appropriate, and warned them to refrain from any act that might jeopardize that objective. Support for Argentina could be offered through affirmation "of the basic constitutional principles of the Charter of the Organization of American States and of the Inter-American Treaty of Reciprocal Assistance, in particular, those that refer to peaceful settlement of disputes." The Resolution also expressed support for UNSC Resolution 505 and the mission of the Secretary-General of the United Nations to pursue a ceasefire. The OAS Resolution was carried by fourteen votes with the same four abstentions as in the previous resolution of 29 April: the United States, Colombia, Chile, and Trinidad and Tobago.

The arguments of Trinidad and Tobago were valid because of the extracontinental nature of the dispute, and because Britain had no *locus standi* before the IAJC, and none of the regional provisions would therefore apply to it. If these provisions had applied to Britain, then Argentina would have been in violation of article 7 of the OAS Charter, which states that every American state has the duty to respect the rights enjoyed by every other state in accordance with international law. Argentina's actions also would have been a violation of articles 15 and 17 unless it could have shown that it had acted in self-defense.

One can argue that in terms of a strict interpretation of the OAS Charter other American states than Argentina acted overtly or covertly in violation of OAS provisions. For instance, the United States may have violated article 16 which says that "no state may use or encourage the use of coercive measures of an economic or political character in order to force the sovereign will of another state and obtain from it advantages of any kind." The United States, by applying economic sanctions and openly supporting Britain, could be said to have violated the principle of nonintervention, in spite of its assertion that Argentina by its first use of force was in violation of international law. One also could suggest that Chile disregarded the principle of nonintervention by assisting British intelligence during the hostilities, an assistance which, of course, the British and Chilean governments have denied. One need not be persuaded by these claims of U.S. or Chilean violation of the OAS Charter to perceive the critical problem: the lack of clarity underlying many of the fundamental legal concepts and institutional mechanisms at the heart of the inter-American system, and the vast ambiguities in the relationships of that system to the wider world of international relations in general and the United States in particular.

Future Prospects

The major problems within the inter-American system revealed by the Falklands War are legal as well as political.[6] Legally, there are serious doubts obscuring the relationship between the UN Charter and the legal instruments of the inter-American system. So far, no principle or method has been agreed to by the Latin American community for hierarchically ordering the norms contained in these constitutive documents. Moreover, even within the regional treaties themselves there are too many unanswered questions on important issues such as the peaceful settlement of disputes, the use of collective defense measures, and whether extracontinental disputes and security threats are to be handled differently from intracontinental ones. Perhaps, one of the most challenging and constructive tasks which the Inter-American Juridical Commission could undertake would be to reexamine and redraft the legal instruments at the foundation of the inter-American system in order to clarify and resolve some of the existing ambiguities. In this work, the IAJC could solicit the collaboration of the UN International Law Commission so as to eliminate, or at least reduce in scope, some of the apparent uncertainties of the relationship between regional law and the UN Charter. But while such efforts may be legally and philosophically appealing, they are likely to encounter substantial political opposition from within the Latin American community. After all, no matter how displeasing they are to the legal mind, ambiguities are prized by statesmen as valuable sources of freedom of action and moral justification.

Functionally, the OAS needs to develop better mechanisms for the peaceful settlement of extracontinental as well as intracontinental conflicts. In the past, one mechanism that has proved useful on several occasions, at least at the level of intracontinental disputes, has been the Inter-American Peace Committee. The IAPC was formed at the 1948 Bogota Conference when the representatives of the Dominican Republic asked for a reactivation of Resolution XIV of the Second Meeting of the Ministers of Foreign Affairs at Havana in July 1940. Resolution XIV had requested the Governing Board of the Pan-American Union to set up a committee composed of representatives of five countries. According to the Resolution, this committee had "the duty of keeping constant vigilance to insure that states between which any dispute exists or may arise, of any nature whatsoever, may solve it as quickly as possible, and of suggesting . . . the measures and steps which may be conducive to a settlement." This Resolution was reactivated at the 1948 Bogota Conference because there was a perceived need for informal methods of peaceful settlement whose flexibility would permit their use without the political risks attendant in the procedures of the Pact of Bogota.

Immediately upon its creation on 31 July 1948, the committee was faced with a number of conflicts that needed resolution. In spite of its early effectiveness, however, the IAPC ran into difficulties. The tenth Inter-American Conference, which met in Caracas in 1954, attempted to resolve these by adopting a new IAPC statute that provided for rotating membership for the committee. According to this statute, a party directly involved in a conflict could request the committee's aid, but the committee could intervene only with the consent of all parties to the dispute. Still, the IAPC has had partial success. In 1961 the governments of Honduras and Nicaragua requested the committee's assistance in implementing an International Court of Justice advisory opinion dealing with a boundary dispute between the two countries. In response to this request, the IAPC sent a commission that resolved many of the outstanding problems, and ensured the peaceful transfer of the territory in question.

Unfortunately the IAPC has not been used since that time, and its legal and institutional status is not clear today. There is great need, however, for a mechanism such as the IAPC that would institutionalize and give specific substance to the norms for peaceful settlement of disputes outlined in the OAS Charter. Even more informal mechanisms could be very valuable, too, if they were perceived as legitimate and were to be used on a regular basis by inter-American states rather than as sporadic last-minute reactions to imminent outbreaks of violence. Thus, there are rich possibilities presented for OAS fact-finding and mediating missions, as well as for the recent initiatives undertaken by the five-nation Contadora group (Mexico, Panama, Colombia, Costa Rica, and Venezuela) to launch peace negotiations between guerrilla factions and Central American governments. Interestingly enough, these efforts have been endorsed unanimously by the European Community's ten leaders, including Great Britain. On the other hand, more ambitious proposals such as those that often have been put forth to establish an inter-American peace force have been unacceptable to governments and are likely to continue to lead nowhere.

Extracontinental threats and disputes will continue to pose severe functional challenges. Efforts by the OAS to mediate conflicts between a member state and an outside power are frustrated by the bonds of Latin American solidarity; few, if any, outside powers trust the OAS to exercise the required impartiality and objectivity in mediating such conflicts. Perhaps it is the United States, rather than the OAS, that is best suited to play this special conciliatory role by virtue of its dual position as a leading OAS member and a superpower with vast responsibilities for the maintenance of international order.

But if the United States is to play a constructive part in the peaceful settlement of extracontinental disputes, it will have to restore its credibility within the OAS. American credibility has suffered from the Falklands War, as well as from past abuses and sheer neglect by the United States of its southern neighbors. A common Latin American complaint is that whenever the extracontinental threat is international communism in any of its forms, the United States is quick to lead the OAS in action; if the threat is of a different type, however, the United States will try to restrain and immobilize the OAS, even though the matter at hand may be of great concern to the Latin American community. Similar complaints and frustrations resurfaced with vigor during the Falklands War. One scholar of international affairs has captured the ominous mood in Latin America during the critical months of April, May, and June 1982:

> The Inter-American System, which had been painstakingly forged under U.S. leadership for almost a century, was under attack by many of the Spanish-speaking nations who questioned whether a "Latin American system" that excluded the United States might not better serve their needs. Thus, there was talk of moving the OAS permanent secretariat to Central America, and of transferring some of the military organs of the Inter-American System to a South American country such as Venezuela to remove them from overwhelming U.S. influence. The impact was especially strong on the organs of the inter-American military system, such as the Rio Treaty (the 1947 Inter-American Treaty of Reciprocal Assistance), the Inter-American Defense Board, the Inter-American Defense College, the periodic military conferences and exercises, and the complex network of U.S.-controlled military-assistance groups and arms suppliers.[7]

While the feared rupture did not take place, the lesson for policymakers should not be lost—the United States must not take the inter-American system for granted. It may not be in the

United States' best interests to make Latin America the center-piece of its foreign policy, but the United States needs to take more seriously regional concerns if it is to regain its credibility in the area. While the OAS needs the leadership and support of American power and initiative, the United States also needs an effective OAS that can help to maintain order and negotiate peaceful change in a region of critical importance to the United States.

Notes: Chapter 10

1 See John C. Drier, *The Organization of American States and the Hemisphere Crisis* (New York: Harper & Row, 1962), p. 16.
2 For a detailed description of the many conferences, see Samuel G. Inman, *Inter-American Conferences: Historic Problems* (Washington, D.C.: U.S. Printing Office, 1965).
3 Drier, *The Organization of American States*, p. 22.
4 For an illuminating discussion of these issues see Bryce Wood, *The Making of the Good Neighbor Policy* (New York: Columbia University Press, 1961).
5 See G. Ireland, *Boundaries, Possessions and Conflicts in South America* (Cambridge, Mass.: Harvard University Press, 1941).
6 See A. Haffa and N. Werz, "The Falklands conflict and inter-American relations," *Aussenpolitik*, vol. 34 (February 1983), pp. 185–201.
7 Jack Child, "Abstention or intervention?," *Orbis*, vol. 26 (Summer 1982), pp. 311–17 at p. 315.

PART THREE

Looking to the Future:
Strategic, Military, and Political
Implications

11

The South Atlantic Conflict: Strategic, Military, and Technological Lessons

DOV S. ZAKHEIM

The South Atlantic conflict was a strange little war. It was fought in one of the most remote parts of the world. Its prize was real estate that may have been worth less than the asset value of the forces committed to defend it (or to seize it, for that matter). The combatants were a power whose glory days had long since passed—by its own reckoning—and a power whose days of glory were at times more imagined than real. The battles harked back to an earlier era—involving big naval task forces, amphibious assaults, and forced marches. Those whose job it is to plan for future conflict undoubtedly never conducted a "Falklands/Malvinas war game" prior to that conflict. More to the point, it is unlikely that they would do so now that it has been fought.

Yet this war was surely fought, by two governments fully in possession of their collective faculties. Like all wars, this one has its military lessons and its political lessons as well. This essay will attempt to recount some of these, and indicate the interaction between the political and the military. (For geographical reference see Figures 2 and 3, pp. 184–5.)

The South Atlantic Conflict: Politico-Military Implications

As remote and unlikely a war as the South Atlantic conflict was, perhaps because it was so remote and unlikely, it offers a host

159

of politico-military lessons that are applicable to crises and contingencies that the United States and other Western powers are likely to face during the remainder of this century. The first, and most important, of these lessons relates to the role of maritime forces in modern crisis management and warfare. A second concerns the importance of allies and of available geographic footholds along the lines of communication between a country and the scene of its military activities. A third lesson relates to the sale of arms to other states. A final lesson concerns the interaction between domestic politics and military effort taking place overseas: the management of government relations with the press, the public, and opposition parties. Each of these issues will be dealt with in turn.

Deterrence, Defense, and the "Unforeseen Contingency"

It is commonly agreed by all who have thus far evaluated the South Atlantic conflict that the outbreak of hostilities was due to a fundamental Argentine miscalculation of the consequences of their seizing the islands.[1] At this point, however, agreement comes to an end. Sir James Cable, whose seminal volume *Gunboat Diplomacy* was translated by the Argentine Navy in 1977, has recently asserted that

> what was needed years ago was not a garrison or a naval presence capable of defeating all-out attack, but sufficient forces in place to make serious fighting inevitable. This would have convinced Argentina—and mere words unsupported by visible preparations never convince anybody—that the Falklands could only be seized at the cost of war.[2]

Cable points out that even lesser measures might have deterred Argentina. For example, had the Ministry of Defense's announced intention to send naval task groups to the islands "been implemented earlier, successive visits by separate task groups would at least have demonstrated resolution and capacity".[3]

The Franks Report, the official U.K. government post mortem on the outbreak of hostilities, implicitly rejected Cable's would-have-been solution in light of the very complex set of factors surrounding the future of the islands, factors over which the U.K. government had only partial control. The Franks Report has been described as an "extraordinary document," whose evaluation of the government's behavior during and prior to the crisis leaves room for considerable interpretation, and whose frankness regarding British intelligence apparatus and structure is unique.[4] The British were confronted by an unyielding island population that refused to consider even the possibility of a transfer of sovereignty, by an equally determined Argentine government, and by fiscal constraints and political priorities that had forced an ever greater concentration of resources on the U.K. contribution to the defense of Western Europe. Added to these factors were the ongoing negotiations with Argentina, and the cycle of tensions, Argentine threats, and British counteractions—all well below the scale of all-out hostilities—that had been intensifying since 1965. As the Franks Report noted, by 1982 there appeared to remain only one solution that might satisfy all parties, a leaseback arrangement with Argentina; and the prospects for that solution were diminishing rapidly.[5] As all other policy options diminished, the "dilemma" between containing the dispute by diplomatic means and maintaining a commitment to defend the islands continued to sharpen:

> The Islands were always at risk, and increasingly so as Argentina's military capability grew stronger; but a British decision to deploy to the area any additional warships, whose secrecy could not always be assured (as it had been when two frigates and a nuclear powered submarine were deployed during a 1977 crisis over the islands), also carried a risk, depending on its timing of *frustrating the prospect of negotiation.* (emphasis added)[6]

Thus, according to the Franks Report, a solution such as that proposed by Cable might actually have brought about the very circumstances that the government was desperately hoping to avoid, namely, an even more determined Argentine position leading to an invasion. On the other hand, of course, the invasion did take place anyway. Furthermore, the Franks solution—continued negotiation and retention of the ice-patrol ship *Endurance,* whose announced withdrawal in June 1981 certainly influenced Argentine assessments of British resolve—likewise might not have been the answer either. For that solution begs a larger question that the Argentines may have posed and that, in any event, they answered wrongly: That question was not, *would* Britain defend the islands, but *could* it do so?

This issue was raised in an article by Lawrence Freedman, who asserts that "It may be that the underestimation [of British reaction] was not so much of British anger and readiness to take up the challenge as of its actual capacity to retake the islands by military means."[7] To buttress his contention, Freedman notes the seeming Argentine nonchalance about the timing of its invasion. A delay until after the Easter holiday would have made it more difficult for Britain to assemble a task force, since a major deployment to the Indian Ocean was scheduled for the following several months. Such a delay would have also enabled Argentina to receive more deliveries of new arms, including French Super Etendard aircraft, which can carry antiship Exocet missiles. Argentina thereby could have improved its military position vis-à-vis any task force that might have been sent south by the British. Finally, such a delay would have made it almost inevitable that Britain would have been forced to retake the islands during the South Atlantic winter, a most daunting prospect.

Freedman provides no prescriptions for the United Kingdom as to how it might have disabused Argentina of its notions about British capability to fight and win. Surely, continued deployment of the *Endurance* would not have done so. Nor would infrequent naval visits; at most, that might have led the Argentines to plan their invasion for July or August, as Freedman states they should have.

What, then, should Britain have done; or could it have done? Perhaps more significantly, for those seeking political-military lessons from this conflict, what actions are required in order to prevent similar aggression from taking place in a context where long-standing negotiations have proved fruitless and where parties to the dispute, to whom one of the negotiators has long-standing commitments, have a *de facto* veto over any negotiated outcome? The issue could apply to a host of situations, including the Middle East. There are, of course, no pat answers to these questions. But the conflict may have pointed to approaches other than those pursued by the United States before 1980, and by the United Kingdom before the Argentine surrender at Port Stanley.

Naval Forces in Modern Crisis Management

"Gunboat diplomacy" is a concept that conjures up images of colonial powers browbeating helpless natives by means of a small show of force. In fact, as Sir James Cable and the studies in the 1970s by Barry Blechman and Steven Kaplan have demonstrated, such tactics have by no means been discarded in the late twentieth century. Their effectiveness, however, is another matter. Some, like Blechman and Kaplan, have argued that the long-term impact of the redeployment of naval forces in response to a crisis is difficult to measure, and may be quite limited. Others have argued that the success of such redeployments is unmeasurable, because success is defined as the prevention of any adverse action occuring: by definition, nonoccurrence produces no data points.

In no case since World War II, however, have naval forces as large as the task force deployed from Britain to the South Atlantic initially for crisis management, actually been committed to full-scale naval hostilities. Thus, until the South Atlantic war there was no way of demonstrating that naval redeployments permitted a calibrated response to crises that *began* with naval presence but ended in force. Without an explicit readiness to resort to force, in the event mere presence failed, presence was inherently meaningless. The absence of such a resort to force may have been responsible for the increasing skepticism with which many observers viewed the deployment of naval forces in a crisis, even if those forces were powerful aircraft carriers.

Certainly, even the deployment of the large British Task Force, as a last resort, did not force Argentina to agree to Britain's demand to return to the negotiating table. At bottom, therefore, as Freedman notes, what was at issue was Britain's military credibility: Would it fight, and if so, could it win? Since the Royal Navy did fight, and win, the lesson for future potential aggressors may well be what Mrs. Thatcher has hoped it would be: states will take necessary military action to protect their interests, however far off those interests may be. Moreover, Britain's behavior in the South Atlantic may have restored the credibility of gunboat diplomacy for crisis management, since ships will have been seen to fight as well as wave the flag. The future of such diplomacy will, of course, continue to depend also upon perceptions that a state can provide the wherewithal to back up its "gunboats" with viable and timely force when necessary. To create such perceptions, however, requires other than the mere stationing of a few small naval units in potential crisis areas.

Planning Forces for "Unplanned" Conflicts

It has become *de rigeur* among military systems analysts to postulate precise sets of assumptions about the nature of conflict, and then to plan forces whose capability in wartime are highly sensitive to those assumptions. Such force planning has always been difficult with respect to maritime and rapid development forces (in the case of forward deployed maritime forces the two are synonymous), whose inherent advantages lie in their flexibility to cope with a variety of crises, rather than in their optimal performance in any one conflict. Because "flexibility" cannot be measured in terms of effectiveness, analysts have often discounted it entirely, and correspondingly have assigned lower priority to the need for additional maritime forces relative to other, more precisely defined requirements. Keith Speed was dismissed as First Lord of the Admiralty because he contended that maritime requirements were wrongly being assigned lower priority by John Nott, then British Secretary of State for Defense.[8]

If any conflict could be labeled "unplanned" it was the South Atlantic War. The Franks Report acknowledged as much.[9] It is impossible to assert that, had Britain undertaken a program to maintain, operate, and develop more flexible forces for long-distance operations—a large proportion of which would have been maritime—the Argentine invasion might not have taken place. Even such a program might not have altered perceptions based on over a decade of determined British efforts to scale back all non-European military activity and commitments. Nevertheless, such a program, including more frequent exercises that demonstrated rapid British response capability outside NATO, even if such exercises were not held in the South Atlantic, might have caused the Argentines to think again. Their planners might not have concluded, as Freedman speculates, that Britain could not win a limited conflict. Moreover, a determined British effort to increase its out-of-NATO capabilities and presence would likely have created a planning atmosphere inside the Ministry of Defense that would have led at least to the retention of *Endurance* in the South Atlantic, and possibly to the sorts of "presence" visits that Cable has cited as necessary.

In this regard, it is noteworthy that the decision to scrap *Endurance* was made by the Ministry of Defense over the protestations of Lord Carrington at the Foreign Office. While at first blush it might have been expected that the roles between the two ministries might have been reversed, in practice the cry "send a carrier" has more often been that of foreign ministries in response to crises than that of military planners.

Ultimately, in the case of U.K. action in the South Atlantic, considerations of cost effectiveness, driven by measures of effectiveness that could easily be quantified, overcame political imperatives. Only in a climate where it would have been recognized that some measures of effectiveness must encompass other than purely statistical considerations (and, as noted above, who can measure the value of presence, when its effectiveness is defined in terms of preventing things from happening?) could a more vigorous British effort to pursue flexible military programs geared to "out-of-area" contingencies possibly have taken place.

It is, therefore, highly significant that the experience in the South Atlantic appears to have fostered a climate in British military planning circles that stresses a more vigorous effort to pursue flexible military programs geared to "out-of-area" contingencies. While not in any way rejecting the primacy of its European commitment, the Ministry of Defense in its own evaluation of the South Atlantic conflict has pointed to a large number of actions that are obviously directed at improving the flexibility, adaptability, and responsiveness of its forces in general, and its maritime units in particular.[10]

One such action is the reevaluation of the cost effectiveness of certain naval forces. The example in question is the fate of the carrier, or "through deck cruiser," *Invincible*. The ship was the first of a class of three units, whose cost had risen dramatically since the inception of the project. Operating cost for the ships also appear to have been higher than anticipated. A second ship, *Illustrious*, has been completed; and construction of a third, *Ark Royal*, has already begun. Given Britain's primary naval mission of contributing to the protection of the Atlantic sea lanes in the event of a conflict with the Warsaw Pact, the marginal cost of a third Harrier carrier did not seem to justify the marginal effectiveness that such a ship offered to the successful pursuit of that mission. Her Majesty's government, therefore, determined that it could not afford to operate all three ships. As a result it undertook an effort to sell the oldest of the three, *Invincible*, and found a buyer in the Australian government, whose own large deck carrier, *Melbourne*, was nearing retirement.

Before the transfer could take place, the crisis broke in the

South Atlantic. The *Invincible* played a critical role supporting Harrier operations, as it was the only other truly air capable ship apart from the older carrier, *Hermes*. Within weeks of the war's end, the government announced that Australia had agreed not to press ahead with the purchase; the ship will remain part of the British fleet.

The cost of operating *Invincible* has not been reestimated downward. No announcement has been made of changes in British plans to operate the other two ships of the same class. Moreover, Britain remains committed to operating two older amphibious ships, the *Fearless* and the *Intrepid*, whose retirement, again determined by cost considerations, had only been forestalled in March, two months before the war began. It was not marginal cost considerations therefore, but the revised British estimate of *Invincible's* effectiveness measured against the opaque, but nevertheless real, demands for flexibility in "unforeseen contingencies" that saved *Invincible*.

It is unlikely that those analysts for whom measures of effectiveness obtain their validity in direct proportion to their susceptibility to quantification will ever accept the proposition that the marginal utility of flexible maritime forces, such as multipurpose carriers and surface units, justify their costs. Nevertheless, the South Atlantic experience should give them pause. A greater commitment to maintaining and exercising the responsiveness inherent in maritime forces might have averted the crisis altogether. The employment of those and other rapidly deployable forces led to its successful (from the British perspective) conclusion.

Cost effectiveness critically depends upon the choice of *appropriate* measures of effectiveness. Deterring and coping with unforeseen problems simply requires capabilities whose effectiveness cannot easily be quantified, but are no less real. Those measures differ in both kind and degree when applied to the viability of developing programs for the acquisition, operation, and deployment of flexible, rapidly deployable maritime (and other) forces, such as those which won the war in the South Atlantic.

Of Allies and Access [11]

For many Europeans, and indeed Americans, the "Alliance" is a code word for the NATO organization, or the North Atlantic Alliance. Few Europeans think of bilateral U.S. ties with individual European states in the context of a conflict, primarily because there is little interest in supporting American operations outside Europe. There is also little enthusiasm for addressing non-European situations in which individual European states might become involved. Such "regional" contingencies are meant to take place only among Third World states.

The South Atlantic conflict demonstrated that bilateral alliances are still extremely important. It showed that the dependence upon individual allies for access to facilities along extended lines of communication is not merely a problem for the United States alone. It highlighted the fact that America's bilateral relations with her allies, in addition to the multilateral relationship that defines the NATO alliance, are critical to any coordinated Western effort to cope with threats outside the NATO area. And it demonstrated that America takes its bilateral ties seriously, and that American support for an ally can be meaningful politically as well as militarily.

Britain clearly required the goodwill of the United States—apart from any material support it might have received—if it was to prosecute its South Atlantic operations successfully. That goodwill was the key to America's willingness to tolerate an intensive level of operations on Ascension Island, which supported a number of Vulcan bombing runs against Port Stanley airfield, provided enroute bases for refueling of Harrier aircraft, and served as a way station for naval forces steaming further south. Without Ascension it is unlikely that Britain could have prevailed in the conflict.

The importance of American support on Ascension Island has been ignored in a number of accounts. For example, the two articles entitled "The Falklands War" and "Military Lessons of the Falklands Campaign" that appear in *Strategic Survey 1982–1983*, do not even mention the island facility.[12] On the other hand, former British Secretary of State for Defense John Nott stated that the RAF moved over 5,800 people and 6,600 tons of stores through Ascension in over 600 sorties by CC-130 and UC-10 aircraft.[13] Moreover, it is inconceivable that any bombing raids would have been conducted without the use of Wideawake, and the availability of the airfield and its surrounding facilities to the large number of tankers (ten) required for each single raid.[14] Layman was informed during his stopover at Ascension that Wideawake Airfield had replaced Chicago's O'Hare Airport as the world's busiest.

Of course, America also announced it would provide the

United Kingdom with material support. That support amounted to roughly $100 million in sales, for which the United Kingdom had to provide payments under the normal terms of such agreements. Perhaps more important than the magnitude or even the details of those sales, however, was the psychological impact of the U.S. announcement. Argentina stood branded before the world as an aggressor by a state that clearly had sought to cultivate its goodwill. Furthermore, by its decision to take sides, the United States added further credibility to the British claim that aggression simply could not be tolerated as a means for solving long-standing diplomatic disputes. The use of military force by the British, and the American support for that force, demonstrated to other potential aggressors that actions, not mere words, stood behind fundamental Western principles of justice and fair play.

Selling Arms: Who Are Your Friends?

Arms-producing states that sell their wares abroad have always assumed, explicitly, or implicitly, that such sales would not result in their having to defend against the systems they have sold. Sales are meant for "friendly" states, or at least, states that are not "unfriendly." Western states, including the United Kingdom, have pointed to arms sales as a means of fostering their own interests abroad, and as a surrogate for their having to commit their own forces to conflicts in distant locales. In addition, the sale of arms is often integral to the survival of a state's domestic armaments manufacturing sector, and is viewed as a key source of export revenue.

The South Atlantic crisis demonstrated in a most graphic way that there is no guarantee that the vendor nation will never face its own weapons, or those of its allies, in future combat. British forces found themselves operating against Blowpipe and other systems produced by their own industries. Moreover, French systems continued to be delivered to Argentina until the invasion actually occurred. Indeed, after the war broke out Argentina tried desperately to acquire more of those systems both from France and from other suppliers of Exocet missiles and other systems. While no evidence was ever produced to verify constant reports of arms and spare parts reaching Argentina, such transfer was possible given the markets that had been carved out in Latin America.

The fact that Argentina employed Western systems, many of

which were also potentially available from states other than those which produced them (even if in fact it failed to acquire them), points to the great need for caution when selling arms to other states. That lesson might easily have been applied somewhat earlier, in the event of a confrontation between Iranian and U.S. forces, had the hostage crisis continued. The loss of F-14 and other U.S. systems after the fall of the Shah drove home to at least some Americans the need for selectivity and caution when selling arms abroad. The South Atlantic conflict should leave no doubts on this point.

Finally, acquisition of a foreign system allows the purchaser to learn that system's strengths and weaknesses. The transfer of British defensive systems to Argentina created opportunities for the Argentines to train and perfect tactics for anticipated combat by using their own, virtually identical, systems as proxies for the British. Prior to the attack on the *Sheffield*, Argentine pilots reportedly trained against their own Sheffield-class ships that, like the British Type 42x, were armed with the Sea Dart missile.[15]

If there are any policy disputes between vendor and buyer, the vendor should be cautious despite the pleas of arms manufacturers. Spare parts inventories may have to be carefully controlled; key subsystems may have to be excluded; and sales may have to include restrictive clauses to prevent unauthorized transfers to third parties. Arrangements with allies may be necessary to assure similar behavior on their part. Such cautions should by no means be seen as a restriction upon arms sales. To the contrary, it is simply a manifestation of what the relationship of sales should be to national policy: sales are a vehicle for national security policy, and should be governed by that policy, not, as was sometimes the case in the past, vice versa. Those who were shot at by Blowpipes or Exocets are unlikely to forget the experience soon, if they were lucky enough to have survived it.

Winning the War at Home: The Lesson of Public Support

Many Americans, still recalling the Vietnam experience, have been prone to question the likelihood that public support could ever be elicited for any conflict other than one that threatens the survival of the nation. To a lesser extent, the Suez experience left similar impressions among many thoughtful British observers. The South Atlantic conflict demonstrated quite

conclusively that there was little merit to the "simple ...
assumption that democratic societies have a low level of
tolerance for war, with national will being snapped with each
casualty and lurid media coverage." Freedman notes that things
might have been different in other circumstances: had Britain
not maintained the initiative; had the war turned into a
stalemate; had allied criticism been more vociferous; had the
war not been so far away; had British soldiers not been dying
in Northern Ireland; had the issue not been one of democracy
against dictatorship, but one involving "shadowy notions of
national interest."[16] Yet Freedman misses the entire point of
public support for the government during the war.

The intensity of public support for the government went
beyond mere polling results. In its basest manifestation, fans
hounded Argentine footballers from the playing fields of their
English home clubs. More interestingly, the public outcry over
"too much" media objectivity for employing Argentine footage
demonstrated an impatience with television efforts to report on
the war along the lines that the U.S. media reported Vietnam.[17]
It was public support that spurred the rapid mobilization of
industrial resources for the war effort, and the successful con-
version of civilian assets to military capabilities that may have
been the difference between victory and stalemate.

Public support for the war should have been *lower* because it
was in a "far away place," as indeed Vietnam was (as was
Czechoslovakia before it, in 1938). Again, public attitudes to the
United States verged on hostility, in part because the United
States was perceived as "letting Britain down." Finally, the
entire South Atlantic issue was one that clearly did not involve
an obvious national interest; it was precisely for that reason that
the government could never bring itself to devote greater
resources to the defense of the islands. What Freedman misses
is that the matter was not one of national interest but of national
pride: the British public was not prepared to tolerate the blow to
national pride that the Argentine invasion represented. The
lesson of the conflict, perhaps its most important political
lesson, is that patriotism remains alive and well in the Western
democracies.

Implications for Military Operations

Two conflicting impulses tempt the military analyst studying the
South Atlantic conflict. On the one hand, what transpired in

and around the Falkland/Malvinas Islands in the summer of 1982 included the "first truly naval confrontation since the Pacific conflict in World War II."[18] As such, the conflict could be seen as a cornucopia of lessons for those seeking to plan naval strategy, tactics, and forces for other possible scenarios that might arise during the latter part of the twentieth century. On the other hand, however, the South Atlantic crisis could be dismissed entirely as an artifact of a bygone era. In this view, it would bear little real relationship to the demands of conflict that would likely arise in the event that hostilities commenced between, for example, the world's two great power blocs, NATO and the Warsaw Pact.

The truth, of course, lies somewhere in between. The South Atlantic conflict was *sui generis* in some respects, but the validity of some lessons is not diminished by that fact. In particular, the conflict's outcome appears to have significant implications for five major facets of strategy operations and tactics: (1) the role of naval surface forces; (2) the relevance of the amphibious mission; (3) the potential contribution of Special Operation Forces; (4) the coordination of land- and sea-based operations; and (5) the critical importance of logistics. The following sections will address each of these facets.

The Continuing Importance of Naval Surface Forces

Ever since the battles between Louis Johnson, Truman's Secretary of Defense, and the carrier admirals over the future of the carrier fleet, experts have argued over the validity of maintaining large and costly surface naval forces in the age of the bomber and submarine.[19] The debate has bifurcated into two issues: the viability of the aircraft carrier in particular, and the utility of surface ships in general.

The debate over both carriers and surface ships intensified in the aftermath of the sinking of the Israeli destroyer *Eilat* by a Soviet-built Egyptian Styx antiship missile. Proponents of the view that modern fleets should emphasize aircraft, submarines, and small patrol boats argued that the *Eilat* incident proved the inherent advantage lay with the antiship force. They pointed to the tremendous disparity between the cost of a large surface warship and the cost of the small number of missiles that could sink it. Proponents of large surface fleets, such as United States Navy spokesmen, argued that the Styx incident vindicated the concept of "defense in depth." A powerful aircraft carrier, itself capable of surviving multiple hits by enemy missiles, would be afforded several layers of additional protection, both from aircraft deployed from its decks, and from highly specialized escort ships whose purpose it was to shoot down enemy bombers and missiles.

Continuing efforts by the United States Navy to build larger, more capable, and more costly carriers and escorts, coupled with improving accuracies on cruise missiles, and the deployment of even larger numbers of these missiles aboard Soviet ships, submarines, and bombers, further fueled the debate on the wisdom of acquiring large aircraft carriers. At the same time, the navy's implicit decision to concentrate all its firepower in its carrier force and to relegate escorts to purely defensive missions, led some analysts to criticize the level of expenditures being applied to ships whose mission foreordained their rapid demise once hostilities opened at sea.

The South Atlantic conflict certainly did not put to rest the arguments on either side.[20] But the war demonstrated that surface ships could survive, even in the face of determined and capable opposition. Furthermore, it indicated that nations operating in hostile environments, at the end of long lines of communication and in the absence of friendly land bases, could not hope to complete successful military operations without adequate defense-in-depth and the "cover" provided by sea-based aviation. The Sea Harriers operated by the Royal Navy and the GR3 Harriers flown by the Royal Air Force enabled the U.K. surface forces to survive determined assaults by the Argentine Air Force. The absence of early warning, however, was manifest virtually every time a British surface ship was sunk. Moreover, British forces were fortunate that the absence of electronic countermeasures aircraft was not a liability since the Argentines did not employ many of the weapons of electronic warfare available to other military powers.

To be sure, the sinking of the *Sheffield* and other British surface ships did point to their continued vulnerability. But the loss of a ship, like the loss of a tank on land, does not signify the uselessness of that system. What is remarkable is not how *many* British ships sank, but how *few* of them did—a testimony to the imaginative employment of limited air defense resources for defense in depth. The Argentine tactical aim was to sink the carriers *Invincible* and *Hermes*.[21] Freedman notes the degree to which the careful positioning of British warships forced the Argentines to fly profiles too low to enable their iron bombs to detonate.[22] *Strategic Survey 1982-1983* reaches a similar conclusion.[23] Too much should not be made of this point, however, since the Argentines may have miscalculated the optimum release point for their weapons. Britain did not have at its disposal the modern radar systems, target identification systems, data management systems, and electronic warfare units that, for example, would have been available to a United States Navy task force operating under similar circumstances. And, as the U.S. Navy report on the conflict rightly indicated, "A well-rounded complement of aerial surveillance aircraft, interceptors, anti-submarine aircraft and all-weather attack bombers would have made all the difference" to the survival of a larger part of the surface fleet.[24]

The Amphibious Mission

The amphibious mission has been synonymous with the United States Marine Corps since its birth in 1775. Its modern expression comprises carefully timed operations that involve pre-attack "preparation" of the landing site by naval aircraft and guns, highly synchronized landings of troops, vehicles, helicopters, and support forces from a variety of landing ships and craft, and the seizure of major beachheads as preparation for a sustained offensive. The Marine amphibious landing, as it is familiar both to military specialists and to avid viewers of war movies, reached its zenith during the Pacific island hopping campaign of World War II and the Inchon landing of 1951.

Since then, however, and particularly since the advent of the cruise missile, the Marines and their mission have been subjected to much of the same criticism that has been directed at carrier forces. Beginning in the 1970s, critics argued that the Marines were sentimentally tied to a mission that simply could not stand up to the cold reality of modern warfare. The World War II island hopping campaigns were a thing of the past. Critics contended that past Marine campaigns had little meaning in relation to a major war on the European continent, where Marines seeking to assault beaches in slow moving landing ships and craft would find themselves literally looking into launchers of highly accurate cruise missiles. The Marines would never reach any beach, much less seize it.[25] Needless to say, whatever critique applied to the U.S. Marines was presumed to apply, *ipso facto*, to all other similar units, whose size was a fraction of that of the U.S. force.

173

The realization by U.S. strategists that there is a world outside Europe altered the way in which they viewed the Marines. The Corps formed an integral part of the Rapid Deployment Force and likewise is a prime element in the new U.S. Central Command. The South Atlantic conflict, however, yielded the operational proof that even the most meticulous tables of operation and equipment could not provide; the landings on East Falkland demonstrated that the amphibious mission was alive and well.

Just as the British surface force performed well without the luxury of many defensive and offensive systems integral to American surface units, so too the British landing by the Royal Marines' Commando Brigade was bereft of many capabilities that would be a critical element in an equivalent landing by United States Marines. The British actually employed few specialized amphibious units, since they did not have many. At the start of the operation, the United Kingdom had only eight amphibious ships available—*Fearless*, *Intrepid*, and six smaller logistic landing ships (LSLs). As noted earlier, the two prime dock landing ships, the *Fearless* and *Intrepid*, actually had been slated for retirement until a prescient reprieve by the British government several months before the conflict retained them in the force. The Royal Marines' Brigade had no specialized tank landing ships such as U.S. LST classes, and no multipurpose amphibious ships, such as the massive (39,000 ton displacement) LHA-1 class, which can by itself carry all the men and equipment for a battalion landing team, as well as the aircraft and landing ships to support it.

British forces were hampered by a shortage of helicopter landing spots on ships and, due to the destruction of three of the four available CH-47 helicopters, the British suffered from a shortage of heliborne lift as well. Finally, although U.K. naval guns performed admirably in providing fire support for the landing units, they were limited by gun caliber and therefore range and power. Nevertheless, the significance of British naval gunfire is revealed in the following recollection of the commander of the Argentine Fifth Marine Battalion: "Naval Artillery had tremendous precision... They fired at an impressive speed... We were hidden well enough, but if we so much as lifted our heads, we would be decapitated."[26] Due to careful planning, dedication, and as a consequence, erroneous Argentine assumptions about prospective landing sites, the British landed without initial opposition, despite the loss of two key logistic landing ships.

The South Atlantic experience thus clearly underscores the relevance and importance of the various improvements that the United States has applied to its own amphibious forces since the 1960s. The United States has refined its concept of "vertical envelopment," which incorporates landings inland by outsized cargo and troop helicopters, such as the CH-53E, in conjunction with conventional landings ashore. The United States is also introducing the air cushioned landing craft (LCAC), a high-speed boat that can carry troops, or even a tank, for about 200 nautical miles at speeds in excess of 40 knots.

Conscious of its own lack of sea-based firepower support for landing units, the United States Navy is reintroducing the four IOWA class battleships into the fleet after nearly two decades (and in some cases, nearly three decades) in mothball status. These ships, with their 16 inch guns, will provide longer range and more potent firepower support than anything the British were able to field in the South Atlantic. In addition, the battleship's cruise missile armament opens up new tactical possibilities for the landing forces. Long-range cruise missiles could be targeted against enemy strongholds, airfields, and command centers well before the landing force comes within 200 miles of the shore. At that point, it could seek to establish air superiority while deploying long-range LCACs. As the force approached the shore, the shorter-range landing forces could operate under both air cover and supporting fire from the 16 inch guns.

It is expected that carrier-based aircraft would provide the above noted "air superiority" and "air cover" for U.S. landing forces. However, the Marines have been the first to recognize the potential of the British Harrier as an aircraft that could fit easily into the integrated air/ground landing embodied in the U.S. amphibious assault operation. The Harrier's versatility renders it the only plane that can move with the Marines through every single stage of an amphibious operation: from the ships, to the initial assault, to operations on bare strips of land, and finally combat, once initial objectives have been taken.

One lesson of the South Atlantic conflict, therefore, is that these weapons developments for amphibious forces, many of them costly, are well justified. The amphibious mission remains viable, even in the late twentieth century, given the availability of improved systems, and of ample ingenuity of the kind that the British recently demonstrated when their forces landed on, and took, East Falkland.

Special Operations Forces

The South Atlantic conflict again reaffirmed the value of the proper use of Special Operations Forces, those elite sea, air, and land units that can conduct unconventional warfare operations, operate behind enemy lines, and train the forces of other states in counterinsurgency operations.

The British Army's Special Air Service (SAS) units and the Royal Marines' Special Boat Squadron demonstrated the versatility of these forces. They provided tactical intelligence for the landing units on both South Georgia and East Falkland, and were able to relay their findings in a timely manner to operational commanders. They carried out a series of raids that misled the Argentines as to the actual location of the major landing. They also successfully carried out sabotage missions. In one such operation, an SAS raiding party, supported by naval gunfire, destroyed an ammunition dump, stores, and eleven aircraft. In all cases, these forces suffered few casualties, and their "unconventional warfare" activities are acknowledged to have had a major influence on the outcome of the battle.[27]

The United States has long operated four Special Forces: the Army's Green Berets, the Navy's Sea-Air Land (SEAL) units, the Marine Corps Reconnaissance units, and the Air Force special forces. At one time an aura of romanticism seemed to surround these forces, particularly during the early 1960s, when the Kennedy administration's planners seemed infatuated with the Green Berets. In recent years, however, both the size and scope of U.S. special forces suffered from post-Vietnam budget reductions. U.S. forces could, of course, provide the same catalytic support for regular force operations as the British forces did for their own regular units. But Special Forces are far from inexpensive. They require costly training, including language proficiency (often in dialects unique to particular regions), and unique weapons systems. For this reason, the Reagan administration, while committed to reviving the capabilities of these forces, has proceeded with caution in funding only modest force level increases for the Special Forces. Funds are being devoted as well for the research and development necessary to provide these special units with the weapons and equipment that will enable their missions to succeed.

Logistics

Armchair strategists often overlook the importance of logistics; professional soldiers, at least those who have conducted successful operations, rarely do. It is pointless to plan a daring operation if supplies are unavailable or to mount an assault when ammunition quickly runs out. To the credit of the British, they were able to overcome the hazards posed by extremely long lines of communication and successfully, if barely, kept their forces sufficiently well supported to maintain the tempo of battle necessary for victory. Once again, the lesson was an old one whose validity was no less current for its age: logistics is a necessary condition for success on the battlefield.

The contrast between British and Argentine logistics management was particularly stark. Argentina, favored by geographic proximity, could not distribute adequately the stores of munitions and weapons that it had stockpiled on the islands soon after it seized them. As a result, some units were short of equipment that was in fact available in supply dumps elsewhere on the small islands.[28] In addition, Argentina was not able to maintain a constant pace of resupply once the British exclusion zone came into force. While the clandestine flights into the Falklands by small supply planes were small victories for the Argentines, their payloads were by far insufficient to have sustained their forces indefinitely against a determined British attack. According to one report, from 2 to 30 April, the period prior to the British assault on the islands, Argentina transported 500 tons of supplies and 1,500 persons from the mainland. From 1 May, when the British landing began, until 14 June, Argentina was only able to transport 304 persons and 70 tons of supplies.[29]

The British logistics management problem was an entirely different one. Distance posed the most formidable barrier: a line of communication stretching some 7,000 nautical miles, broken only by the small Ascension Island, whose runway and storage space were extremely limited, and whose facility was jointly operated and managed by United States forces. Still another problem was that which attends any amphibious assault—managing the transfer of logistics from ship to shore in a hostile environment. As the beachhead grew, the problem became more manageable, but even after initial landings, the timing and mix of combat and support landing operations remained especially demanding for the logisticians.

Britain employed a particularly ingenious solution to cope with its logistics problem: it called upon civilian assets, converted them rapidly to military use, and brought into play plans that had been formulated well before the crisis broke. Not every state may be able—or need—to deploy its civilian resources with the same rapidity. Interestingly, the Argentine Navy employs merchant tankers in place of replenishment oilers, and included two such tankers in the Task Force it had organized in late April to counter a possible British assault on the islands or the mainland.[30] Every state contemplating operations at remote distances (and there are others apart from the United States that have done so in the recent past) must pay heed to the demands of logistics if its forces are not to wither on the battlefield "for want of a bullet."

Coordination of Land- and Sea-Based Operations

The South Atlantic conflict was not, strictly speaking, a "naval war." It could be more accurately termed a "maritime conflict." The distinction is not trivial. Naval conflict involves only sea-based forces, whether they operate on or under the sea, or in the air. "Maritime operations" include land-based forces that operate against targets at sea, as well as sea-based forces—such as Marines—whose operations are conducted primarily on land.

The British forces demonstrated that land-based units can successfully complement those which operate at sea, given a clear allocation of missions, suitable training for maritime operation, an appreciation of the technological limitations of the assets available, and the successful integration of command and control of both types of forces. A notable example of British efficiency in conducting maritime operations at long distances, apart from the ship-to-shore movements of men and materiel noted above, was the employment of Vulcan bombers to strike the Port Stanley airfield. The Vulcans were only able to complete the mission from their bases in Ascension Island to their targets in Port Stanley as a result of carefully planned refueling operations along their 3,300 nautical mile route. By successfully threatening the airfield (though not actually inflicting as much damage as the United Kingdom had hoped) the Vulcans both struck a blow at Argentine morale and helped initially to limit the flow of supplies to the beleaguered island.

The Argentines' most notable effort in this regard was, of course, the series of air strikes that they undertook against the British Naval Task Force. Argentine pilots displayed great courage in flying operations at the furthest reaches of their planes' combat radii, and in conducting successful strikes against the surface ships. Had the Argentines operated more modern aircraft, and benefited from electronic support measures, their rate of success against the British would likely have been considerably higher.

As technology enables aircraft to fly longer missions—at higher speeds and with greater payloads—the opportunity for land-based air defense of maritime sea lanes, as well as for land-based strikes against distant maritime targets, will continue to grow. It is noteworthy, in this regard, that a recent U.S. Navy/Air Force memorandum provides for expanded training in combined maritime operations, including antiship, maritime reconnaissance, and airborne early warning missions.

Other Operational Findings

While the role of surface naval and special forces, of amphibious operations, and of logistics in modern maritime combat are among the most noteworthy aspects of the South Atlantic conflict, other lessons deserve brief mention.

Training, leadership, and high levels of morale are essential to successful military operations.

British forces scored positively on all three counts; the Argentine record was, at best, mixed. The air force was well trained and highly dedicated, and, not surprisingly, turned out to be the most serious threat to British success. The surface navy remained in port once the cruiser *General Belgrano* was sunk. The army, whose officer corps was professional, but whose enlisted men were conscripts, betrayed the greatest failings in all areas: morale was poor, training was limited, and, by all accounts, there was little positive leadership provided by officers to their men.[31]

Adequate medical services are critical to morale, and are a boon to the professionalism of a fighting force.

British medical teams preserved the lives of 90 percent of British casualties; about 90 percent of the injured returned to their fighting units within six months of the conflict. The return of these troops added to the cadre of British veterans who would be a vital source of training and expertise to new recruits. The benefits in terms of morale when fighting men see that they are not being abandoned when injured are incalculable.

Technological Developments

Technological lessons are, of course, difficult to winnow from operational lessons, since the proper use of advanced technology enhances the chances of operational success. The South Atlantic crisis was not a high technology war as the 1982 conflict in Lebanon was. Nevertheless, high technology systems were used, and it is somewhat misleading to imply that because, for example, in one instance a 4·5 inch gun was able to shoot down a Skyhawk aircraft, older systems could in some way substitute for weapons incorporating newer technologies.

Despite the relative absence of electronic countermeasures and counter-countermeasures, the British did employ other forms of countermeasures, notably chaff. Both sides used highly complex aircraft. The British employed the Harrier, whose vectored thrust engine is certainly not a simple technology; Argentina employed the Super Etendard. Both sides used "high technology" missiles to shoot at their targets. The British also employed a variety of electronic communications equipment, as well as specialized equipment for SAS and SBS, both of which fall within the class of "high technology." Finally, the British employed nuclear-powered submarines for antiship missions, the first time that SSNs have been operated in wartime.

Aircraft

The Harrier. The British Harrier V/STOL aircraft was accorded the greatest prominence of any weapons system operating during the South Atlantic conflict. As already noted, it was the only source of on-site air cover for the landing forces, and provided air-to-ground support as the assault progressed. Its most publicized exploits involved its aerial combat with Argentine fighters: twenty-three Argentine planes were shot down by Harriers, while no Harriers were lost as a result of these dogfights.

Nevertheless, while these statistics are certainly impressive, they are somewhat misleading. The Harrier was operating against aircraft that were at the limits of their combat radii. Their endurance and freedom of action were therefore highly restricted. In addition, they did not benefit from avionics or weaponry as modern as those of the Harrier. In particular, the Harrier's effectiveness was significantly enhanced by the infrared homing AIM-9L Sidewinder missile. The Argentines did not themselves employ an equivalent heat-seeking missile.

Perhaps a more significant indicator of the Harrier's utility is the measure of its readiness and sortie rates during the conflict. The forty-two Harriers achieved 95 percent availability at the outset of each day and flew 99 percent of all planned missions. These statistics point to the responsiveness and versatility of the V/STOL plane, and justify the determination of the Marine Corps to acquire the AV-8B Harrier on the grounds that V/STOL type aircraft could more rapidly respond to the time-urgent demands of the ground commander for aerial firepower on a fast changing battlefield.

Super Etendard. For its part, the Argentine Air Force demonstrated the capability of the Super Etendard aircraft, which France operates as a carrier-based system, but which flew from Argentine land bases. The combination of Super Etendard and Exocet missile was probably the greatest threat to the British naval force. The plane's inertial navigation system and attack radar permitted it to fly attack profiles at very low levels, pop up to fire, and then exit rapidly. Because the aircraft can be refueled while in flight, it did not suffer from the same constraints that affected other Argentine planes flying at the limits of their combat radii. Unlike the American A-7E, however, which the U.S. Navy considers comparable to the Etendard, the latter did not carry iron bombs. Nor did the Etendards benefit from target-locating assistance in three of the five missions that the small squadron undertook.[32]

Missile Systems

Exocet. The important role of this subsonic sea-skimming missile already has been noted several times in this essay. Exocet's low-level flight profile creates new demands upon both surface naval anti-air radars and the guns and missiles that they direct and/or control. It is noteworthy that the Argentines also attempted to employ Exocet in its land-based variant, despite having to employ a makeshift battery in order to do so. Nevertheless, one land-based Exocet reportedly did score a hit during the campaign.

Rapier. A number of different missile types were employed by the British to defend against incoming attack aircraft. Of these, the most modern was the Rapier system, a relatively lightweight missile employed against low- and medium-altitude targets. The missile appears to have performed reasonably well, enabling the British to shoot down fourteen Argentine aircraft (and possibly six more).

Rapier did not conclusively prove itself to be a capable system for an expeditionary force, however. It appears to have suffered from the dampness of the sea journey. It may have had electronic interference from the Royal Navy Identification Friend-or-Foe Radio Transmissions. Rapier also proved difficult to deploy quickly from ship to shore, and was unavailable to defend the forces that landed at Bluff Cove and were subjected to a surprise attack by the Argentine Air Force.[33] Finally, the Rapier was not subjected to serious countermeasures, thus leaving unresolved the question of its capabilities in the kind of conflict that could take place in Europe.

Sea Wolf. Sea Wolf is a radar-controlled short-range defense missile that can be fired in bursts of two. Its operation in the South Atlantic was its first exposure to wartime conditions. The Sea Wolf, emplaced aboard three ships, proved to be extremely effective, achieving five kills for six launches. All of the kills were aircraft; Sea Wolf was not employed against Exocet, though it has an antimissile capability. In November 1983, however, a Sea Wolf missile shot down an Exocet during a test firing. This was the first time that the low altitude Exocet had been shot down by a close-in naval missile defense system.

Sea Wolf nevertheless failed to provide last-ditch weapons defense during the conflict. The United Kingdom has acknowledged as much, and is seeking a different type of close-in system.[34] One possible lesson of the war may be that missile systems, however capable, do not provide the responsiveness and speed required for close-in defense. On the other hand, the radar-guided Vulcan/Phalanx gatling gun system provides the U.S. Navy with the kind of defense that the British needed in the South Atlantic.

Sea Skua. The Sea Skua is a helicopter-launched antiship missile that had not been certified for fleet use prior to the South Atlantic conflict. Developed for employment by Britain's lightweight Lynx naval helicopter, Sea Skua performed impressively, scoring from four to eight hits out of eight shots. The United States has introduced an air-launched antiship missile, the Harpoon, which has a longer range than Sea Skua, but performs the same mission. Its viability was clearly validated by the Sea Skua's success in the South Atlantic.

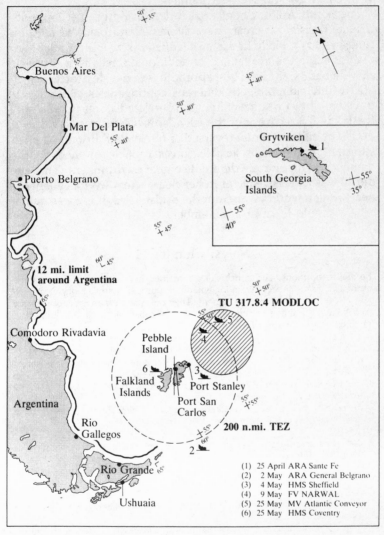

Figure 2 South Atlantic Ocean
Approximate positions of ship sinkings, the total exclusion
zone (TEZ) and RN carrier operating area (MODLOC)

that arises when planners focus on only one scenario, however demanding it might be. Such an emphasis tends to overlook the importance of flexibility, which is the *sine qua non* for coping with crises not foreseen by planners.

The South Atlantic conflict also demonstrated that an unanticipated crisis can create new demands and place a strain on forces which initially had been planned for meeting a particular need. Failing the availability of additional forces to meet these new demands, the next best approach is to develop forces which are readily adaptable to different contingencies. Britain was forced to draw on some of her NATO-related assets to prosecute the battle for recovery of the islands. Nevertheless, because of decisions either recently reversed or forestalled, Britain retained sufficient numbers of flexible forces capable of meeting the demands of an entirely different combat environment. That she did so was a decisive factor in her clear victory over a gallant foe nearly half a world away from the British Isles. It is a lesson that others should learn and remember.

Notes: Chapter 11

The views, opinions, and conclusions contained here are solely those of the author and do not reflect the endorsement or approval of any agency or department of the United States government. They are based on analysis of material available to the public and should in no way be construed to prejudge or affect the official Department of Defense evaluation of the conflict.

1 See Lawrence Freedman's exhaustive review of British/American literature on the war, "Bridgehead revisited: the literature of the Falklands," *International Affairs*, vol. 59 (Summer 1983), pp. 445–52, and Simon Collier, "The First Falklands War?: Argentine attitudes," ibid., pp. 458–64, for a survey of the Argentine literature.
2 Sir James Cable, "The Falklands conflict," *United States Naval Institute Proceedings*, vol. 107 (September 1982), p. 74.
3 loc. cit.
4 For an assessment of the report see William Wallace, "How frank was Franks?," *International Affairs*, vol. 59 (Summer 1983), pp. 453–8.
5 Lord Franks, et al., *Falkland Islands Review: Report of a Committee of Privy Counsellors*, Cmnd. 8787 (London: HMSO, 1983), p. 77.
6 ibid., pp. 19, 77, 91.
7 Lawrence Freedman, "The War of the Falkland Islands, 1982," *Foreign Affairs*, Fall 1982, p. 199.
8 Speed's account, which argues that his views were vindicated by the South Atlantic conflict, appears as *Sea Change: The Battle for the Falklands and the Future of Britain's Navy* (Bath: Ashgrove, 1982).
9 Franks, et al., *Falkland Islands Review*, p. 88.
10 *The Falklands Campaign, the Lessons*, Cmnd. 8785 (London: HMSO, 1982), pp. 34–5.
11 The title of this section is borrowed from a paper devoted to the subject. See

Dov S. Zakheim, "Of allies and access," *Washington Quarterly*, vol. 4 (Winter 1981), pp. 88–96.

12 *Strategic Survey 1982–1983* (London: International Institute for Strategic Studies, 1983), pp. 116–24.

13 John Nott, "The Falklands campaign," *United States Naval Institute Proceedings*, vol. 119 (May 1983), p. 120.

14 See Michael Moodie, "Six months and three wars," *Washington Quarterly*, vol. 5 (Autumn 1982), p. 31, and Captain C. H. Layman, R.N., "Duty in bomb alley," *United States Naval Institute Proceedings*, vol. 119 (August 1983), p. 39.

15 See Dr. Robert L. Scheina, "The Malvinas campaign," *United States Naval Institute Proceedings*, vol. 119 (May 1983), pp. 107, 112.

16 Freedman, "The War of the Falkland Islands, 1982," pp. 209, 210.

17 See Edgar O'Ballance, "The other Falkland campaign," *Military Review*, January 1983.

18 United States Department of the Navy, *Lessons of the Falklands: Summary Report* (February 1983), p. 1.

19 For a discussion, albeit somewhat biased in favor of the "carrier admirals," see Paul B. Ryan, *First Line of Defense: The U.S. Navy since 1945* (Stanford, Calif.: Hoover Institution Press, 1981), pp. 12–14.

20 For a discussion of the fact that, as George and Coughlin state, "everyone seems to be claiming that the conflict in the South Atlantic vindicates his line of strategic thought," see Bruce George, M.P., and Michael Coughlin, "British defense policy after the Falklands," *Survival*, vol. 24 (September/October 1982), pp. 201–2 (from which the quotation is borrowed); Commander Kenneth R. McGruther, U.S.N. "When deterrence fails: the nasty little war for the Falkland Islands," *Naval War College Review*, vol. 36 (March–April 1983), p. 47; Jeffrey Record, "The Falklands War," *Washington Quarterly*, vol. 5 (Autumn 1982), pp. 45–6; Norman Friedman, "Lessons learned and mislearned," *Orbis*, vol. 26 (Winter 1983), p. 939.

21 For a discussion see Major General E. H. Dar, Pakistan Army (Ret.), "Strategy in the Falklands War," *United States Naval Institute Proceedings*, vol. 109 (March 1983), pp. 132–4.

22 Freedman, "The War of the Falkland Islands, 1982," p. 205.

23 "Military lessons of the Falklands campaign," p. 122.

24 *Lessons of the Falklands*, p. 2.

25 A comprehensive critique appears in Martin Binkin and Jeffrey Record, *Where Does the Marine Corps Go from Here?* (Washington, D.C.: Brookings Institution, 1976).

26 Scheina, "The Malvinas campaign," p. 116.

27 See George and Coughlin, "British defense policy after the Falklands," p. 206, and *The Falklands Campaign*, p. 18.

28 *Lessons of the Falklands*, p. 47.

29 Scheina, "The Malvinas campaign," p. 109.

30 ibid., p. 105.

31 For a discussion of the importance of training see Record, "The Falklands War," pp. 46–7, who notes the contrast between British troops trained to conduct operations at night and in cold weather, and the Argentine forces who had been poorly trained for night and bad weather combat. Most British advances on the ground were conducted at night. For additional perspectives see Admiral Stansfield Turner, U.S.N. (Ret.), "The unobvious lessons of the Falklands War," *United States Naval Institute Proceedings*, vol. 119 (April 1983), p. 56. For a personal account of life and morale in "bomb alley," as San Carlos Water was called, see Layman, "Duty in bomb alley," pp. 35–9.

32 See Dr. Robert L. Scheina, "Super Etendard: super squadron," *United States Naval Institute Proceedings*, vol. 119 (March 1983), p. 135, and Scheina, "The Malvinas campaign," p. 114.

33 See J. P. Robinson, "The use and effectiveness of air defense systems in the Falkland Islands," (Hughes Aircraft Company Weapons Systems Laboratory, unpublished, November 1982), pp. 12–13, and George and Coughlin, "British defense policy after the Falklands," p. 205.

34 *The Falklands Campaign*, pp. 33–5.

35 For a recounting of Argentine views of the impact of British SSN operations, see Scheina, "The Malvinas campaign," pp. 107, 116–17.

12

Anglo-Argentine Rivalry after the Falklands: On the Road to Antarctica?

CHRISTOPHER C. JOYNER

The Falkland Islands War of 1982 generated heated debate over military, political, economic, and legal issues. Even so, scant serious attention has been focused upon possible geostrategic implications of the conflict. This appears to be the case particularly with regard to the Antarctic, a region where both Great Britain and Argentina have espoused conflicting territorial claims of sovereignty and purported administrative jurisdiction. Several major questions are posed. Given the Falklands military crisis of 1982, what geopolitical ramifications, if any, can be inferred about ongoing Anglo-Argentine activities in and around the Antarctic continent? What justifications under international law have been made for each state's respective territorial claims in the region, and to what extent are their legal positions incompatible with each other? What genuine merits to legal title have accrued to Great Britain and Argentina vis-à-vis their respective claims over portions of Antarctica and select circumjacent island groups? Is the current Antarctic regime sufficiently stable to withstand the political challenge of a disruptive outbreak of Anglo-Argentine rivalry over Antarctica? Finally, what is the likelihood of conflict over Antarctica, and what factors could operate either to precipitate or to deter a possible military confrontation between the two powers? This essay seeks to address these queries by examining both Argentina's and Great Britain's historical experiences in the Antarctic region, ascertaining the nature of their territorial claims there,

189

and assessing the relative prospects for cooperation or confrontation in the wake of the 1982 Falkland Islands War. Consequently, this study will attempt to provide a better understanding of the historical nuances and legal complexities surrounding Anglo-Argentine rivalry in the region not only for the Falkland Islands situation in particular, but also for the broader Antarctic context in general. (See Figure 3.)

Argentina's Activities in Antarctica, 1834–1958

Exploration and Development

Argentina historically has regarded the Antarctic region as strategically significant. Serious concern persists about the ostensible need to protect the Argentine mainland's southern flank from attack and possible blockade. The South Atlantic Ocean and the Antarctic continent are seen not merely as distant, frigid, ice-covered wastelands; rather, they are perceived as embodying an all too near springboard from which hostile military activity could be launched against Argentina's national security.

No doubt, Argentina's security anxieties stem not only from geographical realities, but also from historical experience in the area, perhaps most emphatically the long-standing dispute with Great Britain over the Falklands. Since the British occupation of the Falklands in 1834, the Argentine government has been willing neither to recognize legally Great Britain's territorial claims nor to accept politically any proclaimed British administration over the area. Furthermore, Argentina views its disputes with Great Britain over the Falkland Islands and portions of Antarctica as one and the same. Both the Islas Malvinas and other Antarctic-related claims have been treated politically and legally by Argentina as if these areas were sovereign national territory. For example, schoolchildren are taught from early ages that these areas are integral portions of the Argentine homeland; the population of these regions, particularly that of the Malvinas, is included in Argentina's national census returns; and island residents visiting Argentina are treated as Argentine citizens, being liable for call into the military service and required to carry Argentine passports.

Prior to 1900 Argentina expressed only passing interest in the Antarctic. In 1903, however, the Argentine gunboat *Uruguay* successfully completed Argentina's first voyage through Antarctic waters, in the process rescuing the Nordenskjold expedition from the Snow Hill Islands. The following year, in February 1904, at the invitation of the Scottish National Antarctic Expedition, Argentina assumed official control over the meteorological observatory on Laurie Island in the South Orkneys, and has maintained its operation continuously since then.

Although Argentine Antarctic activities remained dormant over the next two decades, in 1927 interest in the region was renewed. A radio transmitter was installed at Laurie Island, and Argentina first enunciated its claims officially in a statement delivered to the Universal Postal Union: "The Argentine territorial jurisdiction extends in fact over the continental area, the territorial sea and the islands of Tierra del Fuego, the archipelagoes of Estado, Ano Nuevo, South Georgia, and to the Polar lands not yet delimited."[1] Argentina initiated more extensive Antarctic-related endeavors during the 1940s beginning with the creation by government decree of a permanent National Commission on the Antarctic (Comision Nacional del Antartico) on 30 April 1940. Two years later the Argentine naval transport *Primero de Mayo* undertook a highly visible Antarctic expedition, visiting Deception Island, Melchin Island, and Winter Island en route. The *Primero de Mayo* deposited on these islands bronze tablets bearing inscriptions which proclaimed Argentine annexation of all lands lying within the area south of latitude 60° south and between longitudes 25° west and 68°34′ west.

The election of Juan Peron in 1946 stabilized Argentina's domestic situation, giving the government an opportunity to elevate Antarctica as a principal focus of Argentina's political, military, and diplomatic concern. That year, a significant governmental expeditionary program was initiated in Graham's Land (later Palmer Peninsula), and concurrently, a vigorous domestic publicity campaign was launched to make the Argentine people more Antarctica-conscious. By November 1946 sufficient cartographical evidence had been accumulated to suggest that Argentina tacitly had accepted sectorization of its claim to the Antarctic continent, consisting of a territorial wedge emanating outward from the South Pole between 25° and 74° west longitude, bounded to the north by the 60° parallel.

Of related significance was Argentina's posture in negotiating the 1947 Inter-American Treaty of Reciprocal Assistance (the Rio Treaty). Perusal of this regional security compact reveals three interesting pertinent provisions. First, "an armed attack by any

State against an American State [would] be considered as an attack against all the American States" (article 3(1)). Second, the area applicable for the treaty's designated jurisdiction specifically included the South Pole, as well as longitudinal boundaries designed to encompass Argentina's Antarctic claims (article 4). Third, the Peron government appended to the treaty text a formal reservation which retained Argentina's national rights over claims in the Antarctic-circumpolar region. As a consequence, the "American Antarctic" effectively became subsumed under the Rio Treaty's security umbrella. Moreover, a commitment was made by the parties, including the United States, to resist "aggression" against Argentina by an "extracontinental Power" (ostensibly read by the Argentine government to mean "Great Britain").[2]

Before entry into force of the current Antarctic Treaty regime in 1961, Argentina's activities regarding the circumpolar region assumed an increasingly nationalistic hue. In 1951 the Antarctic Institute (Instituto Antarctico Argentina) was created and placed under the policy aegis of the Ministry of the Army. Four years later, on 28 June 1955, new national legislation, the "Provincialization of the National Territories," was promulgated. This new law formally incorporated Argentina's South Atlantic territories into provinces of the national federal domain. On 28 February 1957 the Argentine government proclaimed the establishment of "The National Territory of Tierra del Fuego, the Antarctic and the Islands of the South Atlantic." Including the Islas Malvinas, this new national territory was reaffirmed as an integral part of the Argentine homeland, and, supposedly, was to be administered from its provincial capital of Ushuaia in Tierra del Fuego.

Argentina's Claims to Legal Title

In light of the above observations, Argentina's assertions to legal title over territories in the South Atlantic-Antarctic are predicated upon certain historical, geographical, and geological considerations peculiar to the area. From the Argentine viewpoint, for instance, Argentina's uninterrupted maintenance since 22 February 1904 of the weather station on Laurie Island in the South Orkneys constitutes sufficient effective occupation under international law to advance a bona fide claim meriting territorial sovereignty over the Antarctic region. Surely not unrelated in this respect is the allegation that certain symbolic acts were performed during the course of Argentina's receiving the Laurie Island outpost from the Scottish jurisdiction in 1904: namely, after the completion of formal transfer of authority the Argentine flag was raised over the station as a gesture of national ownership. In addition, an Argentine citizen present at the occasion performed a stamp cancellation ceremony, purportedly to demonstrate establishment there of a post office, a factor which under international law generally is considered to indicate administrative jurisdiction and sovereign control over a territory.

Argentina's continuous operation of the Laurie Island facility over eight decades is not at issue. Serious questions arise, however, as to whether such presence on a single relatively insignificant islet can constitute a degree of *effective* occupation sufficient to legitimize Argentina's concomitant claims to the Malvinas/Falklands, South Georgia, the South Shetlands, the South Sandwich group, and several hundred-thousand square miles of land space on the Antarctic mainland. Legally, one cannot but harbor grave doubts about such an assertion.

Concerning symbolic acts as evidence of effective occupation, no legal credibility is attached to them without actual prolonged settlement. Argentina has gone to considerable lengths to highlight its claims in the circumpolar area by performing several intermittent ceremonial acts implying administration, such as placing property plaques, designating postmasters, coroners, and local magistrates, issuing postage stamps commemorating the claimed territories, delivering children there, and declaring a national "Antarctic" holiday. All this notwithstanding, international law regards such activities as mere forms of "fictitious occupation," without any real legal foundation. Consequently, Argentina's symbolic acts of sovereignty in the region are regarded by most legal commentators as just that: symbolic acts, not facts.

Perhaps more interesting from the legal historian's vantage point is Argentina's reliance upon the Latin American doctrine of *uti possidetis juris* to bolster its Antarctic-related claims. It was argued that legal title to possessions in the Western hemisphere does not spring from occupation and settlement of *res nullius* lands in the New World, because appropriate legal title already had been granted by the pope to the Spanish throne in the fifteenth century. In 1493 Pope Alexander VI issued his famous Bull *Inter Caetera*, which drew a line from Pole to Pole, extending 370 leagues from the Cape Verde Islands. Concurrently, the pope declared that all lands lying west of 46° longitude belonged to Spain, and those situated east of the demarcation belonged to Portugal. This papal division of the New World was formally agreed to by Spain and Portugal in 1494 in the Treaty of Tordesillas. In effect, then, modern legal titles over territories in Latin America are deemed to have been transferred from the Spanish and Portuguese Empires to their legitimate heirs, who were created through the attainment of national independence. The historical essence of *uti possidetis juris* has been aptly described as follows:

When the Spanish colonies of Central and South America proclaimed their independence in the second decade of the Nineteenth Century, they adopted a principle of Constitutional and International Law to which they gave the name of *uti possidetis juris* of 1810. The principle laid down the rule that the boundaries of the newly established republics would be the frontiers of the Spanish provinces which they were succeeding. This general principle offered the advantage of establishing the absolute rule that in law no territory of old Spanish America was without an owner. To be sure, there were many regions that had not been occupied by the Spaniards and many regions that were unexplored or inhabited by uncivilised natives, but these sections were regarded as belonging in law to the respective republics that had succeeded the Spanish provinces to which these lands were connected by virtue of old Royal decrees of the Spanish mother country. These territories, although not occupied in fact, were by common agreement considered as being occupied in law by the new republics from the very beginning. Encroachments and ill-timed efforts at colonisation beyond the frontiers, as well as occupations in fact, became invalid and ineffective in law. The principle also had the advantage, it was hoped, of doing away with boundary disputes between the new States. Finally it put an end to the designs of the colonising States of Europe against lands which otherwise they could have sought to proclaim as *res nullius*.[3]

Thus, Argentina maintains that its title to territories claimed in the South Atlantic and Antarctica flows directly and irrefutably from the uncontested Spanish title, recognized and sanctioned by Pope Alexander VI in 1493–4.

It is arguable whether the doctrine of *uti possidetis juris* retains substantial legal applicability as a tenet of contemporary international law. As one study curtly put it, "Because modern international law does not recognize the authority of fifteenth-century pontiffs to bind nations five centuries later, this theory carries little weight today."[4] The Papal Bull of 1493 long antedated creation of the sovereign nation-state system and the Eurocentric corpus of international law. Moreover, *uti possidetis juris* fails to square properly with the legal establishment of non-Hispanic states in the New World, as well as the more recently evolved principles of decolonization and self-determination. Furthermore, except for Latin American states, succession from original Spanish rights has neither commanded widespread respect nor attracted international acceptance, either in practice or in principle. This apparent lack of contemporary legal recognition indicates that *uti possidetis juris* contributes little, if any, legal support for Argentina's South Atlantic and Antarctic claims.

Turning to factors of geography, Argentina (as well as Chile) has advanced the contention that a state's propinquity (that is, proximity or contiguity) may enhance its claims to legal title. Argentina is the state located closest to various South Atlantic islands and Antarctic lands; having the most proximate location supposedly conveys a special right vis-à-vis legal possession, particularly when the notion of sectorization is applied to national claims on the continent. The sector theory, adapted from the Arctic experience, defines claimants' territorial boundaries according to longitudinal lines that converge on the South Pole from baselines originating either from mainland perimeters of the claimant state (for example, Argentina) or from a section of the Antarctic coast "discovered" or "occupied" by the claimant state (for example, Great Britain).[5] Though not recognized internationally, sectorization has been adopted and implemented by claimants to Antarctica as a means of neatly dividing up the continent.

While Argentina's proximity to the Antarctic is geographically evident, it is insufficient by itself to justify a legal title. Mere propinquity is not, nor is it likely to be, respectfully regarded in international law as a definitive criterion for asserting title to sovereignty. Moreover, while the sector method of demarcating claims in Antarctica has been used by claimant states as a convenient apportionment device, it has not been accepted as a universal principle or a rule of law. Legal opinion overwhelmingly concurs that polar sectorization through propinquity serves primarily as a political convenience for the involved parties; but as a steadfast, acknowledged norm of international law, sectorization and its basis for title has been repudiated in substantial measure.[6]

A third aspect of Argentina's legal argument aims at establishing claims to portions of the circumpolar region upon geological and geomorphological grounds. Put simply, "the highlands of Antarctica must be regarded as a continuation of the Andes."[7] Geomorphological evidence actually has revealed that a regionally submerged mountain chain does exist, of which the Falkland Islands, Shag Rocks, South Georgia, the South Sandwich Islands, and Graham Land are parts protruding above water. This so-called "Antillan Loop" is believed to be an integral segment of the Andean chain, linking together Tierra del Fuego with the mountains in Graham Land.[8] Perhaps not surprisingly, the Argentine legal view holds that Graham Land geologically is an extension of the Andes system, and, moreover, that the various island groups associated with it are joined to South America by a prolonged continental shelf area. Consequently, Argentina believes that its claims of sovereignty over these juxtaposed territories have priority over those of other states.

While Argentina's geomorphological reasoning may be appealing, its legal deduction proves fallacious, at least by the international community's standards. While not discounting theoretical contingencies, practice in international law has mandated that efficacy, rather than purported geological contiguity, should be the overriding determinant of legal title. As stated by Professor Van der Heydte,

> The natural boundary lines of any application of the rule of contiguity are drawn, precisely, by its very origin from the general principle of effectiveness. Admitting the existence of such a rule, we only assert the existence of an individual case of applying the principle of virtual effectiveness as defined above. It is proper, therefore, to speak of contiguity only as far as one can speak also of virtual effectiveness.[9]

To accept the notion that Argentina's continental shelf prolongation legally constitutes appropriate contiguity relative to circumpolar territories undercuts the traditional international legal framework affecting territorial sovereignty over land; it also displaces relevant considerations of the law of the sea, particularly those principles concerning territorial delimitation of coastal states, the exclusive economic zone, the legal status of islands, and various high seas freedoms. Additionally, application of Argentina's geological contiguity position tends to disregard an obvious fact of geography: the lack of sufficient adjacency required to exercise a claim of contiguity. It is at best difficult to accept that Argentina can qualify as a state "adjacent" to Antarctica, unless some 450 miles of ocean space and pack ice are construed to be a transcontinental bridge. In short, J. Peter Bernhardt put it well when he concluded, "Applying the contiguity principle to the Antarctic would be an unwarranted extension of an already overstretched idea."[10]

Concluding Observations

Argentina historically has shown considerable interest in the Antarctic, and since the early 1900s the government often has attempted to demonstrate the legitimacy of its claims through manifold symbolic displays of sovereignty. Further, beginning in the 1940s, the Antarctica-Falklands issue assumed saliency in Argentine domestic politics, engendering at times an ultra-nationalist fervor. Especially sensitive and acute for Argentines is the issue of foreign colonialist domination, allegedly exemplified by the perceived intervention of Great Britain into Western hemispheric affairs and the former's refusal to recognize Argentine territorial claims in the region. As a diplomatic counterpoise to the British presence in the South Atlantic-Antarctic, Argentina contends that its valid legal claims to title have been acquired regionally through succession from the fifteenth-century Spanish Empire, relative proximity to the area, and geomorphological contiguity of the Andes chain transoceanically with the Antarctic Mountains. Nonetheless, when viewed within the context of contemporary international law, Argentina's claims to sovereignty at best appear to be tenuous, anachronistic, and polemical; at worst, they may be challenged on grounds of being perfunctory, contentious, and perhaps, even nugatory.

Great Britain's Antarctic Activities 1675–1962

Exploration and Development

Great Britain's presence in the Antarctic has been evident for more than two centuries. The earliest discovery of land in the area is believed to have been South Georgia in 1675 by the British merchant Anthony de la Roche. A century later the island was "rediscovered" by the English Captain James Cook, who on 17 January 1775, claimed its possession for King George III and named it South Georgia in the king's honor. In that same month Captain Cook also reportedly discovered and claimed the South Sandwich Island group for Great Britain.

The early nineteenth century witnessed numerous British expeditions into the Antarctic. In February 1819 William Smith discovered the South Shetlands and claimed them for the British Crown. The first sighting of the Antarctic coast, probably along the northern extremity known as Trinity Peninsula on Graham Land, is credited to Edward Bransfield, a Royal Navy officer, in 1820. The South Orkney Islands were discovered and claimed for Great Britain by George Powell in December 1821. Captain Henry Foster of the Royal Navy explored and claimed parts of the Antarctic mainland in 1828–9 and deposited a copper cylinder on Hoseason Island, declaring it a British possession in the name of King George IV. Three years later, on 21 February 1832, Captain John Biscoe circumnavigated the continent and visited part of the Palmer archipelago. Claiming the area in the name of King William IV, Captain Biscoe mistakenly called it Graham Land, apparently convinced that he had actually discovered portions of the mainland. Between 1841 and 1843 Sir James Clark Ross circumnavigated the continent, charted some 500 miles of coastline in Victoria Land, and discovered Ross Island and the northern edge of the Ross Ice Shelf. On 6 January 1843 Ross landed on the eastern shore of Palmer peninsula, claiming Ross Island and all "contiguous lands" for the British crown.[11]

Save for whalers, scant British interest was shown in Antarctica over the next fifty years. However, between 1895 and 1905 seven major national expeditions set out for Antarctica, two of which were British-sponsored: the British Antarctic Expedition of 1898–1900 under C. E. Borchgrevink, and the larger British National Antarctic Expedition of 1901–4 led by Captain R. F. Scott. In the following years, private expeditions by British subjects contributed much in the way of scientific discovery and Antarctic cartography. Foremost among these were Captain Scott's second expedition (1910–13) in the Ross Dependency, and the exploits of Sir Ernest Shackleton (1907–9, 1914–17, and 1921–2) who claimed possession of the Ross Dependency for Great Britain. During this "Heroic Age of Antarctic Exploration," Great Britain formally announced its claims to portions of Antarctica. In 1908 and 1917 the British government promulgated two Letters Patent, setting out boundary delimitations for the British claims which became subsequently known as the Falkland Islands Dependencies.

From 1923 to 1939 the Discovery Committee, a British-based organization, produced more accurate maps of the Dependencies and gathered information useful to Great Britain's whaling industry. Significantly, a series of survey voyages also were sponsored under the committee's direction, leading to enhanced oceanographical studies of the Southern Ocean, two circumnavigations of the Antarctic continent, and recharting of the coasts of South Georgia, the South Orkneys, the South Shetlands, and the South Sandwich Islands.

British appreciation of the Antarctic's strategic importance was accentuated by World War II. Accordingly, during 1943–5 "Operation Tabarin" was undertaken to secure military bases at Deception Island and Graham Land, ostensibly to preclude an "Antarctic coup" by either Argentine or German forces. In 1945 these stations were transformed into the Falkland Islands Dependencies Survey (renamed the British Antarctic Survey in 1967) under whose aegis British exploration and scientific activities in the region have since been conducted. In 1962 Britain established through an Order-in-Council the British Antarctic Territory. Effective since 2 March 1962, the territory as designated would comprise all lands and islands lying south of 60° south latitude and between 20° and 80° west longitudes, encompassing all British-claimed territories within the area set out in the Antarctic Treaty of 1959. The Falkland Islands Dependencies were reduced in size to only South Georgia, the South Sandwich group, and various oceanic rock formations, all located north of the Antarctic Treaty perimeter.[12]

Great Britain's Claims to Legal Title

Of all states who had serious interest in the South Atlantic-Antarctic area prior to 1900, none was more active than Great Britain. The historical record speaks for itself, particularly in terms of British discovery and exploration efforts. Those explorers who laid claim to various territories in the South Atlantic and Antarctic for Great Britain were officers in the Royal Navy, duly commissioned and officially assigned to make these voyages in the name of the king. This undeniably imparts some measure of governmental legitimacy to British claims in the region. Even so, the issue to be addressed here is the extent to which British allegations of sovereign control over Antarctic territories merit valid title under international law.

Under contemporary international law six methods of acquiring title to territory are recognized by states: occupation, accretion, prescription, voluntary cession, conquest, and treaties of peace. Historically, discovery represented the paramount means of securing title to vacant lands. Since the eighteenth century, however, discovery alone has been deemed insufficient to effect a claim of valid legal title; it must be followed by "effective" occupation, ostensibly demonstrated through permanent settlement and responsible administrative jurisdiction. It is largely on the grounds of discovery and consequent effective occupation that British claims to Antarctic territories are predicated. These claims have been formally stated as follows:

> by reason of historic British discoveries of certain territories in the Antarctic and sub-Antarctic; by reason of the long-continued and peaceful display of British sovereignty from the date of those discoveries onwards in, and in regard to, the territories in the dominions of the British Crown; by virtue of their formal constitution in the Royal Letters Patent of 1908 and 1917 as the British Possession called the Falkland Islands Dependencies: the United Kingdom possesses, and at all material dates has possessed, the sovereignty over the territories of the Falkland Islands Dependencies, and in particular the South Sandwich Islands, South Georgia, the South Orkneys, South Shetlands, Graham Land and Coats Land.[13]

The central question therefore becomes how effective Great Britain's occupation has been, and whether or not it has been sufficient to warrant legal recognition as full and complete sovereign control. When set against the accepted criteria for effective occupation, the recorded British experience since 1675 in the region leaves room for doubt as to whether legal conditions for conferring British sovereignty have been fully met.

International law through state practice has defined effectiveness of occupation as "the objective manifestation of a continuous development of control commencing with discovery and subsequent inchoate title and continuing by permanent settlement and administration."[14] If this is so, the British claim suffers noticeably from the absence of any permanent settlement on all save one of their territories, the Falklands, which have a local population of about 1,800. South Georgia and the South

Sandwich Islands are virtually uninhabited, and the South Shetland Islands, the South Orkneys, and Graham's Land are populated only by a chain of small meteorological stations. The few "residents" there are neither indigenous peoples nor British colonists, but scientists assigned to operate the facilities.

The South Polar area, of course, is incredibly inhospitable; Antarctica is the coldest, driest, windiest, and remotest place on earth. Given these extraordinarily harsh environmental conditions, the suggestion has been made that special consideration ought to be made for Antarctica-based claims; because normal "effective occupation" is essentially impossible in Antarctic conditions, less stringent requirements for effectiveness should be applied. This is not the place to debate the "exceptions" polemic; others have done that more authoritatively, without universally conclusive results. What must be posited, though, is that effective control for securing recognized sovereign title in the Antarctic would necessitate at least "actual continuous and peaceful display of state functions," if not directly through permanent settlement, then indirectly through "effective" administration.[15]

Administratively, British claims to legal title were clearly spelled out in the King's Letters Patent of 1908. This royal proclamation publicly declared formal organization of the Falkland Islands Dependencies, consisting of the Falkland Islands, South Georgia, the South Orkneys, the South Shetlands, the South Sandwich Islands, and Graham's Land. As British commentators are quick to note, the Letters Patent did not make a claim of British sovereignty; such an assertion was presumed already extant and deemed legitimized, principally because no overt foreign challenge to it had been made during the nineteenth century.[16] The statement, it is argued, simply confirmed Great Britain's previous circumpolar claims and consolidated them under a unitary administrative structure.

As a suitable vehicle for substantiating British sovereign control in the Antarctic, the Letters Patent of 1908 has some critical deficiencies. First, although predicated upon title to territory secured by discovery, portions of some lands included in the Letters Patent had been discovered or initially surveyed by nationals from states other than Great Britain. For example, Admiral Thaddeus Bellingshausen of Russia extensively explored the South Sandwich group during 1819–21. In 1838–40 a French expedition under Dumont d'Urville surveyed and charted the South Orkneys, South Shetlands, and Graham's

Land. The Belgian Antarctic Expedition commanded by Adrien de Gerlache in 1897–9, the Swedish Polar Expedition of 1901–4 led by Otto Nordenskjold, and the French Antarctic Expedition of 1903–5 under J. B. Charcot all performed noteworthy explorations in the Graham Land area. Hence, considerable foreign discovery and exploration activity occurred in British-claimed areas, apparently without the seeking or securing of official British advice or permission.

A second difficulty associated with the Letters Patent of 1908 is that such a unilateral declaration looms inadequate for demonstrating national sovereignty over a territory. The proclamation was merely a Royal Prerogative, designed to modify administrative boundaries of a non-self-governing territory, and to set up an appropriate supervisory structure. Consequently, the Letters Patent of 1908 must be viewed purely as a domestic measure, intended to facilitate Great Britain's governance of claimed lands over 8,000 miles away. Obviously, such an intention presupposes the legal right to govern. But the Letters Patent neither substantiated the claims nor validated sovereign title; legally, it merely presumed the claims' validity.

Third, as stated in the 1908 Letters Patent, the enumerated "Dominion" island groups are described as being "situated in the South Atlantic Ocean to the south of the 50th Parallel of South latitude and lying between the 20th and 80th degrees of West longitude." Interestingly, if interpreted literally, those geographical coordinates would encompass several islands offshore Chile and Argentina in the lower Patagonian zone, south of the 50th Parallel. In order to assuage possible political misunderstandings, particularly by Argentina, a second Letters Patent was issued on 28 March 1917. This proclamation, while reaffirming the intent of the 1908 document, clarified Great Britain's claim to include "all islands and territories whatsoever between the twentieth degree of west longitude and the fiftieth degree of west longitude which are situated south of the 50th Parallel of south latitude; and all islands and territories whatsoever between the fiftieth degree of west longitude and the eightieth degree of west longitude which are situated south of the 58th Parallel of south latitude."

Hence, island groups or rocks located within the territorial waters of Argentina and Chile were excluded from British appropriation. Even so, like its 1908 predecessor the 1917 Letters Patent must be regarded under international law as only providing a domestic declaration of policy; it did not embody either validation or substantiation of Great Britain's claim to sovereign title over these territories.

Also relevant to Great Britain's assertion of title is the fact that its claim to the Ross Dependency and Australian Antarctic Territory were made by Orders in Council in 1923 and 1933 respectively. At that time, the former territory was placed under the jurisdiction of New Zealand and the latter under the governance of the Commonwealth of Australia. Parenthetically, it is interesting to speculate on the legal complications that would be generated if Great Britain's claims to its Antarctic territories someday were adjudged by an international tribunal never to have been legally sound. New Zealand's and Australia's claims to territory in Antarctica then could become liable to challenge, and their legal status would become relegated to that of adopted offspring, spawned from an illegitimate parentage.

Notwithstanding the above critique, there is no doubt that during this century the British government has evinced substantial confidence in the accepted legality of its claims in the Antarctic region. This self-assurance was shown in December 1947 when Great Britain offered the opportunity to Argentina and Chile of adjudicating rightful title through the International Court of Justice. Similarly, in April 1951 and again in February 1953 Great Britain renewed its offer to Argentina and Chile, but all these offers proved fruitless. Finally, in May 1955 the British government submitted a unilateral application to the Court. Directed specifically at Argentina and Chile, the British Antarctica Cases Application averred:

(1) that the legal titles of the United Kingdom to the Falkland Islands Dependencies, and in particular to the South Sandwich Islands, South Georgia, the South Orkneys, South Shetlands, Graham Land and Coats Land, are, and at all material dates have been, superior to the claims of any other State, and in particular to those of the Republic of Argentina;

(2) that, in consequence, the pretensions of the Republic of Argentina to the South Sandwich Islands, South Georgia, the South Orkneys, South Shetlands, Graham Land and Coats Land, and her encroachments and pretended acts of sovereignty in those territories are, under international law, illegal and invalid.[17]

Perhaps not surprisingly, Argentina and Chile refused to accept the International Court's jurisdiction in the matter, and Great

203

Britain's petition subsequently was removed from the Court's consideration.

Concluding Observations

Great Britain has had ample and long-standing historical interest in the South Atlantic and the Antarctic. British subjects were among the earliest and most active explorers and cartographers of the region. In terms of pre-1900 discovery and exploration Great Britain must then rank extremely high, if not paramount, among states attracted to the area.

However, valid title and justifiable sovereign claims under modern international law are not predicated upon discovery and exploration alone. Substantial settlement, complemented by a genuine intention to occupy the region permanently, are necessary for a state to perfect legal claims and sovereign title to territory. These essential requirements appear to be lacking in the British position. Admittedly, the British government historically has regarded selected parts of the Antarctic duly and legally as British, and since 1908 it has sought through administrative acts to portray the exercise of a legitimate title to these territories. Nevertheless, these administrative actions presuppose the reality of a clearly recognized, uncontested British title to those lands, something which never has been acknowledged unequivocally by the international community, even up to the present day. In sum, Great Britain's claims in the Antarctic region suffer legally from three obvious shortcomings: (1) these lands never have been permanently settled; (2) consequently, they never have been effectively occupied; and (3) finally, British claims never have been legally recognized. When viewed within the context of contemporary international law, South Georgia, the South Shetlands, the South Sandwich Islands, the South Orkneys, and Graham's Land therefore might be regarded as *terra nullius* more than as bona fide British territorial possessions.

The Antarctic Treaty Regime, 1961 to the Present

The Antarctic Treaty

The regime presently governing activities on the Antarctic continent was created in 1959 by the Antarctic Treaty. A diplomatic outgrowth of the 1958 International Geophysical Year, the

Antarctic Treaty entered into force on 23 June 1961, after ratification by all twelve signatory states. Seven of these (Argentina, Australia, Chile, France, Great Britain, New Zealand, and Norway) had made prior legal claims to the region; the remaining five (Belgium, Japan, South Africa, the Soviet Union, and the United States) had neither claims nor the intention to declare any. The treaty has functioned well since 1961, being regarded as a milestone in Cold War diplomacy. It provides for demilitarization, denuclearization, and peaceful use of the continent. Moreover, freedom of scientific research, information exchange, and cooperation, as well as on-site inspection and the obligation to settle disputes peacefully, are guaranteed.

Perhaps most important for this study, however, is article IV, which relates specifically to territorial claims. This provision directs that no acts or activities occurring while the treaty is in force should "constitute a basis for asserting, supporting, or denying a claim to territorial sovereignty," or "create any rights of territorial sovereignty" on the continent. Furthermore, no new claims or enlargements of existing claims to sovereignty are to be asserted while the treaty is in force. Finally, existing claims and interests are safeguarded by a proviso that nothing contained in the treaty should be interpreted as a "renunciation" by any party of "previously asserted rights," "claims," or "basis of claim to territorial sovereignty in the Antarctic." Article IV legally froze the *status quo ante* of various sector claims made to Antarctic territory south of 60° south latitude, without qualifying or clarifying the legitimacy of the claims' character under international law. Today, that same situation persists regarding the overlapping set of Argentine and British claims to the region.

Potential Sources of Anglo-Argentine Rivalry in Antarctica

Antarctica can be described as a vast frigid desert, a wind-swept barren, ice-clad wasteland. Why, then, should anyone really care about activities in the region, much less about possible Anglo-Argentine rivalries there? Undoubtedly, this is a view commonly shared by the vast majority of laymen, and by a considerable number of government policymakers. The answer to this query has to do with the potential presence of natural resources, both living and nonliving, and the prospects for their eventual commercial exploitation during the remainder of this century.

Regarding nonliving resources in the Antarctic, most information on the availability of substantial mineral deposits is primarily speculative. If the geoscientific notion of "continental drift" is accurate, and the earth's land masses were at one time conjoined into a "super-continent," then minerals found in the southern portions of South America, Africa, India, Australia, and several associated Pacific island chains conceivably could exist in Antarctica as well. So far, only trace findings of these minerals have been discovered; nonetheless, several studies have suggested that there may exist in Antarctica commercially recoverable deposits of coal, copper, gold, uranium, silver, nickel, manganese, cobalt, tin, beryl, platinum, molybdenum, and phosphates. In addition, there has been great interest in potential hydrocarbon fields located within Antarctica's continental shelf, particularly beneath the Weddell Sea. As early as 1974, at least one U.S. government study reportedly said that as much as 45 billion barrels of oil and 115 trillion cubic feet of natural gas potentially might be found there.[18] The Weddell Sea lies within the sectorial region claimed by both Argentina and Great Britain.

As for living resources, the South Atlantic-Antarctic ecosystems teem with marine life. In the circumpolar waters there are significant stocks of seals, whales, fin fish, squid, and penguins. The greatest opportunity, however, may lie with a small shrimp-like crustacean called krill (*Euphasia superba*). If the projections that have suggested annual harvests of 100 million metric tons were fulfilled, krill supplies could help to meet the world's burgeoning demand for protein.[19] The most extensive krill concentrations swarm around certain circumpolar island formations, namely, Bouvet Island, the South Shetlands, the South Orkneys, South Georgia, and the South Sandwich group. Save for Bouvet, which is claimed exclusively by Norway, the other island groups are disputed by Argentina and Great Britain. In sum, Antarctica's resources are potentially of tremendous significance, even if today they are undeveloped because of harsh environmental conditions, difficulties of technological access and extraction, and high operational costs. Finally, it must be noted that a major portion of these natural resources are found seaward from the South Pole at 25° through 75° west longitude, north to 60° south latitude, virtually coincident to the disputed territories historically and legally claimed by both Argentina and Great Britain. Should exploitation of Antarctica's living or nonliving resources eventually become commercially profitable, the stakes of Anglo-Argentine rivalry in the region could arise accordingly. Interestingly enough, it was reported in 1982 that the possibility of petroleum deposits offshore the Falkland Islands might have helped to precipitate the Falkland Islands crisis.[20]

If past national behavior is a prologue to future international relations, the unraveling of Anglo-Argentine rivalry over Antarctic natural resources would not come as a great surprise. Indeed, given the protracted, highly sensitive territorial dispute over South Atlantic and Antarctic territories, patently exacerbated by the recent Falklands military conflict, some observers might regard such a British-Argentine confrontation as logically inevitable in the near future. Yet, for the foreseeable term such a resource war between Great Britain and Argentina seems unlikely to occur. Deterring such a conflict is the continued availability of relatively inexpensive mineral commodities, hydrocarbons, and fishery protein from traditional, non-Antarctic sources. Additionally, the inaccessibility of Antarctic resources, complicated by the harsh physical environment, makes present commercial exploitation of the region economically unattractive, and will likely continue to do so throughout the rest of this century. Perhaps paramount in preventing Anglo-Argentine resource competition in the circumpolar region is the political character of the contemporary Antarctic Treaty regime and the respective roles each government has assumed in maintaining it.

The Consultative Party Mechanism

The Consultative Party System is integral to sustaining Anglo-Argentine peaceful coexistence in the Southern Ocean, as well as for the functioning of the Antarctic Treaty regime. As provided for in article IX of the treaty, the Consultative Party Group is composed of the twelve original parties to the treaty, plus four new entrants, Poland in 1977, the Federal Republic of Germany in 1981, and India and Brazil in 1983. The Consultative Parties meet biannually to formulate regional policies, which they develop through consensus in the form of "recommendations." The Antarctic Consultative Party Group serves as the governing body for the Treaty regime. Argentina and Great Britain are principal actors in this consultative process. They have enjoyed Consultative Party status since the treaty's entry into force in 1961, and have participated together regularly and actively, even during the 1982 Falklands War, to fashion policy recommendations under the treaty's auspices. Present indications suggest that they will continue to cooperate together in Consultative Party negotiations, in spite of the vehement territorial dispute in the area that has clouded Anglo-Argentine relations for over a century.

Given the climate of discord, especially in the aftermath of the Falklands War, one is prompted to speculate why either Argentina or Great Britain should continue to sit down with each other at the same negotiating table and participate in discussions aimed at establishing oversight policies for territories which they both claim to be their own. The answer to this seemingly paradoxical question is found in political pragmatism: the current Consultative Party system serves both Argentina's and Great Britain's national interests in the region better than the absence of a formal regime. The present system also appears to them preferable to other conceivable alternative regimes. Among these less desirable options would be the internationalization of the Antarctic as part of "the Common Heritage of Mankind;" transition of the region into a trusteeship territory under the United Nations' supervision; or reversion of the continent to *terra nullius*, so that it would be open to national claims and unrestricted exploitation by all states.

Thus, for the time being, Argentina and Great Britain appear politically willing to support the Treaty regime. They both reap the full diplomatic benefits of Consultative Party status, such as priority assessment, policy input and direction, representative voice, and consensus vote, without incurring the risks and costs associated with bilateral disputes. Further, they are both members of a relatively small decision-making body of sixteen who have assumed legal responsibility for political and environmental supervision of Antarctica. This status carries international clout, particularly as the vast majority of the world community remains barred from ever gaining Consultative Party membership. Despite past exploration investments, declarations of title, and strategic considerations, the Consultative Party process today is deemed more palatable by Argentina and Great Britain than other imaginable schemes; and, barring some dramatically unsettling political development, this pragmatic attitude seems unlikely to change before the treaty becomes eligible for review in 1991. In short, the Consultative Party process remains the strongest administrative cement sustaining pacific Anglo-Argentine coexistence in the

Antarctic. It has ameliorated nationalistic tensions and anti-pathies over disputed territories, even if it has left in limbo the contradictory legal claims.

Conclusion

The Falkland Islands War of 1982 highlighted the tension between Argentina and Great Britain over South Atlantic territories, but it also reminded the international community that Anglo-Argentine rivalry in the region goes far beyond the Falklands/Malvinas archipelago. It encompasses the islands of South Georgia, the South Orkneys, the South Shetlands, the South Sandwich group, as well as a substantial segment of Antarctica. Anglo-Argentine rivalry is neither of recent vintage nor of fleeting duration. Historically, it has been protracted, intransigent, ultranationalistic, and violent. The seeds for future conflict between Argentina and Great Britain have been sown in Antarctica's frozen turf.

With regard to international law, both Argentina and Great Britain have purposively designed legal arguments substantiating their respective claims to sovereign title over selected territories in the region. None of these arguments, however, is sufficiently compelling to warrant award of clear and unequivocal title to either party. Given the politico-legal arrangement for the Antarctic during the past two decades, both Argentina and Great Britain appear willing to accept the status quo and forgo pressing their claims. Were they to act otherwise, they would be bringing about an unravelling of the Antarctic Treaty regime and forfeiting the privileged Consultative Party status they now enjoy.

The Falklands War revealed that, at least for Argentina and Great Britain, lands in the South Atlantic are worth a considerable measure of military, economic, diplomatic, and human capital. For the foreseeable future, it seems safe to predict that neither Great Britain nor Argentina will attach such high stakes to Antarctica and its indigenous resources. Nevertheless, another prediction also seems certain. As worldwide industrialization proceeds and population growth persists, finite natural resources will dwindle. Accordingly, commercial interest in exploiting Antarctica's resources will increase on the part of both Argentina and Great Britain, and the international community as a whole. One can only speculate about how Argentina and Great Britain will respond to that situation.

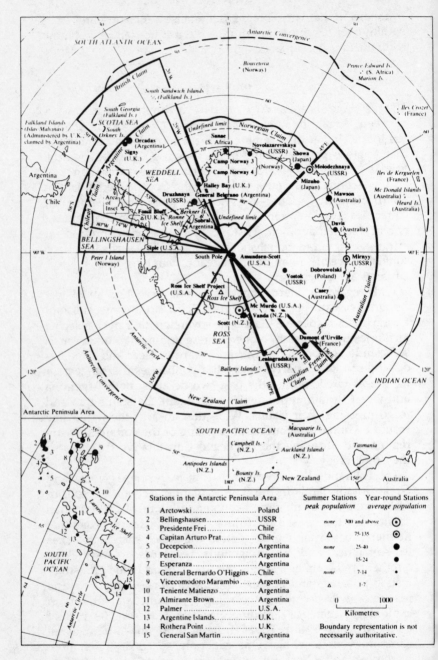

Figure 3

Whatever their reaction will be, it will affect greatly any future exploitation opportunities in the Southern Ocean and Antarctic regions. More importantly, it will indicate whether geopolitical conflict or peaceful accommodation will prevail over the cold continent.

Notes: Chapter 12

1 Letter to the Director of the Universal Postal Union, 14 September 1927, reprinted in U.S. Naval War College, *International Law Documents*, vol. 46 (1948–9), p. 218.
2 See Robert D. Hayton, "The 'American' Antarctic," *American Journal of International Law*, vol. 50 (1956), p. 588.
3 This quotation is from the dictum of the Federal Council of Switzerland which served as an arbiter in the Colombia–Venezuela boundary dispute, as quoted in J. B. Scott, "The Swiss decision in the boundary dispute between Colombia and Venezuela," *American Journal of International Law*, vol. 16 (1922), p. 428.
4 Note, "Thaw in international law? Rights in Antarctica under the Law of Common Spaces," *Yale Law Journal*, vol. 87 (1978), p. 814, n. 43.
5 ibid., pp. 822–3.
6 ibid., p. 823, n. 90.
7 Lincoln Ellsworth, "My flight across Antarctica," *National Geographic*, vol. 70 (1936), p. 35.
8 E. W. Hunter Christie, *The Antarctic Problem* (London: Allen & Unwin, 1951), p. 263.
9 F. A. Van der Heydte, "Discovery, symbolic annexation and virtual effectiveness in international law," *American Journal of International Law*, vol. 29 (1935), p. 470.
10 J. Peter Bernhardt, "Sovereignty in Antarctica," *California Western International Law Journal*, vol. 5 (1975), p. 342.
11 Facts are cited in *Antarctica Cases* (United Kingdom v. Argentina; United Kingdom v. Chile), ICJ Reports, 1956, p. 11.
12 See Christie, *The Antarctic Problem*, for a discussion of these events.
13 *Antarctica Cases*, p. 37.
14 Bernhardt, "Sovereignty in Antarctica," p. 322.
15 The Island of Palmas (Miangas) Arbitration, 2 R. Int'l Arb. Awards, 1928, p. 829.
16 Christie, *The Antarctic Problem*, p. 240.
17 *Antarctica Cases*, p. 37.
18 "Frozen assets?," *Wall Street Journal*, 21 February 1974, p. 1.
19 Barbara Mitchell, "The politics of Antarctica," *Environment*, vol. 22 (1980), pp. 12–13.
20 Jack Anderson, "Argentina eyes Antarctic too," *Washington Post*, 12 April 1982, p. C-15.

13

The Falkland Islands Crisis and the Management of Boundary Disputes

DAVID A. COLSON

From a practitioner's perspective, the Falkland Islands crisis is an example of how not to control, or resolve, a sovereignty dispute between states. Yet, the same underlying sovereignty question at the heart of the Falklands crisis is found in many parts of the world. There are many land borders which remain to a significant degree unsettled. To name only a few, unsettled land boundaries include China–Soviet Union, Chad–Libya, Iran–Iraq, Sudan–Ethiopia, India–China, Vietnam–China, Venezuela–Guyana, and Peru–Ecuador.[1] Also, as a result of the establishment of zones of maritime jurisdiction extending 200 nautical miles from the coast into the ocean, more than 300 maritime boundaries await resolution. In about 20 percent of these cases, there is an actively contested dispute between the neighboring states; of these, in about half the cases the problem is more difficult because a sovereignty dispute over land territory makes it impracticable to address the maritime boundary issue.[2] Many of these maritime boundary situations have the potential for creating an international crisis of major proportions. One need only mention those of the East and South China Sea, of the Aegean, and of the Persian Gulf to indicate the global nature of the matter. States have an interest in seeing these problems dealt with responsibly.

This essay has two purposes. First, it will identify and discuss three situations where states have put aside doctrine and successfully resolved or controlled a sovereignty dispute by negotiating a functional solution. Second, the role of interim measures will be discussed. If sovereignty disputes are to be resolved without war, no principle may be as important as that which holds that interim measures taken to manage the problem pending its resolution must be without prejudice to the basic position of either side to the dispute. This discussion will shed some light on issues relevant for any future negotiations about the status of the Falklands.

The Falklands crisis has reaffirmed the point that sovereignty disputes can create wars. Sovereignty disputes have a different character from political or economic disputes. Sovereignty disputes deal with ownership, national pride, prestige, and self-image. Sovereignty includes the right to extract resources from the area concerned. Furthermore, in today's world, sovereign rights over the land territory bring with them the right to adjacent marine resources. All of these factors played a role in the Falklands crisis.

The recent development in international law to recognize or authorize the extension of coastal state jurisdiction over the continental shelf and fisheries and other economic uses of the sea out to 200 nautical miles from the coast has greatly complicated the settlement of land disputes where a coastline is involved. A few examples include: Colombia's dispute with Nicaragua over the sovereignty of small islands in the Caribbean; the Beagle Channel dispute between Argentina and Chile; island disputes between the United Arab Emirates and Iran; the Spratly Island dispute in the South China Sea; the Paracel Islands dispute; the dispute over the Northern Territories between Japan and the Soviet Union; and the Liancount Rock dispute between South Korea and Japan.

In addition, many new disputes have arisen relating solely to the question of how to delimit the maritime area. For instance, the United States and Canada, close friends and allies, with the longest unguarded border in the world, suddenly find themselves with four unresolved maritime boundary disputes including more than 15,000 square nautical miles at issue in the Atlantic and more than 6,000 square nautical miles in dispute in the Arctic.[3]

Furthermore, what once may have been a manageable problem relating to the legal status of a generally unusable small piece of territory, such as a rock or islet, may now have grown into an issue of significantly wider scope because such pieces of territory have become the platform for states to justify claims to wide zones of maritime jurisdiction in international law. The new Law of the Sea Convention seeks to deal with this issue in article 121. Yet, like much of the Convention, this provision is fraught with ambiguity and can be interpreted to support different positions. The present boundary dispute between the United Kingdom and Ireland relates in part to the question of whether the British rock/island Rockall is entitled to be used to extend British maritime jurisdiction.

Thus, the extension of coastal state maritime jurisdiction has created a wide range of problems. But, fundamentally, the ingredients of these sovereignty issues are not new. In the past, states have come to grips with differences over sovereignty, and have negotiated regimes for the legal management of the concerned areas. The three situations discussed below are in concept as different and intractable as that of the Falklands, yet these problems were managed, if not resolved, by the disputing states.

Spitsbergen

Spitsbergen, known also as Svalbard, is an archipelago located about 400 miles north of Norway. Its land area is substantial, measuring about 62,000 square kilometers—about the size of West Virginia. Through the nineteenth century, whaling and sealing vessels occasionally visited the islands, but no government asserted sovereignty. In those days, the islands were widely regarded as *terra nullius*, no man's land. At the turn of this century, coal deposits of commercial value were found. A U.S. company began to exploit the coal, and soon companies from other countries followed suit. A permanent mining population developed on the islands. The growth in economic activity and population in the first years of the twentieth century made desirable the creation of governmental authority.

In 1914 Norway hosted an international conference attended by Germany, the United States, Denmark, France, Great Britain, Norway, the Netherlands, Russia, and Sweden to establish an administration for the islands. The conference's efforts to prepare a treaty proceeded on the assumption that Spitsbergen was *terra nullius*. Thus, the only jurisdictional basis for the establishment of governmental authority over the individuals on the islands was that which nations have over their nationals wherever they may be. There was no territorial sovereign. It was proposed that the islands' administration would be conducted by the several governments acting in concert through joint agencies. The treaty which the conference drafted, and which it almost completed, embraced a comprehensive scheme of civil and criminal jurisprudence. It included the recognition of the rights of persons who had asserted claims to land in the islands; and it also provided for the adjustment of differences growing out of conflicting claims. Underlying this unique and comprehensive scheme of government were finely spun legal theories, some of them undoubtedly a bit too fine. Whether or not this treaty and the legal system it proposed would have worked remains an open question. The outbreak of World War I interrupted the conference, forcing it to set aside the draft agreement.[4]

In connection with the Paris Peace Conference of 1919 a new effort was made to deal with the question of establishing a common governmental authority for Spitsbergen. This effort resulted in a treaty quite different from the 1914 draft. The new accord, which was signed in 1920 and entered into force for the United States in 1925, remains in force today. It provides for the recognition of the sovereignty of Norway over Spitsbergen "subject to the stipulations of the present Treaty." These stipulations are substantial.

The treaty states that Norway must ensure that the nationals of all parties enjoy equal rights of access to the land and territorial waters of the islands for purposes of economic exploitation. The treaty also recognizes the private rights of nationals of the contracting parties. In this regard the treaty establishes an interesting and important precedent. It accords international recognition to private rights which had theretofore been legally undefined. Norway, as the recognized sovereign authority in the islands, was obligated under the treaty to give effect to these private rights by appropriate municipal enactment of laws and regulations consistent with the international recognition of those rights.

The treaty also obligates Norway to provide mining regulations, which Norway did in 1925. Since then, through its internationally agreed responsibility for environmental protection, Norway has adopted rules that further regulate mining activities.

The treaty provides an important arms control function.

Norway may not create, and is obliged to prohibit, the establishment of any naval base or fortification in the archipelago. The territory never may be used for warlike purposes.

The Spitsbergen/Svalbard Treaty continues to function today in a world of changing social strategies and economic interests. It has proved to be a resilient instrument. Adherence to its neutrality provisions by the United States and the Soviet Union is an important component of the overall balance required for global stability. While its solution to the sovereignty question was to recognize that Norway was sovereign, the Spitsbergen/Svalbard Treaty can only be characterized as recognizing that Norway's sovereignty is unique, subject to the provisions of an international instrument to which approximately forty states, including the United States and the Soviet Union, are parties.

Antarctica

A second example is the Antarctic Treaty, discussed in greater detail by Christopher Joyner elsewhere in this book. On the whole, as Joyner points out, the treaty has been a resilient legal instrument. During the Falklands War, despite the fact that both Argentina and the United Kingdom claim parts of the Antarctic continent, that their claims overlap to a significant degree, and that there is an arguable interrelationship of issues, the Antarctic Treaty was unshaken. Throughout the war, meetings within the Antarctic Treaty system proceeded in a workmanlike manner.

The fundamental purpose of the Antarctic Treaty is to ensure that Antarctica does not become the scene or object of international discord. The Antarctic Treaty was negotiated and signed in 1959 by the twelve nations that participated in the International Geophysical Year in Antarctica, 1957–8. Seven of these states—Argentina, Australia, Chile, France, New Zealand, Norway, and the United Kingdom—claim sovereignty over territory in Antarctica. The others—Belgium, Japan, South Africa, the Soviet Union, and the United States—neither assert nor recognize claims of territorial sovereignty in Antarctica, although several of them, including the United States, hold that they have a basis for a claim to sovereignty in the area. Since the treaty entered into force in 1961, fourteen other states have adhered to its provisions. Included among these are Poland and the Federal Republic of Germany which have attained consultative status under the treaty based upon their activities in

Antarctica. Despite the disparate political relationships between these countries, and their legal position on territorial claims, the Antarctic Treaty system has functioned effectively.[5]

When the Antarctic Treaty was negotiated, the major concerns of the parties were the containment of the Cold War and the need to allow scientific research to continue in Antarctica despite the conflicting sovereignty claims. The treaty commits all signatories to prevent Antarctica from becoming an area for international conflict. Under its terms, Antarctica is nonmilitarized, there are open inspection provisions, the dumping of radioactive waste is prohibited, and scientific activities take place in a setting of cooperation.

The treaty did not seek to resolve the fundamental sovereignty dispute. It simply set it aside. A state's participation in the treaty does not affect its legal position on territorial claims. Only those jurisdictional questions foreseen in 1959—those relating to scientific research and expeditions—were addressed. Official observers and exchange scientific personnel, under the treaty, are subject only to the jurisdiction of the contracting party of which they are nationals. The treaty also provides a framework for resolution of other jurisdictional questions. In such a case, the parties are obligated immediately to consult together with a view to reaching a mutually acceptable solution. If this consultative procedure is unsuccessful, the treaty directs a recourse to dispute settlement.

Since the treaty came into force, the Antarctic Treaty system has developed a number of legal norms for conduct in Antarctica. Through the system of recommendations provided for by article IX of the Antarctic Treaty, and through other legal instruments developed within the treaty system to deal with specific situations or special needs, pragmatic solutions have been reached. The parties have found that a mutually agreed approach is more desirable than the chaos, conflict, and legal uncertainty that could result from unilateral action. Thus, just as the Antarctic Treaty was possible because all the states concerned believed it necessary to protect their competing national interests, the same competing interests provide an incentive for cooperation as new issues arise.

The Antarctic Treaty has achieved, and continues to achieve, its original objectives. The development of technology, however, making possible resource exploitation in the hostile Antarctic environment, has required the Antarctic Treaty system to shift its focus to contemporary concerns about environmental protection and resource conservation. In 1980 the Treaty system produced the Convention on the Conservation of Antarctic Marine Living Resources, which is now in force. Presently, the Treaty system is engaged in active negotiations on the question of exploration and exploitation of mineral resources.

The sovereignty question is a matter of extreme sensitivity in relation to the question of mineral exploration and exploitation, as it often is whenever the economic use of an area comes to the front of a diplomatic agenda. The Antarctic Treaty identifies the "preservation and conservation of living resources in Antarctica" as among its principles and objectives. It does not, however, prohibit commercial development. Both claimant and nonclaimant states theoretically regard economic activities as a permissible "peaceful purpose" in conformity with the treaty. Yet the views of the two sides are fundamentally different: the claimant state believes that it has a right to control such activities; while the nonclaimant state believes it has a right to conduct such activities subject only to such restrictions as it may impose upon itself or otherwise agree to. In such a case, unlike those that were foreseen when the treaty was negotiated, the jurisdictional relationship between claimant and nonclaimant states is not resolved by the treaty.

In matters where there is not a common jurisdictional understanding, articles IV and VI of the Antarctic Treaty expressly preserve the positions of claimant and nonclaimant states even though the activities of one state would normally be regarded as legally prejudicial to another's position or interest. Article IV provides that the treaty does not change any party's position concerning its claim of territorial sovereignty, nor its recognition or nonrecognition of another state's claim. It further provides that any activities conducted by the parties while the treaty is in force shall not be the basis for asserting, supporting, or denying either an existing claim or a new claim of sovereignty in Antarctica. Article VI provides that nothing in the treaty shall prejudice or affect the rights, or the exercise of the rights, that any state may have under international law regarding the high seas in the area covered by the treaty. These provisions combine to serve the interest of both claimant and nonclaimant states. They prohibit new claims and the expansion of existing claims. They also permit all states to interpret the treaty's other provisions consistently with each state's position on territorial sovereignty in Antarctica.

Each state is thus assured that activities not covered by express provisions of the Antarctic Treaty, but undertaken within the Treaty system, are not regarded as a jurisdictional plus or minus for either a claimant or nonclaimant state. The fundamental juridical difference between a claimant and nonclaimant state does not disappear; new activities are simply treated as legally neutral. With such an assurance, no party needs to take action in order to balance any perceived juridical equation. In this situation, cooperation, coordination, and consultation between claimant and nonclaimant states are nevertheless essential so as to cause as little friction as possible. The past success of the Antarctic Treaty system gives one reason to believe that it will succeed in managing the problems associated with the exploration and exploitation of mineral resources.

In connection with the Falkland Islands one may note, as Professor Joyner has done, that due to the islands' proximity to Antarctica, if the Treaty system fails to resolve new issues the potential for conflict spilling over to the Falklands is high. Specifically, the Antarctic interests of the United Kingdom and Argentina, and the way in which both states perceive the existing legal regime in Antarctica, will affect their stance on the Falkland Islands and their willingness to reach an accommodation of their competing interests. A disintegration of the Antarctic Treaty system would harden the Argentine and British positions on the Falklands by suggesting that the region's disputes are not manageable by peaceful legal and diplomatic procedures.

The Spitsbergen and Antarctica examples are multilateral approaches to the resolution or management of a sovereignty dispute. They resolve or bypass the disputes by identifying the functional issues at stake and negotiating a solution to them. In the case of Spitsbergen, Norwegian sovereignty was recognized only after the private economic interests were protected; while in the case of Antarctica, a system capable of dealing with practical problems was established while the sovereignty issue was held in abeyance.

The Torres Strait

Functional approaches may also be used to resolve bilateral problems. One example is the recent bilateral agreement between Australia and Papua New Guinea. Their 1978 Treaty on Sovereignty and Maritime Boundaries and Related Matters addresses a set of difficult sovereignty problems and illustrates the fact that boundary disputes are often not one-issue problems.

The area in question, the Torres Strait, is a unique maritime area located between Cape York and the northern coast of Australia and the southern coast of Papua New Guinea. Papua New Guinea was a dependent territory of Australia. The area consists of a considerable number of islands, some large and inhabited, others amounting to no more than small rocks and uninhabited cays. Some populated Australian islands are situated close to the Papua New Guinea coast. In geographical terms alone, it is one of the world's most complex maritime boundary situations. In addition, because Papua New Guineans of the mainland are ethnically distinct from the Torres Strait islanders, the need to protect the livelihood and way of life of the local inhabitants was a major factor to be taken into account in devising a solution to the maritime delimitation problem. Thus, in this case, there were problems concerning differences in cultural heritage and practices of the local population, perceptions about the equity of different divisions of maritime jurisdiction, island sovereignty disputes, differences over fisheries management and utilization, and concerns about navigation responsibilities.

The Torres Strait Treaty is highly imaginative.[6] It should be noted that, as of August 1983, the Torres Strait treaty was not yet in force. Among its novel features are separate seabed and fisheries jurisdiction lines, a Protected Zone in the middle of the Torres Strait, and arrangements regulating the sharing of the catch of commercial fisheries. The treaty points to the fact that complex bilateral sovereignty issues may require that jurisdictional and conceptual arguments be abandoned and functional solutions sought. While such an approach may lead to complex solutions (in this case a treaty of 32 articles and 9 annexes), it also ensures that each matter is dealt with in the light of its unique characteristics. Taken as a whole, the Australia–Papua New Guinea Treaty represents a creative approach to maritime delimitation that equitably takes account of various interrelated issues.

Functional solutions to bilateral sovereignty disputes do not always succeed. For example, the United States and Canada signed an East Coast fisheries agreement and a maritime boundary settlement treaty in March 1979 designed to resolve a sovereignty dispute over some 15,000 square nautical miles of resource-rich ocean created by the extension of jurisdiction to 200 nautical miles by both countries in 1977. Together the two treaties would have provided for the adjudication of the continental shelf and 200-nautical-mile fisheries zone boundary of the United States and Canada in the Gulf of Maine area between the New England States and the Maritime Provinces; and the establishment of a fisheries resource regime to manage and allocate the fisheries between the United States and Canada on the Atlantic coast.

This effort failed because the negotiated fisheries agreement bore no relationship to the economic expectations and political realities in New England. The fisheries agreement was complex, consisting of 25 articles and 4 annexes. It provided for the establishment of a bilateral commission and an elaborate dispute settlement mechanism. It was a work of lawyerly art; unfortunately, it was not a fisherman's agreement, and it failed to attain political support in the United States. Thus, the United States and Canada were left with the sole alternative of a "no-holds-barred" adjudication wherein jurisdiction in the area would be determined by binding third-party settlement procedure. On 25 November 1981 the United States and Canada jointly submitted this boundary dispute to a Chamber of the International Court of Justice for a binding determination of the boundary.

Thus, functional approaches can be difficult to implement because they are inevitably complex. They must deal in some form with the full scope of rights and duties making up the sovereign rights of states. No quick fixes are likely in a negotiation of such matters; long negotiations responsive to local interests are required so that the negotiations succeed from a political as well as a legal perspective. In the end, all sides and interests must be confident that they are better off with the agreement than they are with uncertainty and possible chaos and conflict.

Functional approaches to sovereignty disputes are used when states are not prepared to make a full concession on the ultimate question of sovereignty. Such concessions are rare. There are occasions, however, where the political will exists to concede one's sovereignty claim. The United States recently did so in four treaties in which the United States renounced its claims to sovereignty over twenty-five small islands in the south and central Pacific. The treaties are with Tuvalu, Kiribati, the Cook Islands, and New Zealand in respect of the Tokelau Islands. While the United States claims were virtually without legal merit, they had been maintained over the years despite the strong opposition of allies—the United Kingdom and New Zealand—and the peoples of the region. Continued maintenance of the United States' claims in today's world would have given the United States a claim to marine resource jurisdiction over thousands of square nautical miles of ocean. Nonetheless, in this case the judgment of the United States government (from the Nixon administration forward) was that maintenance of the weak U.S. claim would do more damage to its political position in the region than any perceived benefits from maintaining the claim.

Interim Measures

From the foregoing it may be said that the only limit on designing means to resolve a sovereignty dispute is one's imagination. Any approach that works is the best means of resolving that dispute. What works is a function of political will and time. In this connection, the important problem of how one manages the dispute until a solution is reached must be considered.

Under article 33 of the Charter of the United Nations, states are obligated to seek a solution to their disputes by peaceful means of their choice. This often takes time. During that time, provisions for interim arrangements, or a *modus vivendi*, must operate between states to keep the dispute under control. The dispute must be managed so that events occurring during the period are regarded by both sides as juridically neutral—in other words, those events do not hurt or help the position of either side.

The parties to a dispute are in the best position to adopt pragmatic interim arrangements. Yet, so often, they are unprepared to do so because of perceptions of prejudice to their positions. Where sovereign rights are in question, the simple fact of negotiation, compromise, and agreement with another state on a practical interim arrangement is often regarded as adding an element of prejudice to one's position since inevitably such an arrangement entails something less than a recognition of one's sovereignty. When interim arrangements are formalized, they are almost without exception predicated on compromisory or disclaimer provisions which provide that the arrangements and acts occurring thereunder are without prejudice to the position of the parties in future negotiations or adjudications concerning the legal nature of the dispute.

Nonetheless, in the nature of things, states will often seek to take advantage of their acts and those of their nationals occurring under such a *modus vivendi*. They also will argue that another state's forbearance or willingness to accept the status quo in an interim arrangement is tantamount to acquiescence. The status quo becomes a powerful negotiating tool for one side or the other. Beyond the problems that status quo arrangements pose for negotiators, some conciliators and arbitrators tend to look to the status quo for solutions. Thus, rather than being applauded for statesmanship, the party exercising forbearance under a *modus vivendi* all too often finds itself disadvantaged in later proceedings.

If states are to be encouraged to negotiate rather than fight, the legal neutrality of interim arrangements must be strictly observed. A state must be assured that international law and diplomatic practice will not penalize it for forbearing from the exercise of its claimed sovereign rights prior to the resolution of the dispute. If a state cannot rely on this assurance, and if activities undertaken during the course of the dispute are given legal status by dispute settlement procedures, international law and diplomatic practice will have seriously hindered the efforts of states to deal responsibly with these matters.

Notes: Chapter 13

The views expressed are those of the author and have no official standing.

1 Alan J. Day (ed.), *Border and Territorial Disputes* (Detroit, Mich.: Gale Research Co., 1982).
2 See R. D. Hodgson and R. W. Smith, "Boundary issues created by extended national marine jurisdiction," *Geographical Review*, vol. 69 (October 1979), p. 423.
3 See M. B. Feldman and D. Colson, "The maritime boundaries of the United States," *American Journal of International Law*, vol. 75 (October 1982), p. 729.
4 For a discussion of the 1914 conference and the treaty it drafted see R. Lansing, "A unique international problem," *American Journal of International Law*, vol. 11 (1917), p. 763.
5 For a general discussion of the workings of the Antarctic Treaty system see David Colson, "The Antarctic Treaty system: the mineral issue," *Law and Policy in International Business*, vol. 12, no. 4 (October 1980), p. 841.

6 The treaty has been described in detail in H. Burmester, "The Torres Strait Treaty: ocean boundary delimitation by agreement," *American Journal of International Law*, vol. 76 (1982), pp. 321–49. It should be noted that, as of August 1983, the Torres Strait Treaty was not yet in force.

14

Trusteeship for the Falklands under Joint U.K.–U.S. Administration: A Proposal

MONROE LEIGH

Final resolution of the Falklands dispute continues to elude the international community. The UN and OAS efforts to promote a settlement prior to and during the recent military confrontation have already been examined. With the cessation of hostilities on the islands, there is no reason why these efforts should not continue. Indeed, the major premise of the modest proposal which follows is that any and all UN and OAS efforts to find a solution should enjoy priority of consideration so long as there is any reasonable prospect of success under the direct sponsorship of these two obviously appropriate international institutions. Only if they fail altogether or hopelessly bog down, would I urge an alternative which involves a joint initiative by the United Kingdom and the United States. Nor would I urge this alternative if there were any indication that the parties to the dispute might be able to reach agreement by means of bilateral diplomatic negotiations or by referral of the dispute to international adjudication, either in the International Court of Justice or by binding arbitration.

Thus it is necessary to keep firmly in mind that this proposal is contingent on four principle defaults:

(1) failure of the UN to promote a settlement;
(2) failure of the OAS to promote a settlement;

(3) failure of the parties to negotiate a diplomatic settlement; and

(4) failure of the parties to submit the dispute to binding international adjudication.

If all these defaults occur, the United Kingdom with U.S. support should offer to place the Falklands under a UN Trusteeship pursuant to a provision never heretofore invoked, namely article 77 (1) (c) of the UN Charter, which provides that states responsible for the administration of a territory may "voluntarily" place such a territory under the UN Trusteeship system. Heretofore, article 77 has been invoked only with respect to paragraph (1) (a), dealing with formerly "mandated" territories, such as Southwest Africa and Palestine, and paragraph (1) (b) dealing with territories detached from states as a result of World War II, of which Somaliland is the only example. However, the innovative paragraph (1) (c) has never been actually invoked, though it has been frequently suggested for such areas as Trieste, Berlin, and Jerusalem. As Professor Thomas Franck pointed out in his June 1982 article in the *New York Times*, there is no reason why the UN Trusteeship system should not be used more creatively.

My proposal is a simple one. The United Kingdom, in concert with the United States, should endeavor to place the Falklands under UN Trusteeship under the joint administration of the United Kingdom and the United States. Clearly, such a proposal would fall within the contemplation of article 77 (1) (c) of the Charter. Obviously this proposal raises a number of questions.

The first one is: Why should Britain agree to relinquish an area it has just fought to retain at high cost in lives and in money? To this there are several answers. First, Britain fought not so much to retain the islands as to prevent aggression from succeeding. The islands are not defensible by Britain over the long term—at least not at any reasonable level of military expenditure. Second, although the islands are not economically viable in any circumstances, whether under Argentine rule or British rule, Britain cannot abandon its Kelpers, nor can it forcibly resettle them elsewhere as the Soviet Union did with respect to the Finnish territories ceded to it after World War II. Third, in the long run, a gradual political solution which internationalizes the area is in Britain's interest and not necessarily contrary to the interests of the Kelpers. Finally, the co-trusteeship has a peculiar procedural advantage: it permits the

United Kingdom to take an initiative without thereby forever surrendering the initiative. If British terms for trusteeship are not acceptable to the UN, Britain is free to withdraw the proposal.

A second question is: Why should the United States accept joint administration with the United Kingdom of this remote but constantly threatened territory? First, recent history demonstrates that the United States cannot remain aloof from a dispute which carries the potential for outbreak of war between its oldest and most important ally in Europe and a major member of the OAS, when the latter is prepared to resort to force in violation of the UN Charter, with all the dangers which that action poses for the stability of both the international security system and the regional American security system. Second, on one calculation, the additional burdens beyond those the United States now bears need not be great. The joint administration could be shared with the United Kingdom, with that nation continuing to be responsible for the political, economic, social, and tactical military concerns of the Falklands. The United States' role, under my proposal, would be limited to providing strategic military support to preserve the territorial integrity of the Falklands so long as they would remain under UN Trusteeship, which I would suggest be limited to a term of years—say twenty-five years—at least long enough to permit the passions in Argentina and Britain to cool and to permit the Kelpers to consider the long-term implications of their desolate situation. One does not need to be a mathematical wizard to see that the two to three billion pounds which the British spent in the spring of 1982, would, if divided equally among 2,000 Kelpers, make millionaires of every one of them. This would be enough to purchase handsome estates in Scotland. But this point need not be pressed beyond the suggestion that total monetary inducements to settle voluntarily in another part of the world do not appear to be beyond the range of financial possibility.

The third question that could be raised is whether the UN will accept the offer of a trusteeship for the Falklands. No one can be sure of the answer to this question until the proposal is put to the test. The proposal is fully consistent with the purposes of the UN as set forth in article 1, which include the maintenance of international peace and security, the settlement of international disputes, and the development of friendly relations with respect for the self-determination of peoples. More important, the proposal is consistent with Chapter XII of the Charter, which establishes the Trusteeship system.

The proposal for a Falkland Islands co-trusteeship requires that the status of the Falklands be changed from that of a Non Self-Governing Territory (NSGT) under Chapter XI of the Charter to that of a trust territory under Chapter XII. While there is no prior example of such a change of status, it clearly may be accomplished under the provision in Article 77 (1) (c) which allows "territories [to be] voluntarily placed under the system by states responsible for their administration."

Therefore, Great Britain can turn the territory over to the United Nations Trusteeship System by invoking Article 77 (1) (c). The terms of the trusteeship agreement, which under article 79 must be "agreed upon by the states directly concerned," in this case Great Britain and the United States, will provide for administration by the British and defense by the United States. Since article 81 allows the administering authority to be "one *or more* states" (emphasis added), the trusteeship agreement will designate both Great Britain and the United States as administering authorities.

Notwithstanding the fact that there have been instances of a territory being administered by more than one nation, the proposed arrangement is somewhat unorthodox. However, there are Charter provisions that address the factors which require such an unusual measure. Article 76, which states the principles of the Trusteeship system, holds that while self-government or independence of the territories is a goal, it must be pursued "as may be appropriate to the particular circumstances of each territory, and its peoples and the freely expressed wishes of the people concerned." Advocates of this proposal can argue that the "particular circumstances" of the Falklands, a small island group near a large and threatening nation, require that it be defended by a friendly power. If there is doubt that the power is indeed "friendly," advocates may point to the principle in article 76 that account be taken of "the freely expressed wishes of the people concerned." According to most reports, the Falklanders desire to remain British subjects, and this proposal is one means of ensuring that their wish is granted. It may be advisable to hold a plebiscite on this proposal in the Falklands. Approval of the co-trusteeship by the Falklanders would strengthen the position that article 76 supports the proposal.

Great Britain and the United States may wish to take the additional step of designating the Falklands' trust a "strategic area" under article 82. The Pacific Islands Trust Territory enjoys this status. Article 82 does not specify the additional features of a "strategic area." However, one author has stated that "[t]he strategic trust [Article 82] was devised to allow the Trust Territory to be under Security Council rather than Assembly supervision [and thus subject to the veto] and to permit the closure of areas under national security claims."[1] Under article 83, strategic trusts are administered by the Security Council rather than the General Assembly. The "strategic trust" course should be followed if Britain and the United States anticipate more trouble for their proposal in the General Assembly (from Third World nations) than in the Security Council (from the Soviet Union).

The proposal for a co-trusteeship is a departure from the usual arrangement in which a territory is administered by one nation. However, there are two cases in which territorial administration was shared. These cases suggest certain features that should— and should not be—present in a Falklands co-trusteeship.

(1) The New Hebrides

The Pacific islands formerly known as the New Hebrides (now the independent nation of Vanuatu) were jointly administered as a "condominium" by Great Britain and France from 1914 until July 1980. The treaty between Britain and France provided that separate schools, courts, and police, among other services, be administered by each sovereign.[2] The result of this split was described as a "comic opera atmosphere."[3] Tensions between French and English speaking subjects never ended. Nor did Britain and France see eye to eye on the islands: when rebellion broke out, "France would not let either French or British troops suppress the rebellion before independence [was granted]."[4]

Given the New Hebrides treaty's concern with duality, it seems that there were competing French and British claims of sovereignty and that the condominium was an attempt at a workable compromise. In the Falklands, there would be no such confusion. The United States, as shown by its actions in the British–Argentine war, does not dispute the essential British claim to sovereignty. When drafting the trusteeship agreement, it would be advisable to specify the very limited scope of the United States' duties. All government services in the islands would be British with the possible exception of certain defense roles assigned to the United States by agreement.

229

(2) Nauru

The South Pacific island of Nauru was formerly a trust territory administered by Australia, the United Kingdom, and New Zealand. The trusteeship agreement, however, specified that Australia was the administering authority. According to one author, New Zealand and Great Britain were named as "administering authorities" solely to round out the Trusteeship Council so that it was comprised of an equal number of administering and nonadministering nations.[5] Thus Australia's role was never in doubt among co-trustees. This was emphasized by the Australian delegate to the UN in the course of the General Assembly's debate on the trusteeship agreement when he stated that "the government of Australia will administer the territory until it is agreed among the three governments that one or other of the three governments will assume this function."

Nauru was smoothly governed by Australia until its recent independence, and it provides a good example of the possibilities of a co-trusteeship when only one nation is charged with daily administrative duties. While the Falklands proposal assigns more responsibility to the United States than New Zealand and Great Britain had in Nauru, the Nauru trusteeship remains a solid precedent for co-trusteeship.

Of course, the co-trusteeship proposal may not prove acceptable to the United Nations but there is one additional consideration worth comment. If the majority sentiment in the UN is against acceptance of the proposal, the United Kingdom is perfectly free to withdraw the proposal and proceed by bilateral treaty to set up essentially the same arrangement outside the UN system. The existence of this possibility should militate in favor of UN acceptance.

The question of Argentine reaction to the proposal is reserved for last. One must anticipate that Argentina would immediately declare the proposal unacceptable because it does not recognize Argentina's claim to sovereignty. But the same answer is to be expected from Argentina as to any other proposal which could conceivably be acceptable to Britain. The positions of the two disputants would continue to be irreconcilable. A reconciliation of the conflicting claims to sovereignty cannot be expected for some years to come.

Even if Argentina publicly condemns the proposal, one hopes that it would not pressure the United Nations to reject it. The proposal should be judged by its long-term tendencies. In reality, it would be a first step by Britain toward the relinquishment of that sovereignty which it fought the war to retain. In this sense, it is a first step in the direction which events must move if Argentine aspirations are to be realized.

Typically a trusteeship involves the relinquishment of sovereignty during the period of the trusteeship. The exact provisions on this critical issue would need to be dealt with in the agreement between the United Nations and the "states directly concerned." Or, in default of resolution in the agreement, the sovereignty question would need to be decided at some future date by the Security Council or the General Assembly. It would be foolish to minimize the difficulties involved in the resolution of the sovereignty issue. Nevertheless, I would maintain that there are elements of advantage in the long run to Argentina.

Notes: Chapter 14

1 R. Russell, *The United Nations and United States Security Policy* (Washington, D.C.: Brookings Institution, 1968), p. 241n.
2 League of Nations Treaty Series, vol. 10, p. 34.
3 *The Economist*, no. 275, 1980, p. 14.
4 *The Economist*, no. 278, 1981, p. 37.
5 Russell, *The United Nations and United States Security Policy*, p. 33.

15
Lessons for the Future

ALBERTO R. COLL

The task of drawing lessons from, or ascertaining the meaning of, recent historical events is not easy. Many historians, ranging from Jacob Burckhardt to Herbert Butterfield, have pointed to the need for decades or even centuries to pass before scholars can obtain a balanced appreciation of the significance of a particular historical occurrence. The Falklands War of 1982 is no exception. As David Gompert and Dov Zakheim have indicated, one can see this conflict in at least two different ways. On the one hand, it may turn out to be little more than a strategic, political, and military curiosity devoid of any long-term implications, an isolated exception to the predominant currents of world politics to be remembered and evaluated in the same way as the War of 1812 between England and the United States or the Russo-Finnish War of 1939. On the other hand, however, future students of international politics may see the events of 1982 as confirming and giving added impetus to various currents in international relations, much as the brief Russo-Japanese War of 1905 or the Spanish-American War of 1898 are remembered today. Regardless of the ultimate historical verdict, it is possible to draw some tentative lessons that may serve as helpful guideposts for statesmen and scholars of this generation.

In the realm of political and military strategy several important lessons emerge. First, it is of critical importance for a state facing a crisis such as Great Britain did in April 1982 to formulate a coherent strategy incorporating all of its political, diplomatic, legal, economic, and military resources as comprehensively as possible. The success with which the British did this is instructive. Although perceived by many as a declining economic and military power with little if any political will to recover two barren islands 7,000 miles away, Great Britain turned out to be a formidable adversary largely because of its skill in making the most of its limited assets. Politically and diplomatically the British capitalized heavily on the special relationship with the United States, the strong ties of solidarity with the Commonwealth, and even the distrust of Latin American states such as Chile and Brazil toward Argentina. In the economic area the British were quick to perceive their adversary's great vulnerability as a major exporter with a mounting foreign debt; subsequent British sanctions against Argentina, and successful pressures on the United States and the European Community to do likewise, played a critical role in demoralizing and weakening the Argentines.

Against all odds the British were also successful at the United Nations, especially during the critical month of April when it was imperative for them to gain a diplomatic, political, and moral momentum that would give credibility to their threat to use force if necessary to recover the islands. The skill with which Sir Anthony Parsons steered Resolution 502 through the Security Council without a Soviet veto and with the passive approval of many Third World states has been noted by U.S. Ambassador Jeane Kirkpatrick and others as evidence that it is possible for a Western power to score a victory at the United Nations, as long as the right circumstances are present and they are combined with a vigorous, creative diplomacy.

As Thomas Franck has argued in this book, a very important element of British diplomacy and of the overall British strategy was the appeal to international law and morality. The British successfully used as one of their resources international law, validating the warnings given by Hardy Dillard, Myres McDougal, and John Norton Moore over the last two decades that true political realism requires the incorporation into a state's diplomacy and strategy of notions of legitimacy, in other words, the skillful union of law and power without shortsightedly sacrificing one of these dimensions of strategy for the sake of the other. In the fashion of Metternichian Austria, Great Britain persuaded its allies, both in the Western alliance and in the Commonwealth, that what was at stake in the Falklands crisis was a principle of legitimacy which, if disregarded by the Argentines with impunity, would be fatally weakened, with dangerous consequences for the future security of those states. In the corridors of the UN and elsewhere many statesmen grasped that support for the forceful Argentine takeover of the islands would set a precedent which rapacious neighbors might use in the future to their disadvantage. By linking legitimacy and international law with a broad, long-term conception of national security in the minds of many decision-makers around the world, and harnessing that connection to their own political purposes, British diplomats achieved a major strategic and diplomatic breakthrough in which international law played an important role.

Not to be overlooked, of course, is the military component of British strategy. Although only one of several components in a comprehensive, multifaceted strategy, this was the ultimate guarantor of that strategy's credibility and success. Had the military operations to recover the islands failed, the Argentine flag would have continued to fly over Port Stanley. In addition to the high degree of professionalism, careful attention to detail, and the even quality of leadership and morale shown by the British military at all levels, one is struck by two characteristics underlined by Dov Zakheim in his detailed study of the military aspects of the conflict: tactical flexibility and improvisation. No military strategy can succeed without the support of tactical flexibility and improvisation to compensate for the innumerable contingencies that inevitably dot the course of even the best-conceived plans. This is as true of a Superpower such as the United States, as of a smaller power with limited resources such as Great Britain. The lesson here is clear: in devising ways with which to cope with the Soviet conventional Behemoth in Central Europe, NATO's planners should concentrate on methods for incorporating the highest degree of tactical flexibility and improvisation in their defensive strategy, forsaking perhaps, as the Argentine military should have done, the alluring temptation to rely inordinately on a few standard tactics involving highly expensive weapons systems. Similarly, NATO can learn much from the broad range of military instruments which the British combined to achieve their impressive military victory: from standard naval forces and a professional air-fighting capability to less common but highly effective commando tactics, special forces, sabotage of enemy infrastructure, and propaganda. In contrast to the Argentines, whose military successes rested on the superb courage of their pilots and the functioning of two sophisticated weapons systems (the Etendards and the Exocet missiles), the British relied on a combination of numerous military instruments, in each of which they showed a high level of professional competence and technical proficiency. No discussion of British military strategy, of course, can fail to note that the decision to retake the Falklands was fraught with considerable risks and easily could have ended in a military disaster reminiscent of the ill-fated Spanish Armada or the Athenian expedition to Sicily. Whatever lessons future strategists draw from the British success should not obscure the tremendous vulnerability faced by naval forces in the type of mission undertaken by the British Task Force.

If the coherence and comprehensiveness of British strategy after 2 April 1982 provide valuable lessons for future policy-makers, so do the absence of these qualities—indeed the absence of any strategy—in British policy towards the Falklands during the preceding years. In particular, as Dov Zakheim and Douglas Kinney have observed, British policy was unclear in its objectives towards the Falklands; the confusing signals sent to Argentina during the 1960s and 1970s did not create a clear picture of what Great Britain intended to do with the islands or how vital she considered them to her national honor. Indeed, there was sufficient ambiguity in British policy to suggest to the Argentines that if the ultimate test of force ever came the British, a bit shamefacedly perhaps but not without a sense of relief and gratitude, might yield the barren rocks to their eager claimants. The apparent incoherence of British policy was reinforced, and communicated in a most telling way to the Argentines, by the absence of any meaningful links between British rhetoric on the importance of the islands to the British government and people and the requisite military power to sustain whatever commitment Great Britain was willing to make to preserve the status quo. Even on those occasions when the British government unequivocally explained to the Argentines that the use of force to gain the islands would be unacceptable, the lack of a visible and adequate British military presence in the area persuaded many Argentine leaders that the British did not mean what they said, that they were simply engaging in diplomatic formalism devoid of the substance of power. If, as Walter Lippmann and Hans Morgenthau argued so persuasively, a nation's policy must be commensurate with its resources, it is also true that a policy must be complemented by the willingness, exhibited openly and with ample symbolism, to use the resources available in support of it. This is such a simple truism as to seem almost undeserving of the name of a lesson, yet statesmen seem to disregard it periodically and with costly results; in this case, it cost the British several hundred dead, over two billion dollars, and numerous other less tangible but nonetheless considerable political and economic assets.

Moving from the realm of overall strategy to that of diplomacy, one finds that the 1982 war underlined the severe weaknesses, as well as some of the constructive possibilities offered by the diplomatic mechanisms and institutions of the contemporary international system. At a regional level, the OAS failed to play a constructive role in defusing the crisis. This failure illustrated, as Srilal Perera has shown, two perennial weaknesses of the OAS: its inability to deal constructively with conflicts involving extraregional powers, and its inner fragmentation and divisiveness caused by political and economic rivalries and numerous territorial disputes among OAS members. No amount of legal draftwork has been able to overcome these weaknesses and produce a truly effective inter-American system. In a broader sense, the flaws of the OAS are indicative of those of many regional organizations and of regionalism generally. The consensus and greater integration achieved through regionalism is often at the expense of outsiders, at the cost of a heightened sense of distinctiveness and exclusivity from the rest of the international community. The concomitant of Latin American or Arab solidarity is often a greater recalcitrance to accommodate with Englishmen or Israelis. Thus, regionalism is not necessarily a step in the direction of a more integrated world community; it can be seen also as the way by which various communities linked by common values or a common history join forces to resist absorption into a seemingly alien, cosmopolitan international society. The reservoir of solidarity binding such communities may be sufficient to unite them against outside powers, but not enough to prevent festering intraregional rivalries from breaking out into open violence once the threat or challenge from the outside has receded. In today's international system, even among members of a common regional grouping, the nation-state continues to be the dominant actor, and its interests the primary determinant of the shape and substance of foreign policies.

Universal, as distinct from regional, organizations do not necessarily have better diplomatic capabilities. Inis Claude's analysis of the United Nations' handling of the Falklands War makes this quite clear. In particular, the UN's efforts to achieve a settlement lacked coherence in both substance and style because of the tension within the organization between two contradictory currents. On the one hand, there was a vague desire to restrain the Argentines and let them know that aggression does not pay and cannot be accepted by the international community. This was the essence of the Security Council's Resolution 502. Yet there was also an undefined but strong current of pacifism, illustrated by later efforts, which had an air of desperation about them, to obtain a ceasefire at all costs even if it meant that such efforts diminished any incentives the Argentines had for complying with Resolution 502. The entire episode in all of its tragicomic details revealed once more that vast and perhaps fatal ambiguity at the heart of the United Nations, and of the liberal political philosophy underlying it: to what extent is the burning desire for peace characteristic of modern liberalism reconcilable with the requirements for maintaining and *enforcing* peace in an anarchic world? Can any political institution that is aimed at the preservation of peace operate effectively while making peace, rather than other values, its highest principle of conduct? In the tentative answers to these questions one can discern further lessons from the Falklands War.

The mediation efforts of the Secretary-General indicate the extent to which the United Nations, despite its limitations, can play a constructive diplomatic role not so much through its proceedings in the grand halls and corridors of New York but by throwing its weight behind a sensible, impartial negotiator such as Perez de Cuellar proved to be. The amazing thing about the Secretary-General's mission was not that it failed but that, as Douglas Kinney has pointed out, it came close to success, in fact, closer than that of the U.S. Secretary of State. As Dag Hammarskjold showed during the Congo crisis of 1960, an energetic and creative Secretary-General can use the prestige and credibility associated with his office, if not to settle an international conflict, at least to manage it and prevent it from spreading and drawing in the rival Superpowers. Whether in the case of the Congo or that of the Falklands, where the twin goals were containment and settlement of the dispute, the key to the UN's effectiveness is more the personality of the Secretary-General and the way in which he holds out the prospect of a third-party authoritative settlement and an impartial multinational guarantee of it, than any intrinsic institutional strengths of the UN itself.

Perez de Cuellar's failure, as well as the failures of the American and Peruvian mediation efforts, illustrate that states do not always conduct their diplomacy rationally and in strict accordance with a well-defined conception of the national interest. As Kinney has pointed out, all of the settlements discussed in the course of the three third-party mediations offered to Argentina much more than what, only a year before, she could have obtained through bilateral negotiations with the British. Yet she rejected every one of them. A combination of misplaced national pride, a maximalist diplomacy feeding on what Machiavelli would have described as hopes rather than realities, a lack of a sense of limits, and an overly anxious view of the historical process drove the Argentines to reject terms which, before 2 April 1982, they would have rightly seen as only a short step away from the fulfillment of their centuries-old ambition. The gambles and miscalculations of Argentine diplomacy demonstrate once more the radical changes in political perceptions and expectations brought about by the outbreak of war. Once force is used and it appears capable of fully achieving one's political goals, it is as difficult for statesmen as it is for generals to accept even a partial return to the former status quo in the form of a moderate compromise. War not only alters the perceptions of what is possible; it also heightens expectations of what is rightful and desirable.

Looking to the future, diplomacy may prove capable of providing a settlement satisfactory to both parties. But it will not be easy, and will not occur anytime soon. A "functional" approach to the dispute such as David Colson has suggested can work only if the British make substantial concessions in the direction of granting sovereignty eventually to the Argentines, something which, as of 1984 at least, the Thatcher government did not seem prepared to do. On the Argentine side, the new civilian government, unencumbered by any responsibility for the military's decision to take the islands by force, has some room for flexibility and maneuvering, but even so would most likely reject any settlement that would postpone the handing over of sovereignty to Argentina beyond a "lifetime" period of forty or fifty years. Over the long run there will be great political and economic pressures on Great Britain to yield to Argentine demands. As *The Economist* eloquently put it in one of its editorials, it is absurd for a major Western power to spend upwards of $400 million yearly to protect the Falklands against another Western power with important economic and cultural ties to Great Britain. As desirable as it would be in an ideal world to satisfy the wishes of the 2,000 Kelpers for the indefinite continuation of a British Falklands, prudence suggests that such wishes ought to be disregarded in view of more important considerations.

A British transfer of sovereignty over the Falklands to Argentina could be accomplished gracefully, honorably, and with due regard for the long-term interests of Great Britain. Such a transfer, for example, could make provisions for an equitable share between the two parties of any major economic resources that are discovered or become commercially viable in the future. Generous financial compensation could be offered to those Kelpers wishing to leave the islands, and the Argentines could be persuaded to share the costs of these compensatory efforts. A transfer of sovereignty, especially if scheduled to take effect not earlier than fifteen or twenty years after the end of the 1982 war, would not be seen as a disgraceful British retreat. By then passions should have cooled down in Great Britain and the costliness of a continued British presence should be the predominant concern. Moreover, the cost in lives and money of the 1982 war could be seen not as a futile waste, but as the spirited defense of principles which, as Thomas Franck has argued, have great strategic and political value. Without a doubt, Great Britain's political will and military capabilities are more feared and respected today than they were before 2 April 1982, a point of no small consequence for the credibility of British defense efforts in the North Atlantic against any prospective Soviet threat.

Other possible diplomatic approaches which come short of transfering sovereignty to the Argentines at a date in the near future will not be acceptable to the latter and will fail to defuse political and military tensions in the area. Involving the United States as a military co-protector of the Kelpers and a co-guarantor of continued British rule is equally problematical, regardless of whether it is done within the institutional arrangements of the UN's Trusteeship System or outside of them. Thus, for example, while Monroe Leigh's creative proposal offers many constructive possibilities, and while, as he argues, it has "elements of advantage in the long run to Argentina," it faces two almost insurmountable obstacles. First, the Argentines will not perceive it as sufficiently advantageous; the cultural and historical circumstances explaining such a seemingly rigid Argentine attitude are alluded to by both Alfred Rubin and Douglas Kinney in this book. Anglo-Saxon pragmatists may deplore the unbending nature and apparent irrationality of Argentine perceptions, but they cannot change them. Second, and equally important, the United States will not consent to sacrifice its interests in Latin America and Argentina in order to protect the Falklands militarily. The United States was a hesitant ally of Great Britain when the latter was attacked by the Argentines; it will be considerably less eager to provide continued military support to prop up one of the parties in what, according to the official viewpoint of the U.S. government, is a sovereignty dispute. The replacement in 1983 of the Argentine military junta by a civilian government committed to democracy and human rights makes the prospects of U.S. military involvement in the Falklands even more remote. These are the same obstacles facing proposals that Great Britain grant independence to the Falklands and then proceed, in concert with the United States, to guarantee by treaty their future security.

In the realm of international law, the Falklands War offered some lessons by confirming several important trends in the ongoing development of international law in the late twentieth century. The first of these is the decline, amply discussed by Thomas Franck and Anthony Arend, of the United Nations Charter norms limiting the recourse to violence by states; this decline has been accompanied by the continuing failure of the UN mechanisms for collective security and maintenance of the peace. The creation of authoritative institutions that will provide for peaceful change and the nonviolent accommodation of clashing national interests remains as baffling a problem for international law today as it has been throughout its past. Whether the recurring weaknesses of the *ius ad bellum* enshrined in the UN Charter's prohibition of the first use of force will be compensated for by new legal norms requiring states to seek peaceful means of settlement even after hostilities break out is an open question. Although, as Howard Levie has suggested, the *ius in bello* during the Falklands War presented a much more hopeful picture than the *ius ad bellum*, it is appropriate also to point out that the "Gentlemen's War" of 1982 may be an exception to a broader trend, of which the Iraq–Iran War, the conflicts in Indochina and Afghanistan, and numerous "wars of national liberation" elsewhere are examples, of a growing disregard for the laws of warfare.

The Falklands also confirmed the increasing desuetude into which international institutions for the adjudication and arbitration of disputes seem to be falling, a trend which many scholars have noted over the last decade. Not only do states ignore the decisions of the International Court of Justice (as Iran did in the 1979 hostages case) or those of impartial arbitration panels (as Argentina when it recently rejected a binding arbitration finding against it in the Beagle Channel dispute with Chile). More seriously yet, states seem to be dispensing even with the formalities of bringing disputes before such bodies. Between 1972 and 1980, only six cases were brought before the International Court of Justice; in five of these the states named as parties defendant refused to appear.

The events of 1982 were a sharp reminder of the critical role played in international politics and law by simmering territorial and boundary disputes, of which there are many in today's world threatening to break out into open violence. The lesson here, as David Colson and others have pointed out, is that these disputes need to be taken more seriously by the international community and the parties directly involved. In this connection, a contemporary scholar, David Downing, noted in 1980 that

> Border disputes provide an all too-convenient platform for the expression of international hostility, and waving the flag and waxing lyrical about the nation's sacred soil are time-honoured methods of silencing internal opposition ... But however invidious the role of governments, it cannot be denied that the very existence of ill-drawn borders has played a major role in the fomentation of all this century's major wars.[1]

There are few territorial and boundary disputes which, if they were to lead to war, would not carry the risks of involving the rival Superpowers. Even the Falklands War, fought over two barren islands of dubious economic and military significance, drew in the United States, and easily could have drawn the Soviet Union had a state different from Argentina (closer to the Soviet Union politically, ideologically, or geographically, for example) been one of the antagonists.

Another trend confirmed by the war, and one which helps to explain the volatility and increasing significance of boundary and territorial disputes, is the greater prominence in international law and politics of issues related to the development, management, and allocation of natural resources. The technological revolution of the post-World War II decades has helped to fuel this trend, as has also the rising world demand for food, energy, and raw materials to sustain a growing population and an ever more sophisticated industrial base. The Antarctic Treaty of 1959, the controversial Law of the Sea negotiations throughout the 1970s and 1980s, and the Convention dealing with the commercial exploitation of the moon illustrate the efforts of international law and diplomacy to develop rules for the exploitation and allocation of valuable living and nonliving resources in areas which are becoming increasingly accessible to modern technology. In a sense, the Falklands War was not directly related to these issues; so far, there is a very little evidence of the islands being a reservoir of substantial economic resources. Yet, in another sense, the perception by many Kelpers and by the British and Argentine public that there are vast untapped economic resources in and around the islands contributed to keeping both sides from reaching an agreement before the war. Also, as Christopher Joyner has indicated, the Anglo-Argentine rivalry over the Falklands may have adverse effects over future Anglo-Argentine cooperation in Antarctica, an area where sovereignty disputes among Argentina, Great Britain, and other states is directly related to issues of natural resources. For the foreseeable future, the effective management of such issues, whether in the context of the Antarctic Treaty which becomes open for review in 1991, or the 1982 Law of the Sea Treaty's seabed mining provisions which the United States and other industrial powers are unwilling to accept, will continue to pose for diplomacy and international law some of their most demanding challenges.

Viewed from a broader philosophical perspective, the war also offers important reminders that can be properly described as lessons for the future. In spite of its limited setting, the war was a microcosm of the perpetual fragility of international order, a rich and colorful parable of the cataclysmic and violent character of international relations and of history itself. A distinguished intellectual tradition stretching from Thucydides in the fifth century B.C. to Jacob Burckhardt and Raymond Aron in more recent times has tried to remind us that the essence of international politics is its chaos, its unpredictability, and its recalcitrance to fit into any single mold of intellectual understanding. The recurrent efforts of many statesmen and theorists of international law and politics to ascribe to their subject matter a degree of rationality and predictability that it lacks has been the source of many a disaster. The Falklands War, as well as other events in the long course of this troubled century, suggest that in an anarchic international system states must be prepared for the worst eventualities. Foreign policy must be made with an eye for not only the known uniformities, but also the innumerable surprises which the course of international relations continually produces.

Moreover, the war once again showed that underneath the delicate edifice of modern civilization and the elegant institutions of international law and organization, powerful forces of anarchy and disorder rumble on, ready at any moment to erupt to the surface and destroy the fragile proprieties and restraints of international society. Preeminent among those forces is nationalism which, contrary to the predictions of numerous observers, shows no signs of abatement in the late twentieth century. Argentina's display of intense nationalistic fervor did not surprise anyone, but the same cannot be said of the vast reservoirs of patriotism which Mrs. Thatcher suddenly discovered among a people supposedly too sophisticated to hold such seemingly antiquated values. As suggested by Dov Zakheim, the British fought tenaciously and victoriously mainly for reasons of national pride and honor, sentiments which before 2 April 1982 many observers, and indeed many of the elites in the West, had considered nonexistent and even inappropriate in an advanced industrial democracy with a Welfare State such as Great Britain. Patriotism and national pride will continue to play a critical role in international relations, much to the chagrin of world order theorists. As exasperating and baneful as these social values may seem, they are also an indispensable source of that dynamism and vigor essential for the survival and independence of a community in today's world.

Finally, the war revealed, for anyone too insensitive to have noticed it before, the tragic character of international conflict. The shortsighted obduracy of the Kelpers and the British government in not reaching a pragmatic settlement with the Argentines prior to 1982; Argentina's own impetuosity and bold miscalculation; the exceedingly narrow margin by which the mediation efforts failed to defuse the conflict; the great human and economic costs of the war to both adversaries; and the present predicament of a "Fortress Falklands" in which mounting social problems ranging from alcoholism to unwanted births, and the permanent presence of a large military force, make it very difficult for the islanders to lead the kind of good life for which the war was fought; these are illustrations of a tragedy not uncommon in the history of international politics. It is the kind of tragedy which, even after the Falklands dispute is settled at some future date, is likely to reappear in one form or another in other parts of the world, imposing on scholars and statesmen alike the sober responsibilities of intellectual and political creativity, patience, and catholic understanding.

Note: Chapter 15

1 David Downing, *An Atlas of Territorial and Border Disputes*. (London: New English Library, 1980), p. 8.

Index

Coast fisheries agreement 220–1; sovereignty relinquished 221–2; and trusteeship of Falklands 225–31

USSR: stance on Falklands' War 75, 127

uti possidetis juris 11, 194–5

Van der Heydte, F. A. 196

Vanuata, *see* New Hebrides

Venezuela: support for Argentina 25, 150; history 133; boundary disputes 143

Vernet, Louis: Governor of Falklands 14, 15, 149

Vespucci, Amerigo 9

Victor Emmanuel III, King of Italy 17

Videla, President Jorge Rafael 84

Vignes: Foreign Minister 84

war: international law on 36; laws of 64–76; Hague Regulations on Land Warfare 70

Washington Treaty 137

weapons: Conventional Weapons Convention 68; incendiary weapons 68; technological developments 180–3

Weddell Sea 206

Zakheim, Dov S. 5, 159–88